This Love Is Not for Cowards

THIS LOVE
IS NOT FOR
COWARDS

Salvation and Soccer in Ciudad Juárez

ROBERT ANDREW POWELL

B L O O M S B U R Y

New York Berlin London Sydney

Published by Bloomsbury USA, New York

All papers used by Bloomsbury USA are natural, recyclable products made from
wood grown in well-managed forests. The manufacturing processes conform to
the environmental regulations of the country of origin.

LIBRARY OF CONGRESS CATALOGING-IN-PUBLICATION DATA

Powell, Robert Andrew.
   This love is not for cowards : salvation and soccer in Ciudad
Juárez / Robert Andrew Powell.
      p.   cm.
   ISBN 978-1-60819-716-3 (hardcover : alk. paper)
   1. Soccer—Mexico—Ciudad Juárez.   2. Soccer teams—Mexico—
Ciudad Juárez.   3. Ciudad Juárez (Mexico)—Social life and customs.
I. Title.
   GV944.M6P69 2012
   796.33409721'6—dc23

                                                     2011039004

First U.S. Edition 2012

1 3 5 7 9 10 8 6 4 2

Typeset by Westchester Book Group
Printed in the U.S.A. by Quad/Graphics, Fairfield, Pennsylvania

To my friends who are still there.

The stories you hear in Juárez are hard to believe. Even shocking.
But when you leave they're surprisingly easy to forget.
This is a quality the city has. Some cities are known for seafood.
Some for air pollution. Juárez is easy to forget.

—SCOTT CARRIER

Contents

Prologue

THERE, UP AHEAD, MY FIRST TWO bodies. Dead bodies. Two of the ten or so people killed every day in Ciudad Juárez. The murder rate in this border town is skyrocketing, from three hundred executed in one year to 1,600 the next to 2,700 the year I got here—an all-time record we're definitely going to smash *this* year, the centennial of the revolution. I spot the bodies outside a convenience store down by the airport. First I notice thirty or so *federales*—federal police officers—standing around the parking lot smoking cigarettes, fondling their automatic rifles and snapping cell-phone souvenirs of what turn out to be the cadavers. I pull off the road and proceed to take pictures of my own.

The bodies slump on the ground next to a car parked in the store's drive-through lane. The car is a white Dodge Intrigue with Colorado plates like mine and a soapy For Sale sign scribbled onto its tinted back glass. Two bullets flew through the passenger-side window, one for each person in the car. A surgical hit. Professional. Nobody stops me when I walk right up to the car for a closer look. Blood stripes the tan cloth seat on the driver's side. I'm careful not to disturb the bodies, to taint the crime scene. I can't say the technicians are so concerned. Even if my only knowledge of police protocol comes from television, it's obvious that evidence of the double homicide is being compromised, terribly. The technicians—one of whom wears a black mask to hide his identity—toss around the bodies almost casually. Shattered car windows are knocked out for the heck of it. No one collects fingerprints. No police photos are taken. They'll never catch the killer. They never do.

I'm struck by how untroubled everyone seems. Like it isn't a big deal, two fresh kills baking on the paved drive-through lane of a convenience store. The store doesn't even close. I step inside and buy a bottle of Gatorade, talking for a bit with the clerk who had been serving the dead men, a woman who assures me she saw nothing, absolutely nothing pertaining to their murders. I drive away soon after the bodies are thrown into a white van from the coroner's office. There's a book reading I want to catch at the university, a big affair with more than two hundred people in the audience. Cabernet sauvignon, petite cheese sandwiches, strawberries dipped in chocolate, and no mention of anything like what I've just witnessed.

"This is a city where you can be killed at any time," says Ramón Morales, the main press guy for Los Indios de Ciudad Juárez, the professional soccer team I latched on to after I moved here. "Knowing that, you still have to live as best you can."

I've been in Juárez long enough to understand this casual fatalism, perhaps to even share it. I also understand the sloppy police work. Technicians don't *want* to solve crimes. This is a city where the most popular television news team has stopped investigative reporting. ("My reporters all have families," says the news director.) It's a city where the attorney general rarely prosecutes assaults or murders committed by the Juárez Cartel, preferring to focus her attention on a rival cartel from Sinaloa. ("She's corrupt. Absolutely," a Juárez official tells me.) It's a city where, if the police do a thorough job, if they collect enough evidence to identify the killer, then there's a serious chance they'll be killed in retaliation.

Why put yourself in harm's way? Why step off the line?

Introduction

SIX MONTHS EARLIER . . .

The first time I meet Marco Vidal, he tells me I need to hop on You-Tube. If I want to understand why he willingly lives in the world's most dangerous city and why he plays for the Indios of Ciudad Juárez *fútbol* club and why he feels the Indios are a special team, then I've got to watch what happened after his Indios defeated the Esmeraldas of León back in 2008. Juárez and León (a 440-year-old tannery town in the exact center of Mexico) had played a two-game series, home and home, for the highest of stakes. The losers were to stay in minor league obscurity, earning little money and waiting at least a year for even a chance to change their station in life. The winners would rise into the Primera, Mexico's top league. International TV every week. Big-time paychecks. Home games against glamorous clubs like Chivas of Guadalajara and road trips to such soccer shrines as the 105,000-seat Estadio Azteca, in Mexico City.

Juárez won. Improbably, unbelievably. The Indios beat León 1–0 in a home game played at their small stadium, so close to Texas that an errant corner kick might land in an El Paso railyard. In the second leg, in León, the Indios held on for a 2–2 tie, winning the series 3–2 on aggregate and completing the unlikely dream of the Indios' owner, Francisco Ibarra. Only three years earlier, Ibarra, a construction scion and former television station sports director, had announced he'd bought a minor league soccer team and relocated it to

3

Juárez, and that he planned for the team to rise to the Primera. Few people thought he could pull it off.

The videos are twenty seconds long in one case, one minute long in another, the cinematography all first-generation cell-phone camera. The moment the referee's final whistle blows in León, a festival erupts in Juárez's Chamizal Park, near the stadium. Horns, drums, flags colored Indios red and black. Police cruisers inch through crowded streets, fans rocking one squad car like a teeter-totter. Seven hours of Tecate and tequila later, the party relocates to the airport. Videos show Mayor José Reyes Ferriz on the runway, welcoming the team home. Players squeeze through the security doors into the terminal. Marco's in there somewhere, accepting hugs, handshakes, and kisses. The Indios' mascot, his head an oversize soccer ball wrapped in a red bandanna, dances to mariachi melodies bleated on silver trumpets.

"*Olé, olé, olé! Indios! Indios!*" The chants rocket around the terminal, threatening to lift the ceiling.

"*Va-mos Indios! Va-mos Indios!*" Go Indians! As loud and passionate as Anfield or San Siro. The fiesta overflows into the parking lot, and then onto the six lanes of the Carretera Panamericana, the main road back to the center of town. It takes the players and their coaches and Francisco Ibarra and their new silver trophy forever just to reach the bus, which is surrounded on all sides. Lights flash and twirl on police motorcycles ready to speed the team to a prayer service at San Lorenzo Cathedral, if that were at all possible. The bus cannot speed. It rolls so slowly through the mob that players feel safe climbing onto the roof. They are the Yankees on the Canyon of Heroes, they are astronauts returned from the first moonwalk. Finally at the church, Marco and his teammates parade the trophy up to the altar. Fans turn the pews into bleacher seats, still singing songs and waving flags. A priest steps up to the pulpit. Everyone thanks God for their good fortune.

I've arrived in Juárez in December 2009, too late for the Cinderella story. The Indios are no longer the darlings of Mexican soccer. In fact, they are the worst team in the league. They threaten, if they don't get their act together quickly, to become *the* worst team ever to play in Mexico's top division. The soccer cycle in Mexico consists of two short seasons per year—one in the fall and one in the spring. In the Apertura, or opening season (the fall season), the Indios finished in last place among eighteen teams. I got here just before the start of the Clausura, or closing season. The team is preparing to play every opponent one last time. If they don't win at least eight of those seventeen games, they will fall back to the minors from which they so gloriously escaped. Eight wins. A tall order for a team that won not once the previous season, their third in the Primera.

Substandard soccer is not what drew me to this city. I'm not invested in the survival or descent of the Indios. I've crossed the border, above all, for the city itself. It may sound morbid, but . . . all those murders! Carjackings are way up, too. Kidnappings and extortions have closed so many Juárez businesses that the central shopping district can look like the set of a shuttered Broadway play. I am scared to be here, I'll admit. But I was sort of homeless when I decided to move down. I'd figured all the violence had at least made the city a cheap place to rent an apartment, which was indeed the case.

I don't know what I will find during my time here, along La Frontera. I don't even know what I'm looking for, really. I know only that I want to look. Juárez touches Texas, yet in some ways it doesn't even seem to be on the map. Most stories coming out of the border, to my ears, make Juárez sound like some exotic other, some Kabul. *Playboy* magazine published a feature about life in El Paso, "at the edge of the abyss." Okay. Interesting enough. But what's it like in the abyss?

People do live here. As many as two million people, the mayor tells me. (The exact population is hard to pin down. I've heard maybe only one million people remain, the rest having fled to El Paso or back to Veracruz or, no doubt, illegally to Arizona and California, Denver and Chicago.) Juarenses marry and hold down jobs and raise kids who attend college in town. They are not exactly divorced from Texas or from the United States at large. Marco, an Indios midfielder, is an American. So is the team's vice president and general manager, Gil Cantú. Indios owner Francisco Ibarra lives in El Paso and has applied for the U.S. citizenship his sons already hold. Fly into the El Paso airport, hop in a taxi, and before you even reach downtown you'll see Juárez sprawling from just off Interstate 10. You can't miss the supersize Mexican flag thrust above the valley like a giant middle finger. Juárez is right there. I mean, it's *right there.*

It's an ugly city. Burning tires and improvised slums and poorly built bridges that collapse in spring rains. The weather cycles from snow to dust storms to sun so intense that street vendors sell windshield wipers to replace the ones that melted while you were at work. Employment is the reason everybody is here, including the Indios. Marco and his teammates are men at work in the most violent city going, which is why I've started hanging around their practices and games. Following the team, I figure, will also expose me to the rest of the country, since the Indios travel to away games every other week. Like most Americans, I haven't thought about Mexico all that much. It's there, I know, right below Texas and a few other states. All the cartels and corruption in Mexico matter to the United States, presumably. No other country holds more influence over modern American culture. It's time to look at it. I want to put Juárez and the country that governs it onto my map.

The players and coaches are optimistic about their future when I first start following them. Marco shares stories of the Indios' strong character, of past escapes from certain doom. "You're going to witness the greatest soccer miracle of all time!" Yet it is obvious the violence is taking a toll. Francisco Ibarra has abandoned plans to build a modern stadium in Juárez. Marco's car was stolen at gunpoint. Extortionists threaten players over their home telephones, and one goalie fled with his family after a *ladrón*—a street thug—pointed a shotgun at his head. Worst of all, one of the Indios coaches, in a development I kind of wish I'd noticed before I flew down, has just been murdered. The Indios have been called a civic vitamin, the one good thing that works in Juárez. Yet they're not working all that well. If they can't make it, what does that say for the future of the city? Of Mexico? Of us?

"This shit could all be over in three months," Marco lets slip one of the first times we go to lunch, before the first game of the spring season has even been played.

THERE IS MORE to the YouTube videos than the obvious story they tell: that this team of soccer players makes people happy. The missing context is essential, and it's why I've been ordered to watch the videos by many more people in Juárez than just Marco Vidal.

The championship final was played on the last Sunday of May

2008. That's about a year after the violence in Juárez really blew up. It's also about a year—and this is not a coincidence—from when Mexican president Felipe Calderón took office, promising to crack down on drug cartels. Juárez is Calderón's toughest battle-ground. It's a drug trafficker's dream, a transportation hub with easy access to American markets on both coasts and in the Mid-west. The city has been run for twenty years by the Juárez Cartel, better known in town as La Línea, or "the Line." Around the time Calderón announced his cartel offensive—and is *this* a coincidence?—a rising cartel from the Pacific state of Sinaloa ramped up operations in Juárez, aiming to take over the city.

The home team is fighting back. Cartel warfare killed more Juarenses in the first four months of 2008 than had been assassi-nated in the city all the previous year. Bloody torsos dangled from the Rotary Bridge, near a Wal-Mart and a Starbucks. AK-47s erupted at high noon outside City Hall. More than fifty bodies lay un-claimed in the morgue, which suggests they were outsiders shipped in for battle. Corrupt police flipped to the Sinaloan side. La Línea shot many of the defectors. After the murder of five turncoat officers, La Línea posted a list of seventeen more cops who would be killed "unless they learn."

As the Indios prepared for the final, away leg of the series, gun-men assassinated the number-two man in the Juárez police depart-ment; the chief immediately resigned and fled to Texas. The owner of Marco's favorite nightclub was shot in the head. Three bodies found inside a dusty Oldsmobile were indentified via handwritten note as "treasonous pigs." Five more bodies turned up less than a mile from the border, the bodies decapitated and wrapped in white plastic. An attached message, signed by La Línea, labeled the dead "traitors." On that same day, a viral e-mail warned that the upcom-ing weekend—championship weekend—would be the "deadliest and bloodiest" in the history of the city. Stay out of the bars! Stay at home even during the day. If you must travel, avoid major streets. The e-mail prompted Mayor Reyes Ferriz to cancel a trip to Colom-bia. Americans were warned not to cross the river. Police in El Paso prepared for spillover. The Friday before the game, eleven who ig-nored the e-mail were killed. The Saturday before the game, twelve more were killed.

Yet on Sunday, after the Indios won, *la gente* poured into the streets. The mayor partied alongside the rowdy Indios supporters who call themselves, wonderfully, El Kartel. Boys climbed onto their fathers' shoulders. Players climbed onto the roof of their bus as young women danced in blue jeans and form-fitting red Indios jerseys tied at the waist. *La gente,* the people, proved to be bigger than the cartels. The city showed it was more than just violence. Watch the videos, gringo, and see for yourself. Juárez is home to hundreds of thousands of people who strive only to dance and watch soccer and drink and love.

A beautiful moment. A nice memory.

CHAPTER 1

Opportunity

MARCO VIDAL IS SHORT. HE'S barely five foot five, and light, just 125 pounds. Coaches tend to frown on Marco's size, but in soccer his stature is not necessarily bad news; taller players have been known to envy Marco's low center of gravity. His torso is one solid brick, all power. Wide shoulders taper to forearms that can easily swat a baseball over a fence. His slightly bowed legs bulge with the muscle of a man who paid for his house with his footwork. I've watched him practice for a couple weeks now, always enjoying the experience. He's talkative on the field. *Pass it. You have time. Forward. Back.* He acts like a quarterback of sorts, a field leader. Most notably, he's calm when he gets the ball. That's the admirable aspect of his game. He collects and distributes passes without appearing stressed. His cool lowers the temperature.

It's cold already. Winter. I'd charted the weather before my move, so I knew what to expect in January Juárez, a desert settlement more than a half mile above sea level. It's another thing to actually stand outside as an arctic wind rushes across the practice field. Arctic? Antarctic? *Where is this cold wind coming from?* Snow dusts the squat and cinnamon Juárez Mountains. For the past two hours I've watched Marco and his teammates swoosh around in padded parkas. They wear spandex tights under their shorts. Ears warm beneath half-finished knit hats some players pull down to cover their necks. Marco roams the midfield, specifically the defensive midfield. He rarely pushes forward on the attack. In his three-year career with the Indios, Marco has scored exactly zero goals. Scoring is not in his job description. He's more of a courier,

the link between the defense and the offense. I like to think of him
as a circuit breaker. What he does, very well, is slow the pace, drop
the drama. After chilling everybody out, he moves the ball up
ahead, usually to Edwin Santibáñez, a midfielder with a more offensive mind-set. Edwin then leads an assault on goal, or tries to.
There's no flash in Marco's game, certainly no glamour. He doesn't
seem to do a whole lot out there, actually. I've watched enough soccer to appreciate that Marco's role is subtle, and difficult. He happens to make it look easy.

That apparent ease is why he is often underestimated as a player,
I believe. Throughout his career, whenever his teams have switched
head coaches, Marco has tended to fall out of the lineup. *Do we not
have someone taller than this guy?* Yet after a few weeks of play,
after an injury or poor performance by whoever surpassed him on
the depth chart, Marco is given a chance. He usually makes the
most of it. That the Indios have just hired a new coach, Pepe Treviño, and that the new coach isn't yet sold on his undersize midfielder, is just Marco's lot in life. Treviño played Marco for less
than half of last week's exhibition victory over old nemesis León.
There's a final preseason game coming up this Sunday afternoon.
After watching several intrasquad scrimmages and after talking to
journalists hanging out at practice with me, I'm wondering if the
American will even see the field.

"You ready?" Marco asks. Practice is over. He's wondering if I'm
up for lunch, the next agenda item on the routine we've fallen into.
The Indios' workday starts around ten in the morning, ending about
thirty minutes after noon. Marco showers, gels his black hair into
a fauxhawk, and pulls on his civilian uniform of Dolce & Gabbana
jeans and white Gucci sneakers, the labels large and visible. He
perches Armani sunglasses at his hairline and straps a big white
Diesel watch around his wrist. Hugging his chest, almost always,
is an Ed Hardy T-shirt. Marco wears Ed Hardy nearly every day,
reflexively, as if for his own protection. I want to tell him the Ed
Hardy trend is *sooooooo* played out, but I've already learned that
Mexico is where American fads go for an encore. People still use
the yellow pages down here. The Blockbuster Video near my apartment remains crowded. The other reporters at practice often wear
those khaki "I'm a reporter" safari vests I haven't seen on Ander-
son Cooper in years. And Marco is not alone in his Ed Hardy love.

All the Indios dress alike, as if incapable of individual action. ("I can tell they're soccer players even before I know they're soccer players," says Marco's young wife, Dany.) Wearing his gaudy T-shirts with pride, Marco might share a taco or two with an Armani Exchange'd teammate while they watch European soccer on the clubhouse television. Soon enough, he'll grab his jacket and a winter hat, and he and I will go for a proper lunch.

I need the ride more than the food. I didn't bring my car with me to Juárez. I wanted to settle in the city before importing what is easily my most valuable possession. In my car's absence, I'd hoped to get around on *ruteras*, the cheap and privately owned school buses found in many Mexican cities. Yet on the day I signed a lease on an apartment, the driver of a Juárez *rutera* was shot dead, along with three passengers. One day after that, the driver of another bus was murdered. Extortions, it was explained to me. *Ladrones* have started demanding payments from pharmacies and restaurants and even from mom-and-pop bus drivers. ("There's a new class of criminal taking advantage of the crisis. They know the cops can't stop them or catch them or do anything at all to deter them.") Better to hitch a ride to practice from someone in the Indios' front office, and to catch a ride home from Marco.

"I had an Audi with these great rims that I bought after we made it to the Primera," he says as we slip out of the training complex. He's explaining why my car, which isn't actually all that nice, might still be too nice for Juárez. The Indios' traveling secretary, Gabino Amparán, had his car stolen out of the parking lot of the stadium where the Indios play their home games. Team attorney Mario Boisselier downgraded to a Ford Taurus after his BMW was carjacked, then downgraded further to a dented Toyota with a cracked windshield after the Ford was stolen from him, also at gunpoint. Then it was Marco's turn. "I was stopped at a light, in traffic you know, when this car sped up and boxed me in on the right," Marco says. "A gunman was leaning out the window. Before I could react, there was a gunman on my left, too. The guy on my left barked at me to get out. His gun poked me in the chest. I grabbed my phone with my wallet, like I always do, and the guy said, 'Un-uh, drop everything.' So I dropped everything and they took off in my car."

When he bought the Audi, Marco also gifted Dany a BMW for her daily border crossing to school. Within a week of his carjacking he'd sold her car. Now, like a lot of too-prosperous-to-be-safe-anymore people in Juárez, Marco and Dany both drive the junkiest beaters they can somehow get to start. No exaggeration. The white Mercury we're riding in is at least twelve years old. It is dented in several places. The paint is weathered, the black plastic molding bubbled from too many summers of hot desert sun. A crack spiderwebs across the windshield. Finally: the body, the rims, and the bald tires are covered with so much brown dust, the car looks furry. It's a *fronterizo*, a special and cheaper class of vehicle Marco's allowed to drive only in Juárez; if he tries to take it more than 28 kilometers south of the border, the Mexican government will issue him a steep fine. I ride shotgun as we head to the city's newest shopping mall.

I can tell Marco's an athlete just by watching him drive. He reclines so far back in his seat that a hygienist could clean his teeth. His right hand grazes the wheel with the lightest touch as he navigates city traffic, appearing to barely look at the road. It's not hard to drive a car, of course, but it's clear watching Marco that his relationship with the physical world is more graceful than mine. Sitting close to him, I really notice his strength, too; he could crush me in a fight. (I've also noticed he's so much the metrosexual he shaves his forearms.) His ears jut out enough to be his defining trait. His face—his whole head—is perfectly round and is accented by thick black eyebrows arching into sharp points. I never say it aloud, but sometimes when I look at him I'm reminded of the Count, a character on the television show *Sesame Street*. Marco is twenty-three years old.

We pull onto Mexico 2, a newer beltway encircling the city. The Indios' training complex—two full-size professional fields and a modest clubhouse—hides between a construction depot and one of the many automobile graveyards found on the far southern fringe of the city. We're practically in the Chihuahuan Desert. The rusting cars lurk among endless acres of pale sand dotted with mounds of concrete blocks, mounds of old tires, mounds of spent plastic bottles, and mounds of old clothes, all the mounds spaced out in semi-uniform little ziggurats that remind me of moguls on a ski hill. Thick black telephone lines and electrical cables strap down the city like cargo netting. Occasionally, randomly, we pass subdivisions of the tiniest little concrete homes, the developments fenced in with cinder blocks and topped with rusty loops of barbed wire. More barren desert, more trash, and then a boxy maquiladora where underpaid migrants sew seat belts for nominally American cars. There's Delphi, maker of shock absorbers, brake discs, and diesel engine powertrains. Up ahead is Epson, cranking out computer printers. I feel like a lunar explorer as we roll past these factories to what is becoming the new public center of Juárez. Marco never goes to El Centro, the old, traditional downtown that has grown too dangerous for him to feel safe. I have yet to return there since my first full day on the Mexican side.

I'd flown into El Paso from Miami, where I'm from and where I'd ended up returning after three nomadic years in Colorado, Idaho, and, of all places, Jenesano, Boyacá, Colombia. I'd only been crashing at a friend's in Miami, a friend who was running out of patience with the setup. It was the day after Christmas when I arrived on the border, cold and so late the sun had already set. I went up to my room at an El Paso hotel, stepped onto my little balcony, and stared out at the Juárez Valley. All I could see was Mexico. Even in the gloom I could make out the flat roofs of concrete shacks, squat shoeboxes strung into neighborhoods rising and falling over gentle hills. Streetlights undulated in hazy yellow waves. I tracked a boy bouncing a soccer ball. Down the valley, maybe a half mile farther south, the swirling red-and-white lights of an ambulance crossed an intersection. I couldn't hear a siren, which made the scene seem sterile or unreal, as if the ambulance were a plastic toy gliding along a scale-model landscape.

"I haven't been over to Juárez all year," said the owner of a bodega near the border. I'd forgotten to pack toothpaste, and I wanted to buy a couple cans of beer if I could find any. The bodega was the only place open. "I have friends over there. I used to visit them maybe every month. But not anymore. It's too dangerous."

I entered Juárez the next morning. I took the Stanton Street Bridge, usually fifty cents but free because I got there before nine A.M. I strolled up a gentle incline, the bridge arcing over a dry canal that, to my surprise, was the Rio Grande. *That's the big river?* No one asked for my passport when I descended. No one inspected my backpack, either. I didn't even need to fill out paperwork, because the 28 kilometers in which Marco can legally drive his *fronterizo* are also a special visa-free zone. Knowing that last part already, I didn't expect to see much difference between the two cities. My El

Paso hotel had been staffed by Juarenses. Everyone in El Paso speaks Spanish. Yet there was an immediate disparity when I crossed, something more than customs disinterest.

It was the architecture, the way paint peeled off hundred-year-old storefronts in a manner that recalled old Havana. It was the street vendors selling fried pork rinds drenched in orange "Valentina" hot sauce. It was the police state: It didn't take two minutes for me to see my first convoy of troops, thirty soldiers parading atop three green GMC trucks, every soldier armed with an assault rifle, half the soldiers wearing face masks against the chill or perhaps to protect their identities. El Centro is compact, easy to cover on foot. I stepped into the Juárez Cathedral, crossing myself and blatantly praying for my protection. Back on the street, I haggled down the price of a nativity set a friend in Miami had asked me to find. I was pleased with the purchase; the manger and wood figurines didn't seem like a cheap tourist novelty. There weren't any tourists around anyway, aside from me. Off-duty soldiers at El Paso's Fort Bliss are forbidden to cross the bridges. For the first time in decades of printing vacation maps, El Paso businesses no longer acknowledge Juárez's existence; below the river on their most recent map lies nothing but blank white space. Boosters of Stanford and Oklahoma were invading El Paso for the Sun Bowl football game, the second-oldest bowl game, after the Rose Bowl. Side trips into Juárez have long been the Sun Bowl's primary appeal. Yet I didn't see one college sweatshirt the entire time I walked around.

I saw dental clinics, though many of them were closed. I saw a tuxedo shop. I passed a bar where, I'd read, eight people had been murdered a few months earlier. The Juárez history museum was not open, and looked as if it had been looted. It wasn't the only empty edifice. More than a quarter of the stores in El Centro— maybe *half* the stores in El Centro—appeared to have been abandoned. By city decree, the Mariscal red light district, four blocks of bars and brothels just off Juárez Avenue near the Santa Fe Bridge, has been leveled clean, the owners reinvesting their compensation on the El Paso side of the river. Everywhere I went, puffs of exhaust stung the air, sometimes making my eyes water.

But I also saw women carrying babies in their arms. You have to believe in the future to have a baby, right? I lunched on a burrito *con chile colorado* and a bottle of Mexican Coca-Cola purchased from a storefront no wider than a closet. I talked to people, and they were nice. A man suggested the best neighborhoods to live in. A woman shared general guidelines: "Just don't do anything stupid and you'll be fine. Don't honk your car horn. Don't go to bars or clubs. Stay in at night." I spied another baby, then another one, and still one more. The longer I hung out, the more I relaxed. *This place isn't so bad.* I knew people were being slaughtered here, and that more than a few of the murders had occurred right in El Centro. Yet it wasn't as if life had stopped. The city seemed kind of normal, actually, in a Mexican way. It obviously wasn't paradise, but I've long felt paradise is overrated.

I walked around Juárez for most of the day, meandering up Calle Otumba and down Avenida 16 de Septiembre. When I finally started back to El Paso, I carried with me the nativity set and two bottles of Victoria beer, the light brown cousin of *cerveza* Corona. *I like the energy in Juárez*, I concluded. *I could live here, for sure.* I took the Santa Fe Bridge back, waiting for half an hour in a long line of Mexicans, not realizing until we got closer to customs that there is a special line just for U.S. citizens. I switched to the proper line (is it a line if no one is standing in it?), showed my passport, and declared my purchases.

"What was the purpose of your visit to Juárez?" I was asked. The agent seemed amazed I'd even been there.

"I just wanted to check it out," I replied. "I find it attractive."

"THE WHOLE TEAM is together, with one mission," Marco is telling me. We've made it, appropriately, to Las Misiones, the brand-new shopping center Marco tells me is a demilitarized zone of sorts, considered off-limits for drug violence. It looks like a typical mall. Two stories, glass railings, skylights. Walking on polished marble floors, we pass clothing stores and shoe stores. Major retail outlets include a Sears and a Liverpool, Mexico's Macy's equivalent. There's a fancy health club where Indios players work out for free, and there's the attraction that drives the mall, a twelve-screen IMAX movie theater. The true anchor is the new United States consulate across the parking lot, less than a block away. The consulate is the only place in Mexico to obtain immigrant visas, the first step toward permanent legal residence in the United States.

Applicants from as far south as Chiapas must wait six to eight weeks or longer for their paperwork to clear. They must apply in person, too, so they often stay at one of a dozen new hotels in the consulate district, the new El Centro. Brand-new restaurants serve the area, along with nightclubs patronized mostly by local teenagers. In the shopping-mall food court, Marco waves at three Indios loitering at a table. ("They don't have wives, so they have nowhere else to go.") I tuck into a gordita: chicken, cheese, and green salsa folded into a thick flour tortilla and fried. Marco, the athlete, spoons a cocktail of fresh fruit.

"This is our livelihoods," he continues. "This is our reputations and the reputations of our families. This is everything. Our lives are on the line in the next four months."

When Marco was growing up in Dallas, the plan, always, was to return to Mexico. Marco's father had slipped into Texas intending only to mail a few bucks back to Mexico City. Under-the-table construction paid so well, he stayed longer. And then longer still. Marco's mother and two sisters, all born in Mexico City, moved up with him. Marco joined the family last, an American by birth. His father found a better job as a mechanic. Sister Claudia attended college in Boston. The Vidals upgraded to a two-story brick house in a suburb where American flags fly outside every front door. But when Marco started showing real ability in the competitive youth leagues of Dallas, the family hoped he'd take his soccer talent back to the homeland.

He certainly had talent. He was smart for his age. *Calm.* He played so well that Mexican superclub Chivas offered him a contract when he was just twelve years old. *Twelve!* There was no question of refusing the offer. Marco packed a suitcase with cleats and shorts and the hairspray he needed to maintain his then-puffy mullet. (Think early-period Andre Agassi.) He and his dad flew down to Guadalajara, where they enrolled Marco in the youth system of Mexico's greatest team. Then his dad flew back to Dallas, leaving Marco to fend for himself.

"He'd call me up crying, every night," recalls his mother, Patricia. "I would cry, too. It was very painful for both of us." Twelve is twelve, and Marco was homesick. His mom visiting every other weekend didn't help. Turning thirteen didn't fix the problem. "Every day I would go into my room and just crumble," Marco tells me. "Every day." He stuck it out for a year and a half before fleeing back to Dallas and his family and his old bedroom and the life he knew best.

Marco's talent helped him rebound. He won a title playing for a Dallas men's team when he was just fifteen. He started for the varsity as a high school freshman. At age seventeen, Marco returned to Mexico, joining a team in Monterrey called Tigres. Three years later, at age twenty and without once playing for Tigres in the Primera—*Eres un poco bajito!*—Marco up and quit. He tried out for FC Dallas of Major League Soccer but was cut after four months. "The coach felt he was too short," one of the assistants told the *Dallas Morning News.* Marco took a job at a Dallas radio station, selling advertising. He got serious with his Dallas girlfriend. He was an American living in America dating an American while working for an American company. Without the Primera to aim for, the trajectory of his life seemed set. He could see how it was all going to play out.

"I was very disappointed," recalls his father, also named Marco. "I thought he could make it, but he didn't get his chance."

Then the Indios called. Out of the blue. We're a new outfit, explained Gil Cantú. A minor league team relocated from the central Mexican town of Pachuca. The goal—an audacious goal, yes—is to rise into the Primera. A former Tigres coach now works for the Indios, and he brought up your name. He says you might be a good fit here. You want to come down and try out? You interested?

"Juárez is a city of opportunity," Gil said to me one morning while we watched Marco and his teammates practice. Hundreds of thousands of Mexicans have relocated here to fill jobs at more than three hundred borderland factories. Few of these maquiladora jobs pay a living wage, and turnover at many factories tops 100 percent, meaning the average employee doesn't last a year. Yet when there is absolutely no work in Oaxaca or Zacatecas, a Juárez assembly line has its appeal. Most new arrivals intend to continue on to the United States. Those who can't breach the border often find reasons to stay. "This city gave me a chance," I was told by a systems engineer at a maquiladora. (I'd struck up a conversation when I noticed the Indios jersey he was wearing.) "Juárez has become my home. It's the home of my family. I love this city, and I will fight for it."

Marco didn't succeed with the Indios at first. The team's head coach (a new guy, not the Tigres executive who had recommended Marco) didn't think much of the short midfielder. *Can the kid not grow a couple more inches, please?* Marco passed a whole season on the bench, once again not seeing even a minute of game action. The only reason he stayed with the club, the reason he didn't run back to Dallas and his girlfriend and his job at the radio station, was the creation of Indios USA. Gil Cantú had started up a side project, strictly amateur, a team based in El Paso, where Gil has lived for years. There'd be no salary, but Marco would finally see the pitch.

What happened in El Paso is what has always happened when Marco's been given a chance. He played great. In its first season, right out of the gate, Indios USA won a title, the United States Amateur Soccer Association National Cup. Marco emerged as a team leader, such a star that Gil demanded a spot for Marco in the Juárez Indios' starting lineup. Back in Mexico once more, Marco's poise helped the main Indios club win its fall 2007 season and the right to face León five months later, after the spring season, in that two-game series for promotion into the Primera.

"Those two games were the most important games of my life, obviously," Marco tells me. "We were big underdogs going into the games. But we took it seriously. We went to Monterrey for two weeks just by ourselves, just to train. We . . ." He stops talking for a moment. He puts down his plastic spoon, then looks at me with a nervous smile. "It's making my hair stand on end just to think about it."

As YouTube can confirm, the Indios won the promotion that sent *la gente* of Ciudad Juárez into the streets. Down in León, at the stadium after the decisive game, Marco crumbled into his locker. He cried as hard as a twelve-year-old left alone in Guadalajara. He cried like he told me he'd cried when he washed out with Tigres and believed his career was over. He thought of his family and what they must be feeling. He thought of his dad most of all. Marco was twenty-two, in the tenth year of a professional career plucked from the remainder bin. And now, with the victory over León, he was what he'd always wanted to be: a player in the Primera. At the top, back in Mexico.

Marco bought a house in Juárez with his promotion bonus. His new wife, a Juárez native, came attached to an extended family that all live close by. The immediate goal, Marco tells me, is to save the Indios, to keep the team in the Primera. He wants to stay in the big leagues. He wants to remain in the city that gave him his opportunity.

"I go to Dallas now and it's not home anymore, you know?"

MARCO AND I don't go to lunch every day. I might eat at the Indios' clubhouse commissary and catch a ride home from someone in the front office. When Marco and I do hook up, and when we finish eating, we usually swing by his house to pick up Dany. It's a nice address they share, especially for Juárez. Modern, two stories tall, with a garage and a small yard in the back where Dany's purebred shih tzu can play. This afternoon I try climbing into the backseat so Dany can sit up front, but she won't hear of it. She's twenty-one, just back from her classes at UTEP, the University of Texas at El Paso. Her hair is jet black and straight, shoulder length. She favors skinny blue jeans and severe black stilettos the way Marco favors Ed Hardy T-shirts. Her parents own a bus company that transports workers to maquiladoras every morning, taking the workers home again in the afternoon. She and Marco have been married for eight months.

"Aren't you scared to be here?" she asked when we first met, about a week after I'd arrived. "Yes," I said. "Aren't you?"

I'd spent my second day on La Frontera searching for an apartment. After touring what I had been told were the better parts of town, I ended up choosing Colonia Nogales, one of Juárez's oldest neighborhoods. The other options were way out there, isolated from the city and hidden behind guard gates. I wasn't blasé about my safety, but I didn't want security to consume me. Colonia Nogales is about a mile square, a neighborhood of mature houses in the Mexican style, meaning from the street they appear to be only a wall and a door; everything interesting hides on the inside. Several of the houses are impressively large, real mansions sprawling across as many as seven lots. The other houses are more modest, and are often kind of cute. There are only a few apartment buildings, the largest of which I've decided to live in.

My place is a furnished two-bedroom, one of forty-five identical units dispersed among five rectangular buildings—or barracks, if we're going just on looks. Each building is two stories tall, and each is painted a different, admittedly obnoxious pastel, making the complex look like military housing for an army of Teletubbies. My billet isn't fancy, I'll admit, but it only costs me three hundred dollars a month. (*"Still too much!"* I've been chastised.) There's a small park nearby and a decent burrito restaurant up the street. I can walk to a gym that I've joined, and also to two grocery stores, a butcher, and a full-on shopping mall. Although practice is held too far away for me to taxi, I can at least walk to the stadium where the Indios play their home games.

On the day after I moved in, the front page of *PM*, a bloody tabloid newspaper, featured a photo of a *gasolinero* murdered in the men's room of his station. I'd washed my hands in that same bathroom the day before, which was the day the man was murdered. Not three days later, still in my first week in the city, I tried a torta for lunch. Tortas are a Juárez staple, the functional equivalent of a fast-food hamburger: chicken or ham or beef plus pineapple and avocado on a bun. Not really my thing, but I was glad I tried it. And glad, in retrospect, I left the restaurant when I did. That night, Channel 44—the popular broadcast equivalent of *PM*—showcased the bleeding torso of a man lying outside the same restaurant, shot more than a hundred times by bullets fired from three different guns.

Nothing has spooked me as much as the murder of Pedro Picasso. He was the head coach of the Indios' youth program. He was shot dead, along with his uncle, inside his uncle's cell-phone shop. I learned about his murder on the very day I signed my new lease.

"You know the real story behind that, right?" Marco asks. We're still in his car, not far from my apartment building. We've just zipped under the Rotary Bridge, Dany reminding me that it was only a few weeks ago a body was found hanging from its girders, then smiling because she knows that freaks me out. "It was extortion," Marco continues. "Like I've been telling you about. They targeted his uncle's cell-phone shop. They said if he didn't pay up they would kill him. Picasso happened to be there on the day they came to collect. The uncle refused to pay, so they killed them both."

Marco delivers this analysis casually, like it's no big deal. Everyone around the Indios has been acting as though the murder was just a bad break Picasso suffered, the emotional equivalent of a lost wallet. In the days following my arrival, not even a week after his murder, I never heard Picasso's name mentioned. No one seemed par-

ticularly distraught, even though when I'd ask about Picasso everyone would insist he was a great guy, a humble family man, the last
person to ever get mixed up in the drug game, totally innocent of all
wrongdoing. A tragic loss, in other words. But not tragic enough to
keep anyone from their business.

Marco pulls up to my street, rolling his *fronterizo* to a stop so I
can climb out. I thank him, I help Dany out of the backseat, and I
give her a kiss on the cheek. After dropping me off, they usually proceed to one more restaurant for Dany's first and Marco's third lunch
of the afternoon. A three-hour workday with three lunch breaks—
nice gig. I speed-walk to my apartment, turning the four locks on
my front door and slipping inside before quickly bolting the locks
behind me.

THE INDIOS PLAY their home games at Benito Juárez Olympic Stadium. That cracks me up: Olympic Stadium. There's even a cauldron
welded above the south-end bleachers, waiting to be lit someday by
Mexico's most revered athlete. (Who would that be? Soccer player
Cuauhtémoc Blanco, I'm told.) It's considered Olympic because the
red rubber track circling the field conforms to international standards, yet it's hard to imagine Bob Costas hosting the Summer
Games here for his American audience, relaying the medal count
along with the day's body count. The stadium is a shallow bowl of
concrete, painted red on the outside, the west grandstand shaded by
an aluminum roof. It's not impressive in size, only 23,000 seats,
but it looks a lot more like a stadium than the bleachers-and-
floodlights assembly at El Paso's Bowie High, visible right across
the river. The land upon which the Indios play used to actually be
in El Paso, back when the riverbanks meandered, before concrete
canals were poured and President Lyndon Johnson signed the property over to Mexico in a ceremony marred by a blinding sandstorm.

The seats on the west and east sides of the Benito, as it's sometimes called, are red or white or black plastic buckets spelling out,
when empty, INDIOS and, in smaller letters, UACJ, the initials of the
Universidad Autónoma de Ciudad Juárez, the big college in town, a
regular, respectable school with philosophy majors and literature
majors and a champion track team that trains at the stadium, which
the university owns. The most striking thing about the Indios' home,

if you can look past the cauldron, is the way the stadium's north end frames Franklin Mountain, El Paso's natural landmark, a brown pyramid illuminated at night by a white lone star.

Olympic Stadium first opened in 1980. Back then it was a joke. The Cobras, the only other team from Juárez to ever rise to the Primera (where they stayed for just one season before folding), played on an uneven pitch more dirt than sod. The Indios' grounds crew has solved the turf problem, winning admiration throughout Mexican soccer for a natural grass field that stays flat and green through all of the frontier's intense seasons. Or flat and at least reasonably close to green on this biting January afternoon. It's the Indios' last preseason exhibition. The opponent is Atlante, from down in Cancún, a last-second replacement after the scheduled opponent from Brazil decided not to visit what is being called the deadliest city in the world.

It's Sunday, three days after Marco and I shared our lunch at the mall. Walking to the stadium about an hour before kickoff, I step onto Avenida Malecón, a main street. I fall in behind a ragtag marching band: six bass drums, three snares, and two brass trumpets. Flags and banners trailing the instruments identify the band as El Kartel. Their logo, the letters E and K inside a gunsight, waves on their flags and vibrates on the heads of the bass drums. I even spy the logo tattooed onto the calf of the one man brave enough to wear shorts in the winter cold. Because of the low temperature, the group actually marching is fairly small, maybe fifty people. Most of El Kartel trail in their cars, where it is warm and where they can continue to drink.

"Hey, how's it going?" asks a guy leaning out of a white SUV, a Styrofoam cup in his hand. He speaks English perfectly, like a gringo. "Going to the game, I presume. Get in!"

He slides over in the backseat. "You want some?" he says, offering his big white cup, which is filled with beer, Clamato, Tabasco, and lime, the rim ringed with fiery red salt. *"Los Indios son mi pasión,"* cheers a young woman in the front seat. She's wearing an airbrushed Indios hat cocked to the side of her head. Her fingernails are painted in team colors. Her name is Sofia. She's a student at UTEP, she lives in El Paso, and she is the girlfriend of the driver, a guy who introduces himself as Ken-tokey. All three say I'm lucky to have found them. El Kartel, they insist, is the coolest club anyone can ever join. Of all the booster clubs, or *barras*, that support the Indios, El Kartel prides itself on being the most hardcore.

"I'm going to have to use Spanish to describe some things," Kentokey says. "We're a *barra brava*. We're smoking weed and drinking beer and doing drugs. Cocaine, drugs, pills. Other *barras* are *las porras*—chill. We're not. The songs we sing have swear words and talk about cocaine."

I stick with El Kartel all the way into the stadium. I'd like to write that we stormed the south bleachers, our conquest of the playing field thwarted only by the chain-link fence, the moat, and the line of municipal police dressed in riot gear. But our entry is polite and peaceful. *"Papas! Papas!"* Vendors hawk potato chips stacked in still more Styrofoam cups adorned with lime wedges, the chips drenched upon request in either Worcestershire sauce or, more often, in that orange Valentina hot sauce. A woman asks if I want Indios face paint. When I hesitate—is this a ploy for money?—she says, "Of course you do," and drags red and white wax across my cheeks. *"Vamos Indios!"* Six curvaceous women in body stockings march around the track carrying placards for Tecate, *la cerveza oficial de Los Indios*. Six more women in spandex catsuits advertise the modest homes sold by Grupo Yvasa, the Francisco Ibarra family construction company. A giant Grupo Yvasa soccer ball, two king-size Tecate beer cans, and a colossal nylon cow advertising Lucerna-brand milk deflate as kickoff draws near. Billboards circling the stadium hawk Coke Zero and Gatorade and Total Fitness, the gym at Las Misiones where Marco works out. One billboard features only a black ribbon tied into a bow. I'm grateful to see that last one, which is for Pedro Picasso.

Marco doesn't receive special cheers when he's introduced onto the field. He's not featured on the banners that line Olympic Stadium's outside facade and hang on light posts in the parking lot. That ad space goes to Coco, a bald Argentinean who claims, incredibly, to be only thirty-four years old. No way. After watching Coco hobble around the training pitch, I'd bet my life he's at least forty-two. ("Yeah, he's probably lying about his age," general manager Gil Cantú admits.) Also promoted is King Kong—Alain N'Kong—an African striker just signed to give the Indios punch up front, to score; he netted a laser-beam goal last week in the 2–0 preseason victory over León. Forty minutes into today's game, as the coming halftime is signaled by inflating nylon tunnels connecting the field to the locker rooms, offensive-minded Edwin pushes the ball onto the feet of a striker who darts sideways eight steps before beating the Atlante goalie with a powerful blast. One-nothing, Indios. Beer splashes onto my jacket.

"Toss your beer in the air," I'm ordered. "That's what you do when the Indios score." The second half is all Juárez. The Tribe dominates such intangibles as the time of possession and shots on net. They look really good. That the final score is a 1–1 tie doesn't dampen what feels like a win. Though Marco played only nineteen minutes, he started the game, and looked solid.

I rush with El Kartel over to the locker rooms, near where the players park their cars inside a chain-linked pen. Seven or eight reporters stand inside the pen, voice recorders ready for interviews. El Kartel waits outside. A defenseman comes out first and signs autographs for about five minutes. Marco signs, too, when he emerges. Across the parking lot, on an adjacent dirt field that belongs to the city, kids play their own soccer games. I spy a father holding the hand of a little girl in a pink winter coat. I don't want to insult El Kartel, but I feel chill—relaxed and happy. I've only been in Juárez a few weeks, and I carried a lot of paranoia over the bridge with me, obviously. But as soon as we pulled into the stadium parking lot I felt better. For two and a half hours I wasn't locked in my apartment. I didn't worry about my security. I didn't think about extortion or about being caught in the crossfire of cartel-on-cartel crime. Mostly I marveled at how well the Indios played. Maybe they really will pull off the miracle.

"We're looking better," Ken-tokey agrees. He's a student at UACJ. He also works at his family's junkyard. He doesn't hold a visa to even visit his girlfriend's house in El Paso, but as a boy he lived illegally for twelve years with his father in Louisville. Hence his nickname, which has been twisted a bit for self-evident reasons.

"I smoke a lot of weed," he admits. "I'm basically a pothead." He tells me if I really want to have the Indios experience I've got to ride the bus with El Kartel to next week's season opener in Monterrey. It's an opportunity I can't pass up. "You're going to have the time of your life, man," Ken-tokey promises. "I'm going to be a different dude on that bus, I'll tell you that."

CHAPTER 2

Monterrey

KEN-TOKEY SLIDES HIS FINGERS ACROSS my open palm, finishing the exchange with a fist bump. "Hey man," he says, releasing his words in a choked sort of burst, as if he'd been holding his breath for a few seconds. "I didn't think you'd show up."

He had sent me the logistics in an e-mail. I needed to be at the Olympic Stadium today, Thursday, at four in the afternoon, which it is right now. Bring twelve hundred pesos—for the bus, a ticket to the game, and two nights in a Monterrey hotel. That's about a hundred dollars, a reasonable fee to change my life forever, as Ken-tokey has promised will happen. I'm carrying a duffel bag of clean clothes, a toothbrush, a couple empty notebooks, and some pens. Ken-tokey reaches into an Indios-branded knapsack to pull out a long-sleeved T-shirt featuring the silhouette of Sebastián Maz, a player cut by the Indios when new coach Pepe Treviño assumed command. Maz knows how to score goals. El Kartel was not happy to see him go, or satisfied by Treviño's explanation for the dismissal: that Maz's supposedly bad attitude had been dragging the team down. On the back of the shirt, in large red letters: TREVIÑO VENDE HUMO. Treviño sells smoke.

"Wear this and you'll fit in," Ken-tokey assures me.

Some forty young men—there are maybe twenty females, too, mostly girlfriends—mill about the parking lot, which is otherwise empty save for the bus we're taking to Monterrey. When the Indios first rose to the Primera, everyone in El Kartel followed the team on the road. It took three buses to transport the *barra brava* down to Mexico City to watch the Indios' first game in Estadio Azteca, against Club América. With the Indios playing so poorly of late, only the true hard core of El Kartel remains. I'm introduced to this hard core: Kinkin, Sugar, Chuy, Juvie from Las Cruces, Mike the Capo, Big Weecho, and too many others. The names go by in a blur. Weecho stands out because of his size, which is enormous. He stands six-five and weighs 340 pounds. Ken-tokey presents him to me as a *luchador*, one of those professional wrestlers who wear masks in the ring. "It's true," Weecho admits, "but I'm not supposed to talk about it, you know."

The bus is dented in several places. Its hull has been battered by rocks or maybe baseball bats, or perhaps the whole bus once fell into a ditch. The windows are too dirty for me to see who has already climbed into the cabin. El Kartel trashes its rides so routinely they can secure only the raggediest vehicles: buses with bald tires, torn seats, and a driver who may not be able to stay awake, or sober. "Just don't do anything stupid," I was advised on my first day in Juárez, back when I was checking out the city. I recall that quote as I swallow hard, throw my bag in the hold, and step on board. There's a seat open in front of Ken-tokey and Sofia. He's drinking a Tecate, and he hands me a cold red can of my own. Someone else hands me a bottle of Clamato and a giant Styrofoam cup, telling me to mix the spicy tomato juice with my beer.

"These trips are like fucking addictive, man," Ken-tokey says. "These buses get rowdy. I've seen a girl go down on ten guys back here."

The January sun is already down as we slip out of the city, passing a military checkpoint where Marco Vidal's *fronterizo* would be ordered to turn around. It's too dark to make out even the dunes of the Chihuahuan Desert we are slicing through. I am drinking my *Clamato y cerveza*. Ken-tokey slams his Tecates straight up while Sofia tips a bottle of sickly sweet wine to her lips, her Night Train up and running. None of us are in our seats. Everyone stands, hands gripping the luggage rack for stability. Ken-tokey lights a Marlboro Red. Big Weecho and Mike the Capo tap a vodka punch somebody has mixed in a five-gallon plastic water bottle. Banda music—accordions, fuzzy tubas, the soundtrack of El Norte de Mexico—crackles over the speaker system. My seatmate aligns cocaine on the back of his hand, tapping it out of what looks like a restaurant sugar packet. Ken-tokey switches to marijuana cigarettes. The energy alone is making me high. This bus is rocking. I'm surprised when we stop for food, maybe only an hour in. Roadside flagmen wave us over to a stretch of concrete food stalls sheltered by a high tin roof, a setup that looks like a combination food court and school-bus parking garage.

Juárez claims, with scant credible evidence, to be the birthplace of both the margarita and the burrito. Add the quesadilla to that list. This little pit stop, officially located in the small satellite town of Villa Ahumada, insists it's the first place to ever serve the simple meal of smooth white Chihuahua cheese grilled between two flour tortillas. Big Weecho orders for me, and won't let me pay when I'm handed my cheesy meal, folded and wrapped in a paper towel. I pull apart the tortillas to drizzle on a sauce of cream and green chiles, as instructed. I take a bite and, well . . . it's great. Of course. Obviously. Human DNA is programmed to love it. The quesadilla tastes so good I order two more, my second attempt to pay almost violently rebuffed by the *luchador*.

"Luke, soy tu padre!" Over near a bathroom stall, two Karteleros— Sugar and Chuy—have found a box of long fluorescent light bulbs. Sugar twirls a bulb over his head, acting as if he's Darth Vader and the bulb is his light saber. Chuy, a red-and-black baseball hat turned backwards on his head, raises his light saber for a duel. *Thwack, crash*, the tinkle of frosted glass falling on concrete. Oh, it is hilarious, we decide. Hilarious! Even the quesadilla vendors laugh, as does a man guarding glass bottles of Coca-Cola, as does the woman selling squares of toilet paper for one peso each. Such theatrics are to be expected from El Kartel, which, I'm told, stops here to load up on fat and flour at the start of every road trip. Before motoring on to Monterrey we stop one more time, at an OXXO convenience store just down the road. I watch bags of chips and cookies and even thirty-two-ounce bottles of beer walk out the door under Indios jerseys and jackets. "These guys are crazy, man, it's great," says Weecho, speaking to me in English. He grew up in El Paso and still lives there. "We're, like, you know the word 'hooligan,' don't you?"

Fully fueled, we shoot off into the night. Music videos flicker on television monitors spaced out every six rows of seats. I'm offered more coke, to be inhaled through a rolled-up hundred-peso bill. There is enough smoke compressed into the cabin to give a canary an embolism, or at least a major craving for birdseed. I feel like we're in a nightclub, one that's long and narrow and overcrowded and just happens to be in motion. As we hurtle toward Monterrey, Banda El Limón, to my surprise and also at least a little bit to my relief, gives way to Vampire Weekend. I'm presented with still more coke. Tequila sloshes into the mix. Even as I'm falling into intoxication, I'm not worried about my safety. I'm happy, in a groove, able to see exactly why Ken-tokey is addicted to these trips.

Juárez was founded in the 1600s, a way station for Spanish explorers trekking from Mexico City to Santa Fe and back. El Paso del Norte it was called back then, just one town on both sides of the Rio Grande. In time, a treaty with the United States divided ownership of El Paso between two countries, though the border remained so porous as to be almost theoretical; Mexicans and Americans crossed sides freely until 1917. Prohibition changed the once lawless character of the American side, and altered life on the Mexican side, too. Untouched by temperance, Ciudad Juárez—the city was renamed in 1888 to honor liberal president Benito Juárez—evolved into the real land of liberty. Texas bars and brothels relocated to Mexico to serve Americans drinks, or prostitutes, or even a quickie divorce; Juárez is where Marilyn Monroe legally split from playwright Arthur Miller. The Santa Fe Bridge buckled on Saturday nights with UTEP students and Fort Bliss soldiers strolling over for margaritas at the Kentucky Club and to see the "live girls" dancing at the Hollywood Club. Savvier visitors slipped twenty bucks to random Juárez street cops in exchange for a password that would protect them from the possibility of arrest.

Anything you wanted you could get. Heroin? Coke? An escort to share the drugs with? Just name it. Looser law enforcement on the Juárez side differentiated the city from an El Paso that was growing staid and perhaps even boring. The vast distance between the border and the rest of Mexico also liberated Juárez from a conservative national culture.

"It was a better city than any other in the republic," says my landlady, a woman in her sixties named Guadalupe. "We had freedom. When I was young, I used to go to catechism school. I would come home at two in the morning with my girlfriends, and we would be singing while we skipped down the street. Our families knew where we were and they didn't worry about us. If it was a warm night, people in the neighborhood would be out sleeping in the street."

Those days are over. Every morning I read about at least one or two nightclub shootings from the evening before. Eight people were slaughtered at the "77" bar. Four Americans were shot leaving the Arriba nightclub. Even house parties are growing dangerous: *Sicarios* have begun hunting down targets too scared to visit the bars. Juárez has grown so violent that its Freedom City label has been turned upside down. Mexicans of age (and who hold the proper paperwork) now cross to El Paso to drink at old Juárez bars and pool halls that have reopened safely on the other side.

If they can't cross, like Ken-tokey, they go on the road with El Kartel. No one's going to burst onto this bus and open fire. The long ride to Monterrey is an opportunity to party—hard—with the only lethal threat coming from alcohol poisoning or overdose. Road trips, I recognize, are a responsible way for El Kartel to engage in all the irresponsible things these hooligans like to do.

"No joke," Ken-tokey agrees. "That's exactly what it is. My mom and dad, they feel better when I'm on these buses than when I'm going out in Juárez. There is *nothing* to do in Juárez anymore. Nothing."

I'M NOT FEELING so sanguine some sixteen hours later, when we finally pull into Monterrey. Alcohol and THC spike my bloodstream. Sleep has not been allowed. ("Gringo, wake up! Wake up, gringo!") The bus broke down as expected; it took almost two hours to replace a flat tire. The hoodlum named Kinkin, turning nasty as the sun first emerged on Friday morning, spent hours hazing me. He threatened to beat me up. Later he handed me a cell phone with orders to call my family for the ransom money. I'm so happy when we finally get to our hotel, I don't care that it's dirty and small and located among a warren of auto-body shops. I'd planned to share a room with five or six others to save money. Impulsively, instinctively in survival mode, I invest in a private room. When I open the door to this room, I discover eighteen mirrors hanging on the ceiling, on the headboard, on the walls beside and behind a king-size bed. In the middle of the bed, visible on all eighteen of those mirrors, a very naked man and a very naked woman caress their very naked bodies. I close the door quickly. Back at the front desk, a lady sitting next to a glass bowl of condoms gives me keys to another room. It's unoccupied. I crash for hours.

Marco loves Monterrey. When he played for Tigres—or at least when he tried to play for them—he felt like Monterrey royalty. Fans paid for his meals at restaurants in the Barrio Antiguo, a neighborhood well preserved over the five hundred years since the Spanish discovered the city. After eating, Marco and a teammate or two might stroll to one of the many nightclubs in the barrio, stepping inside for free, a hostess guiding them to tables behind the velvet ropes of the VIP section. Monterrey is prosperous and physically beautiful and a day trip from Dallas. It was nothing for Marco's parents to zip down for a Tigres game to watch Marco warm up, stretch, and then rust on the team's bench.

I may be in love, too. Already. Monterrey is very appealing. It's a big city, the Mexican Chicago. Some four million people live and work here, a population eclipsed nationally by only Mexico City and greater Guadalajara. Rail lines run directly to Laredo, a strategic link with Texas that has helped Monterrey evolve into the industrial hub of Mexico's North. FEMSA, the global brewing and bottling concern, started and remains here. Tec de Monterrey, a school founded by a brewery scion, has evolved into one of the best research universities in the world. Glass skyscrapers rise downtown, but most of the buildings in Monterrey are one or two stories tall, giving the city a livable scale. Emerald mountains frame everything. They're Monterrey's most distinctive physical trait, the Sierra Madre, gentle green folds wrapping the city in a soft hug.

Baseball was Monterrey's first sporting love. Back in the 1920s, executives at the Cervecería Cuauhtémoc—that's the brewery—formed baseball teams to entertain a growing staff of brewmasters and bottlers. These start-up leagues flourished, and became such a part of Monterrey's identity that when the Montreal Expos fell into receivership, Major League Baseball seriously considered relocating the team here. (The Expos ended up becoming the Nationals of Washington, D.C.) I learn this at the Mexican Baseball Hall of Fame, located inside the red-brick brewery. There isn't much to the Hall of Fame: a statue of Fernando Valenzuela, some uniforms of the Yucatán Lions and the Pericos de Puebla. I look in vain for the empty vials of Mexican steroids used by Mark McGwire and Ken Caminiti.

Soccer was the lesser game in Monterrey, at first. The Rayados, the more popular of the two teams in town and the Indios' opponent this weekend, formed after the Second World War, primarily as a social program. "We want our players to be positive role models for our youth," declared a Rayados founder. What the players became in time, above all, were moneymakers for Mexican industry. *Fútbol* trounced baseball everywhere else in Mexico, quickly establishing itself as the national sport. Brewers who slapped the logos of Carta Blanca and Tecate on the backs of team jerseys reaped a windfall in associated customer loyalty. (It's no coincidence that Ken-tokey's favorite beer, Tecate, is the brand advertised on the backs of the Indios' jerseys.) FEMSA, the parent company of the big Monterrey brewer, bought the Rayados outright in 2005. The conglomerate's cash infusion transformed the team from a middling outfit into the best squad in Mexico, and one of the top thirty-five clubs in the entire world. The Rayados won the Primera last season. They've broken ground on a new stadium. Soccer is clearly Monterrey's main sport these days.

Because the Rayados are the defending champions, the first game of the season, even if it is against the Indios, shines in the national spotlight. I discover how bright this spotlight is when I step inside a taqueria near Monterrey's big bus terminal. I order a trio of beef tacos and a bottle of Coca-Cola, which I pour into a squat glass. On a television, a reporter interviews Rayados players as they check in to their hotel. (Home teams, including the Indios when they play in Juárez, commonly stay overnight in a hotel.) Indios players are not interviewed. An analyst uses one of those electronic pens to diagram formations and the probable plays the Rayados will use on corner kicks and penalties. He lists the Rayados' expected starting lineup. The Indios are absent from his discussion. He shares no strategies for stopping Juárez from scoring. In the diagrams and charts, the Indios come across as empty red shirts for the Rayados to dance around.

"Nobody respects us," Ken-tokey told me on the bus. "Everyone in Mexico hates Juárez. They think it's all maquiladoras, all narcos. They feel about us the way Americans feel about Mexicans!"

I proceed from the taco shop to La Puerta, the clubhouse of the Rayados' *barra brava*. The clubhouse is a bombed-out concrete bunker facing a vacant lot, on the outskirts of the Barrio Antiguo. I head over with about a dozen members of El Kartel, and as we get closer to the clubhouse I start to wonder if we're going to, like,

rumble or something. *Barras bravas* are often at war. Postgame
rumbles between El Kartel and a team called Santos have devolved
into rock-throwing riots. Yet there's no apparent enmity between
El Kartel and the Monterrey firm. We're offered beer as soon as we
step inside. Everyone wants to hear stories about cadavers and bullets and torsos hanging from bridges. We're respected, it seems, just
for living in the world murder capital. And maybe because our
team poses no threat.

The clubhouse is furnished with a couple ratty couches. Blue
walls host old posters of Rayados greats, none of whom I recognize.
A dented VCR unspools last season's championship game. Outside,
on a vacant lot, kids in jeans and canvas sneakers kick around a
ball. It's a mellow vibe, a lot more laid-back than I'd expected. The
adrenaline that had spiked on the way over—it's been quite a while
since I was in a street fight—drops back down to baseline. I drink
my free Carta Blanca and watch the game on television for a while,
wondering what's next on the agenda. When it becomes clear everyone is content to chill, I distribute a round of fist bumps, thank our
hosts for the beer, and break away, back to the city.

It's still early evening. The sun has not yet set. I walk down cobble-
stone streets hemmed in by *colonia* buildings painted rich mangoes
and loud pinks. Ornate iron bars protect and perhaps even improve
the glass windows of cafés and boutique clothing stores. Bartenders
post fliers outside rock clubs still several hours from opening. Lots of
towns have a neighborhood like this, several blocks gentrified by
artistic types and/or college students. I know an "arts" district doesn't
thrive without serious urban planning, but Barrio Antiguo feels more
organic than, say, South Street in Philadelphia. It's certainly not a
pure tourism ghetto like Old St. Augustine or Key West. I step inside
a gallery to find a collection of pop art that I enjoy even if it is a little
too similar to Roy Lichtenstein. By the time I step back out the sun
has gone down. Yellow streetlights climb up the Sierra Madre foot-
hills, a rising vista of single-family homes that reminds me a bit of
Seattle. The air is crisp, an invigorating cool that doesn't make my
teeth rattle like they do in January Juárez.

I know there's violence in Monterrey. On the trip from Juárez, at
a convenience store El Kartel ransacked just before we slipped into
the city, I read a local version of *PM*, a newspaper overflowing with
bodies splashed in blood. The television in my room at the sex

hotel broadcasts *narcocorrido* music videos celebrating drug-trafficking culture. I suspect that at least a few skyscrapers in downtown Monterrey were erected in part with laundered cocaine profits, as is the case in Miami. "It's a hard-core drug city here, man," Ken-tokey told me. "Make no mistake."

Yet Monterrey and Juárez feel nothing alike. I watch executives in suits duck into a bookstore to check out the latest titles. Women in wool coats circle the "Lighthouse of Commerce," a monument to moneymaking. Monterrey is the rough energy of Mexico smoothed by the waters of business, education, and the arts. It's what a city in the North can be. It's what Juárez could be, in theory: Juárez is all about making money, too. Yet if the violence in Juárez were to magically disappear—which isn't going to happen—the border would never resemble this gleaming state capital. Cities get divided into classes. Even within cities, neighborhoods split into a yin-yang of beauty versus utility. Monterrey is the yin of El Norte. It's where wealthy executives with Ivy League degrees make decisions. Juárez, the yang, is where those decisions are carried out, the products churned out, the money earned in the maquiladoras shuttled back to Monterrey to pay for free meals for professional soccer players and to buy big houses in the nicer neighborhoods where executives would rather live.

I'm no different. I'd rather live here, too.

"THAT WAS THE hardest game I've ever watched in my life," Marco tells me after the Indios lose to Monterrey by the score of 4–0. "I felt powerless, helpless. It hurt to watch it. It was really painful."

He tells me this over the phone. Marco didn't play in the game. He wasn't on the bench, either. He didn't even make the trip to Monterrey, a last-minute administrative decision that shocked me as much as him. Marco played a big role in the Indios' rise to the Primera. He performed so well that no less than the *New York Times* lobbied for his call-up to the U.S. men's national team. Yet Pepe Treviño, the new coach who sells smoke, is so unimpressed with the small midfielder he inherited that he left the American back in Juárez. *He left him behind?* I knew Marco was falling out of favor with Pepe, but this is absurd. Marco is in shape, he practices like a professional, and he's still the most experienced defensive midfielder the Indios have. It's a horrible coaching decision, I feel. Then there's the economics: The budget is so tight the team wouldn't even comp Marco a plane ticket and a hotel room so he could watch the game on the bench?

I watched the game at Estadio Tecnológico, on the campus of Monterrey Tech, in the company of El Kartel. I'll admit to being drunk by kickoff, so I remember mostly random details: paying seventy-five cents pregame for a hot dog wrapped in bacon and drenched in both chile and melted cheese; clear sun illuminating the green wrinkles of Monterrey's signature mountain, the Cerro de la Silla. Before we could enter the stadium, police ordered us to re-move our belts and leave them on the bus. Those same police incar-cerated El Kartel at the far edge of the arena, a line of helmets and flak jackets separating us from the Rayados fans. During the game, as Monterrey began to pull away, two Karteleros ripped out a plank of bleacher and tossed it into the moat ringing the playing field. They were arrested, as was the oldest woman in El Kartel, a chain-smoking and beer-chugging grandmother. She had lifted up her Indios jersey to flash Monterrey's fans, who graded her breasts with chants of *"chicharrón!"*—a stadium snack of wrinkled and fried pork. Mostly I remember emotions. Frustration at the Indios' poor play. Exhaustion from the sun and the *cerveza*. Resignation at the long season ahead.

"They don't have heart—*corazón*," Ken-tokey mused as we boarded the bus for the ride home. "We get upset when we're tak-ing the bus all this way, eighteen or nineteen hours, and they're flying in a plane and they don't play better for us. You get mad. We'll still support 'em anyway, but if they drop down, we're really gonna be mad at them."

Marco watched the game back in Juárez, at his house. He spent the ninety minutes slumped on a black leather sectional, alone ex-cept for Dany, who gave him his space. Marco usually rooms on the road with Maleno Frías, his best friend, the Indios' starting striker and perhaps the most beloved man in Juárez. Maleno is a big guy, wide and heavy, hulking for a soccer player. He was born in Juárez and grew up in Colonia Altavista, a neighborhood so bloody I've already stopped using a felt-tip pen to mark its murders on a map I've hung in my apartment; in just a month of recordkeeping, Altavista already looks like a red stain on my wall. Maleno has admitted to vague troubles in his past. That he ran with a gang.

That he felt compelled, as a teenager, to flee to El Paso. In Texas he found construction work and a spot on the El Paso Patriots, a semi-pro soccer team. He scored so many goals for the Patriots—a striker's glamorous job is simply to score—that Gil Cantú signed him to Indios USA, where he played alongside Marco. One amateur national championship later, Maleno returned to Juárez as the city's new favorite son. He's the starting striker of a team in the Primera, a local boy with a rough past who has made very, very good.

Members of Maleno's family haven't improved their lives so profoundly. His brother remained messed up in drug dealing and gang life—*remained*, past tense. Not long after I moved to Juárez, gunmen shot the brother in the knee, a warning of some kind, a warning he did not heed. The night before the Monterrey fixture, Maleno's brother was shot again, this time terminally.

"Maleno called me right after the game," Marco shares with me. "I could tell he was upset."

Maleno learned of his brother's murder while still in the locker room, just a few minutes after the game ended. The timing sticks out to me. I track down an assistant coach and ask him when the coaching staff first learned of the murder. In the morning, the assistant admits. On game day. Well before kickoff.

The trip to Monterrey has been eye-opening. A pleasant discovery. It's hard to believe the two cities are part of the same country. Marco loves Monterrey. I love it, too. The Rayados and the city they represent are Mexico at its best. The Indios can't help but embody the country at its worst. That yin and yang. They are lousy soccer players. They appear doomed to descend back to the minor leagues. Yet Maleno illustrates how the Indios are not merely empty red shirts, laundry for the Rayados to run around. The Indios are *of* Ciudad Juárez. The players live in Juárez. Maleno and his brother were born there and were molded by border culture. The problems better teams face—what formation to use, which striker should take penalty kicks—are the least of the challenges the Indios must overcome. *The coaching staff learned of the murder and carried on with business as usual.* Pepe Treviño held on to the information, sharing it with Maleno only after the final whistle had blown.

"We didn't want to upset him," the assistant coach tells me. "We didn't want it to affect his play."

CHAPTER 3

More Than a Club

I'M DRIVING TO CHIHUAHUA CITY with Indios owner Francisco Ibarra. Every few miles I see flowers. They are small and pink and look like poppies, though I'm sure they have a different name and genus out here in the Chihuahuan Desert. There aren't many flowers, which is the reason why I notice them at all. They arrive in tiny patches, or sometimes as a single bloom a few steps off the shoulder. Mostly, endlessly, I see sand. Sand and scrub brush, a vista stretching toward small hills at the end point of our 230-mile journey from Juárez to the state capital. I sit shotgun. Francisco's behind the wheel of his fully armored Ford Explorer, a mobile panic room. Steel plates line every inch of the vehicle. (Almost every inch. *Sicarios* in Juárez have enough experience with armored vehicles by now to have learned that the door locks, the little circles where you stick the key, are vulnerable. If a couple dozen bullets are fired into the keyhole, at least a few of those bullets can reach the driver.) The armor is so heavy that, after I climbed into my seat, I struggled to swing my door closed. The bulletproof windows are too thick to roll down more than an inch. At a toll booth, Francisco can only push his pesos to the attendant, who must stand on her toes to grab the cash. The fuel economy of this tank? Maybe four miles to the gallon. If Francisco presses a button on his keychain, steel bolts shoot through the doors, locking them shut as securely as a bank safe. His bodyguard trails in a second SUV, also armored.

We're headed to the capital to lobby politicians, though that's not the stated purpose for the trip. Officially we're driving a few miles beyond Chihuahua to the small town of Cuauhtémoc, where there are apple orchards, a Mennonite colony transplanted from Manitoba, and a basement-level minor league soccer team Ibarra inherited when he bought the Indios. Ibarra wants to fly the flag, to put in some face time. He'll tell the young players to keep trying, to work hard, and above all not to worry—the Indios aren't going anywhere. From Cuauhtémoc we'll double back to the capital, where Francisco will try, with a sense of desperation, to keep the Indios from going anywhere.

Nothing about Francisco's appearance suggests he's a business leader. There's no corporate in his casual dress. A wrinkled black guayabera embroidered with the Indios logo. Baggy blue jeans. He covers his thin brown hair with an Indios baseball cap, number twelve (Marco's number, though also the number the Indios use to honor their fans, the twelfth man on the field). Francisco is middle-aged, married to a woman he met in grade school. A few extra pounds round his belly and soften the outline of his jaw. If there's anything about his look that indicates authority, it's his beard, a vandyke that gives off a nautical vibe. Put him near water and he could pass for the captain of a shrimp boat. Francisco is nowhere near water, of course. He's in the middle of the desert. He's been here all his life.

"When I was young, I wanted to travel abroad," he tells me. "I wanted to see more of the world. My mother gave me a card. It had a picture on the front and in the picture there was desert. Nothing but sand. Except for this one flower growing. Where God places you, that's where you must do your work."

Sand blows across the highway, swirling close to the blacktop like low-lying fog. The windows of the Explorer are heavily tinted, but the glare is still intense, and I'm glad I remembered to bring my sunglasses. I learned the importance of shades when crossing the Chihuahuan Desert with El Kartel on the long return trip from Monterrey. I dreaded that bus ride, but, aside from the painfully bright sun, it turned out to be not so bad. "The ride back is always easier," advised Mike, the El Kartel capo. "Everybody's tired, nobody has any money left, and the drugs are all gone."

On that trip back, the bus stopped in Chihuahua city at Carnitas el Entronque, a roadside vendor of deep-fried everything. Pig, cow, chicken, and who knows what else bubbled in giant vats of brown oil. Tripe—cow intestines—bobbed to the top of the vats, poked back into the oil by wooden paddles the size of boat oars. When the flesh crackled with crispness, workers used giant metal tongs to pull the meats from the vats. These body parts were served still oozing hot oil. *No quiero, gracias.* No way, Jose. While El Kartel ate, I checked out Chihuahua. The capital is a lot cleaner than Juárez. It's more modern, too. Expensive cars—BMW, Audi, Acura—sparkle in lots lining the highway. Dealership signs battle American chain restaurants for attention. The city looks so gringo that smugglers paid to slip Guatemalans across the U.S. border have been caught dropping them off in the capital and telling them they'd made it to Texas. On the northern edge of town, a series of banners advertise new houses built by Grupo Yvasa, the Ibarra family construction company.

Francisco Ibarra's father moved to Juárez in the 1950s. He was a young man from the coastal state of Sonora, the owner of nothing more than an engineering degree and a hunger to earn his fortune. Juárez was much smaller back then, a frontier, a place where a hustler could try just about anything. (Which it still is. "Juárez is the second world," Francisco tells me. "It's not settled, it's not the first world like El Paso or Mexico City. There are more opportunities.") His father started out selling bread by the side of the road. He saved up enough money to open a food stand, Tacos El Campeón, which remains in the family. He tapped gold when he ventured into construction. His Grupo Yvasa homes are not luxurious accommodations. I spent New Year's Eve in an Yvasa house located in a dirt-road subdivision maybe seven miles from the Indios' practice facility. The house, listed as a two-bedroom with a front yard, looked more like a subdivided studio apartment. A kitchen stove and sink shared a living room with enough space for a couch and a portable television but too small to add even a table. Winter air rushed through gaps between the walls and the ceiling; I've built snow forts that were more substantial. Yet that house and countless houses just like it sold as fast as they could be built. The North American Free Trade Agreement, enacted in 1994, moved Mexico from an agrarian peasant economy to a system dependent upon manufacturing. Jobs harvesting the fields of Michoacán transferred to the maquiladoras along the Texas border. Migrants in search of factory work, hardly wealthy, needed somewhere to live. The poorest squatted in tar-paper shantytowns up in the hills. Those with some means—the house where I partied on New Year's Eve is rented by a nurse from Puebla—moved into the kinds of homes Yvasa slapped together in one subdivision after another. As their business grew, the Ibarras began winning lucrative government contracts to lay highways, pump water, and build still more houses on choice city land.

When Francisco Ibarra was young, his father pushed him to study engineering. Francisco earned a degree, but construction never made his heart thump—not the way a mere sport, soccer, always has. Rather than join Grupo Yvasa, Francisco volunteered with the Cobras, back then the city's new professional team. He broadcast their games over airwaves he rented on a local AM station. Francisco stayed in radio even after the Cobras quickly folded. Grupo Yvasa's fattening bank accounts allowed him to buy a station outright. He diversified from there into television. Francisco anchored sports highlights on the Channel 6 nightly news. He also hosted a weekly sports roundup, then added a show on social issues, *Nuestra Gente*—Our People. Remarkably soon, he found himself managing all of Chihuahua for Televisa, one of the country's big networks. He was encouraged to rise higher, maybe move to Mexico City. He turned the offers down. He had found success in a field for which he had never trained, and had pursued on instinct. He saw no reason not to follow his latest instinct, to bring soccer back to the border.

It wasn't really a business decision, he tells me. Buying a soccer team, like broadcasting, was just something he wanted to do. It was to be his gift to his hometown, which was ready to take the next step in its maturation. Largely because of NAFTA, Juárez had rapidly grown into the fifth-most-populous city in Mexico, yet Juarenses still had to travel all the way to Monterrey to watch the national sport played at its highest level. When Francisco asked his father for money to buy the minor league team that would become the Indios, his father saw no reason not to give it to him. Francisco had a track record of entrepreneurial success. A soccer team looked like a solid investment. Neither man imagined the team might fail.

Everything about the Indios was to be new. Modern. Francisco knew that in a city of migrants, with loyalties forged in other towns, the Indios would start out as everyone's second-favorite team. To create new bonds, he wanted his team to sport a contemporary look.

His logo would not feature medieval shields or Olde English letter-ing. The cartoonish image he chose, in a nod to the native Tarahu-mara who first inhabited Juárez, was a red bandanna wrapped like a sash around a soccer ball. He really likes the way it looks. Keep-ing one hand on the wheel as he drives, Francisco points a finger at the patch on his guayabera, showing me how the logo's soccer ball is angled so it looks as if the ball's black squares are the eyes and mouth of a fan screaming support. Below the ball, the Indios' name is spelled out in all caps, the letters slanted, shaded, and futuristic.

"It's fresh, it's new, it's a new positive image even for kids," he tells me. "It works on so many levels."

Success on the field didn't arrive immediately. The new team played its first season down in Pachuca, waiting for Ibarra to green Olympic Stadium with new grass imported from Phoenix. The owner replaced aluminum bleachers with individual bucket seats. The upgrades cost serious money, yet Francisco viewed the im-provements as mere stopgaps. Only two years after buying the team, as reporters continued to mock his ambitions of rising to the Primera, Francisco announced plans for an entirely *new* Indios home field. A modern stadium, one of the finest in the country. At a press conference, flanked by the mayor of Ciudad Juárez and the governor of Chihuahua, Francisco circulated digital renderings of the new facility. The reporters gawked at a perfect rectangle of natural grass striped with horizontal lines. Some forty thousand individual seats climbing skyward in three tiers. A huge electronic scoreboard to replay game highlights. Two levels of luxury skyboxes provided the truest big-league touch, each box furnished with red leather couches and ottomans, glass coffee tables, flat-screen tele-visions, and white vases sprouting decorative tufts of green grass. Everything was a go, Francisco announced as the politicians nodded their heads. Blueprints approved. Land acquired, permits issued, fund-ing obtained.

It was February 2008. By the end of the year, some sixteen hun-dred people in Juárez would be killed, more than five times the murder rate two years before. The economy tanked as well, world-wide. What businesses were left to rent those skyboxes? Who would dare visit Juárez with all the bullets flying? At the proposed sta-dium site, not a single shovel ever pierced the sandy ground. And yet right then, right when the violence went baroque, that's when

the Indios played their way into the Primera. That's when they defeated León and when *la gente* took to the streets to serenade their
heroes.

Francisco's advisers encouraged him to sell, immediately. With
promotion to the Primera, the club, on paper, was suddenly worth
more than $25 million. Ibarra had spent only about $2 million on
the Indios to that point, and operationally, day to day, the club was
losing money, a cash-flow hemorrhage that would only get worse.
The team would start flying to games as far away as the Guatemalan
border. Francisco also needed to start paying his players major league
salaries. Sell the team, he was told, pocket a once-in-a-lifetime return on investment, and move on. Yet Ibarra refused to sell. As the
violence in his hometown grew worse—much worse—he came to
see his team less as a professional sports franchise than as a vital
social program, the one bright spot in a city growing impossibly dangerous.

"I got in for the soccer," Ibarra tells me as we crest a hill and the
state capital comes into view, "but stayed in for the city, for the
people."

The best teams in Mexican soccer are backed by wealthy companies. Monterrey pays its players with brewery money. Club América
and Chivas and Monarcas and Santos are basically flagships for
their owners, the big television networks. Most of the smaller teams
get by on government aid. Chiapas. San Luis. Atlante used to play
in Mexico City until the state of Quintana Roo paid them to relocate to Cancún. Juárez's Mayor Reyes Ferriz believes the Indios
deserve public support, too. He's diverted thousands of tax dollars
to Francisco's team and has promised to donate thousands more.
"Are they a charity?" Reyes Ferriz asked me when I met him in his
office overlooking El Paso. "Absolutely. They do more good for this
city than almost anyone else." The governor of Chihuahua, though,
sees things differently. "The Indios are not a charity," the governor
has stated, denying repeated requests for financial aid. "They're a
business."

Francisco is driving to Chihuahua city to argue that the team *is*
a charity. In interviews, he always calls the Indios a social project.
He's hung banners at the stadium—Olympic Stadium, the team's
home indefinitely—stating that the Indios are "more than a club."
It's a slogan cribbed from FC Barcelona, the most famous team in

the world, a club that cedes the valuable space on the fronts of their
jerseys to the charity UNICEF. (Or did for years. The team recently
sold out to Qatar.) Francisco doesn't talk about all the money he
left on the table when the Indios rose to the Primera—I found that
out from someone else in Grupo Yvasa. It's not public knowledge
that his father, frustrated by the fiscal bleeding, has withdrawn all
of his financial support, leaving Francisco to save the Indios by
himself. The owner talks only about why he continues to fight for
the team in the face of all economic reason. Indios games, he points
out, are the only time Juárez is mentioned on the national news
without preceding the word "murder" or "execution" or "bloody."

"I hear thousands of daily stories about how the Indios have
helped someone out," Francisco tells me as we roll toward the capital. "These stories are very dramatic. It puts a huge pressure on
me." As he speaks, a motor coach slips past our SUV, the bus
wrapped in an advertisement for a gubernatorial candidate. There
will be a major election on July 4. The governor who won't fund the
Indios will leave office soon thereafter, a victim of term limits.
Francisco's headed to the capital to lobby the men most likely to
take the governor's place, candidates of both major political parties. When Francisco first bought the Indios, he imagined the team
would take up maybe 20 percent of his time. Since the violence
started, the ratio has inverted. The Indios are taking up 80, maybe
90, percent of his day, he says. Most of that time is spent on the
phone with senators and state representatives or, when necessary,
on the highway traveling to Chihuahua city and back. He's searching for a politician—for anyone, really—who views the team the
way he does, and who is willing to spend whatever it takes to make
that vision a reality.

"I feel much responsibility to the people of Juárez," Francisco
says. "A huge responsibility. A responsibility that no one gave me
but myself. When I started Indios, it was just for me. It's not just for
me anymore."

"THE SOCIAL MISSION is probably more important than the soccer,
honestly," says Gil Cantú, the Indios' general manager. The first
time I saw Gil, at a practice the first week I began following the
team, I could tell he was in charge. With Francisco Ibarra out hus-

tling up government support, it's Gil who runs things day to day. He walked onto the practice field looking and acting like the most grown-up guy around. He wears his silver hair slicked back from his forehead until it curls onto his shoulders. His wool coat is the same solid black as his dress shirt, his wrinkle-free flat-front slacks, and the dress shoes he shines to a high gloss. Reporters buzzed around him that morning, recording his thoughts on the future of the Indios, on whether or not head coach Pepe Treviño blows smoke, on the weather itself—freezing cold—and on the general health of the team. His every response appeared in the papers the next day. That first time I saw him, as I admired his straight-up posture and the elegance of his clothes, I extrapolated a host of suave details about his life. I bet his wife is beautiful. I imagined he drove an Italian car of some sort, or perhaps a Porsche. I wasn't yet aware of the upside-down car culture in Juárez, how the last thing anybody would drive is something flashy.

"That game against Monterrey, to be honest with you, that was a disaster," Gil tells me now. I'm back in Juárez, riding shotgun once again, this time in the car Gil actually drives, an old Pontiac minivan with Texas plates. It's a Thursday afternoon, five days after the Monterrey loss and three days before the next game, at home against Santos. The Indios just wrapped a light practice at Olympic Stadium, a venue change from their usual workouts at the Yvasa complex, on the far south side. Gil insists that the team practice at the stadium at least once in the week before a home game. He wants the players familiar with the way the pitch gently slopes for drainage from the center of the field to the sidelines. Marco and his teammates can study the bounce of the ball on the weather-bleached (though still spongy) turf. A lot of the players prefer to practice at the Benito, simply for the commute; the stadium is located a lot closer to home for most of them. With training wrapped up, Marco hops in his *fronterizo* for the ten-minute drive to his house. Gil and I are headed to the border. I'm flying back to Miami in the morning to attend a wedding. I plan to return to Juárez in my car, which will be loaded down with the rest of everything I own. My flight leaves from El Paso, where Gil lives. He's agreed to take me across the bridge and drop me off at a hotel near the airport.

"It was a disaster," he continues, still rehashing the Rayados loss. "The players gave up. Mistakes from three players were unforgivable. Maybe they had a bad day. That happens. When the whole team plays bad, that's a leadership issue."

Gil's full title is vice president of soccer operations. He's part of the four-person politburo—Gil, Francisco, Coach Treviño, and traveling secretary Gabino Amparán—who collectively make the big decisions. Like when to release a player, or when to bring in a new fullback to patch a hole in the defense. Finding talent is primarily Gil's responsibility, and it's the hardest part of his job. The Indios are the poorest team in the Primera. They don't make enough money from ticket sales or merchandizing or beer sales on game days—even with El Kartel in the stands—to pursue the talented but expensive players needed to seriously compete. All morning, I listened to Gil work the phones to Guatemala, where he has a lead on an economical forward. Last night he made a couple calls to China. Gil scours the globe because with the Indios there are complications beyond simple economics. Gil must find players who are talented, affordable, and, above all else, willing to play in Ciudad Juárez.

"I had one player from Atlas loaned to us," Gil tells me as he drives. Atlas is another team in the Primera. "I talked to him on the phone and he said, 'Okay.' And then he called me back and he says he talked to his wife and she said, 'No way.' So he's going to play for a club below the Primera, at a much smaller level. And that's what I've got to confront. I tell you, brother, I'm so busy."

We're on a highway that follows the curve of the international border. The boundary fence, a tall black grille, shades a berm just off the shoulder, on our left. Our immediate destination is Zaragoza, one of the four bridges connecting Juárez and El Paso. This will be my first visit to this particular bridge. The Zaragoza was built to serve the American trucks picking up car batteries and seat belts at NAFTA maquiladoras. It's also a favorite bridge of everyday international commuters like Gil, who's purchased a credential that allows him to pass through customs quicker than other drivers. Even with his speed pass, the fifteen-mile drive from the Indios' training complex to Gil's house in El Paso can take an hour and a half on days when the bridge is clean, meaning traffic isn't backed up. If there's a bust? If customs spots a pickup truck with cocaine sewn into the seat cushions or tucked behind its door panels? Add another hour or even two.

"It's not that dangerous in Juárez," Gil opines, slipping into what is obviously his recruiting sales pitch. "Just live in good neighborhoods, stick to main roads. You can live here just fine. Ask Edwin [Santibáñez, the offensive midfielder]. He's been with us the whole time, and he's fine. Ask Marco—he's been with us for years and he's fine, too. We tell them we're right next to El Paso, where their wives can go shopping. No other team can offer that. We tell them they'll be safe if they take proper precautions, but some of them, their wives step in. We lose so many [prospects] so often I no longer count. South American, Mexican. They turn us down right away or their agent says, 'You know what, I'm not going to let him play in Juárez.' But Juárez is not only violence, I tell them. There are good sections of town."

I don't know about that. Judging by the map on my wall, I'd say nowhere in Juárez appears immune from the killing. There are obvious trouble spots, like bloody Colonia Altavista, where Maleno Frías grew up. But I've read about murders in Campestre, an upscale community built around a golf course. Colonia Nogales, where I live, is supposedly one of the better parts of town, yet two people have been murdered already on my very street (though thankfully not on my block). The Mexican grocery chain S-Mart is the Indios' main sponsor, their logo the biggest image on the team jerseys. Someone shot two people outside the S-Mart closest to my apartment, where I continue buying my tortillas. These murders have not been isolated incidents. A car waiting in line for gas at the station two blocks from my home was pumped with bullets fired by automatic weapons, the driver slain as morning commuters whizzed down López Mateos. Five diners were assassinated at a Chinese restaurant across the street from that gas station. It's very hard to deny that Juárez—everywhere in Juárez—is violent like nowhere else.

Before I got here, I figured all the players on the team lived in El Paso, for safety. None of them actually do. Not one. Crossing is too much of a hassle. There was one kid in the Indios' youth program who tried commuting for a while. The youth teams play their games immediately after the regular Indios games, in stadiums emptied of fans. So many kids are trying to climb up through the

system that their jerseys display absurd numbers as high as 168 or
even 217. They don't interact with the players on the big club very
often, but sometimes they'll be at the training complex at the same
time, practicing on the other of the two full-size fields. I was sitting
on the bleachers one morning when a kid named Jorge approached
and asked if I spoke English. He told me he was from Phoenix. His
dad had played professionally for the Cobras, and he, Jorge, had recently dropped out of high school to follow his father's path. Even
though his father was Mexican, Jorge didn't speak any Spanish. That
seemed more tragic to me than his decision to drop out of school.

"Have you seen any bodies yet?" he asked. He'd seen two, and he'd
only been with the organization about a month. He saw his first body
in the street outside the house he shared with some other prospects.
The second body landed on the very doorstep of that house. Jorge had
to hop over the body to get outside. His parents immediately moved
him to El Paso. Jorge told me the commute wasn't working out that
well. A little while later he quit the team altogether.

This makes Gil the only one in the organization who pulls it off.
(Francisco Ibarra lives in El Paso, but he's not a regular commuter;
he's visited the practice compound only once this season.) Although Gil was born in Monterrey, he's an American citizen, and
has been for a while. "You can really see your tax dollars at work in
El Paso," he has told me. "You see it every day in things like trash
pickup, electricity, water. You can live in a very comfortable way. I
got an offer for another job down in Cancún, but I don't want to
leave El Paso."

More than ten thousand cars and trucks cross the Zaragoza
Bridge every day. When we pull up to the bridge, I notice the road
forks in two. Gil steers his passenger car to the left, away from
maybe two hundred tractor trailers lined up on the right. There are
a lot of cars ahead of us. Gil's Pontiac rolls to a stop because of the
traffic, so I grab my duffel bag, get out of the minivan, and tell Gil
I'll see him on the other side—he's not allowed to take a passenger
with him through the express line. A pedestrian walkway arcs
over the Rio Grande. The river is mostly dry, just a small stream of
water I could probably leap across if I had to. As I walk, I study the
long line of trucks. Swift. Mesilla Valley Transportation. A couple
flatbeds carrying neat stacks of two-by-fours. The trucks (and also
the passenger cars) are backed up as far as I can see. This isn't the

clean bridge Gil was hoping for. I veer to the left with the passenger cars. As I approach the gates where customs officers inspect each car before letting it into El Paso, I notice that all but one of the seven tollbooth-ish bays have been cleared. Steel gates affixed with stop signs have been lowered across every lane, preventing any cars from moving forward. Only one car remains in a bay, a white Ford Taurus. I count sixteen officers standing around the car, staring at it. I think we have a bust. No one's getting through for a while.

No one behind a wheel, that is. I'm one of only ten pedestrians on the bridge, and I pass through customs quickly, without incident. Gil is so far back I can't even see him, so I walk over to a parking lot, prepared to wait for a while. BIENVENIDO A LOS ESTADOS UNIDOS DE AMERICA, states a sign. I'm back in my home country, for the first time in a month. I smell the air. *Is it any different?* I see only sand and blacktop and a couple scrubby trees without leaves. No stores or houses have developed the land near this bridge, so it's hard to make a comparison between the countries. I wait more than an hour for Gil to clear customs. When he finally pulls up, I open the passenger-side door and reclaim my front seat. Gil and I drive into Texas together.

"Juárez is a city where you find a job easily," he says, sounding like he's still on his sales pitch. I'm astonished at his focus. "You find a school easily. You have the blessing of being close to the U.S., which really is a blessing. And Juárez is a beautiful land, a beautiful atmosphere. And the people are a warm people, always willing to receive a person regardless of where they're from. That's the difference of Juárez. Once you get here, you feel from here, like you've been living here forever."

We merge onto I-10, traveling at high speed for five minutes until we exit the highway at Lee Trevino Drive, named after the professional golfer. We roll past gas stations and budget hotels, heading deeper into the safety and security of El Paso, where Gil, for all his kind words about Juárez, has lived for years. He pulls his Pontiac into the parking lot of my hotel, turning to ask me when I'm coming back. Will I need to be picked up at the airport? I'll return in a week, I reply, and thanks, but a ride won't be necessary. I'm driving back in my car.

"Your car?!" he cries. "You're bringing back your car? To Juárez? Are you crazy? They'll hunt you like a deer! They'll figure out where you live and your routine. You'll be nervous every night, brother. I would not do that if I were you!"

I'VE GOT AN evening to kill in El Paso. Wonderful. How exciting. After I check in at the hotel, I stroll a few blocks down a wide commercial street called Montana Avenue. I like walking around cities, but there isn't much for me to see out here, marooned near the airport. I find an elementary school. I find strip-mall cell-phone and clothing stores and a gas station parked next to a Burger King. I enter the restaurant and buy a Whopper, ordering in Spanish like everyone else. I take my time eating. When I finish, I duck into the gas station to buy a can of Bud Light and Clamato for tonight (I'm acquiring a taste) and a small protein shake to save for breakfast before my six A.M. flight. I wince at the bill: seven dollars, for what would cost me no more than three dollars in Juárez. All this safety costs money.

"There's a little violence in El Paso like anywhere else," Gil said in the car. "But I don't need to put bars on my windows or anything. It's a very safe place. It's a very good city. It's calm. When I want action I take my wife and kids to Disneyland and that's it, brother."

El Paso *is* safe. City officials constantly—and I mean *constantly*—repeat that El Paso is the third-safest city in the entire United States. Bring up the ongoing bloodbath in Juárez and they'll ask what is this Juárez of which you speak? Is it a city in Mexico or something? Then they'll point out that in El Paso last year not even ten people were killed, a fraction of 1 percent of the annual slaughter taking place in—what city was that again? Juárez?

It certainly is quieter in El Paso. Walking back to the hotel from the gas station, I don't feel the slightest threat. My stomach is distended slightly, unclenched for the first time in a month. Which doesn't make me feel good, necessarily. *It's boring in the United States.* That's my impression upon my return. Isn't that a queer way to feel? *I wish I was back in the world murder capital, where life is—what—spicier?* Maybe I just wish I wasn't in El Paso. It's not even eight o'clock and the town is asleep. People in Juárez stay in at night because of the cartels and the killing. People in El Paso stay in by choice, I guess because they have nothing better to do.

Montana Avenue and the airport and my hotel all sit high on a ridge that rises quick and steep from the bed of the Rio Grande. Looking over the ridge, Juárez is most of what I see. Yellow streetlights mark López Mateos and Manuel Gómez Morin and other avenues I'm pleased I can identify on sight. I see the soccer stadium. Even in the dark I can make out the mountain exhorting me in Spanish to READ THE BIBLE, IT'S THE TRUTH. A wind starts in the valley. It blows over my apartment in Colonia Nogales. The wind rushes across the river, past the guard dogs of the Border Patrol, up and over I-10 before it buffets my jacket and my face. I wince to protect my eyes. Gil doesn't want to live down there, in Juárez. He doesn't think I should even drive down there. Francisco Ibarra *does* want to live there, but, for his safety, he now lives in El Paso just like Gil. Before Francisco was born, his mother had suggested she give birth in Texas. Why not? American citizenship might come in handy someday. "No!" Francisco's father barked. "We are Mexicans!" Francisco never even studied English, and still can't speak it. Yet he now lives in the United States. In El Paso. Across the river from where his flower was planted.

I'M IN MIAMI when the Indios host Santos. The game is touted as a geographic rivalry, *el clásico del norte*, but Santos's home city of Torreón and Juárez don't really have much in common, and with almost five hundred miles between them, the two teams aren't exactly crosstown rivals. Still, it's a game everyone has been anticipating. Santos is a good club, but they're not a *great* club, of, say, Monterrey's caliber. Like the Indios, Santos is relatively new to the Primera. Newer teams are the most likely to fall back down to the minors. If the Indios are going to be the squad that stays up, Santos is exactly the kind of team they need to beat. It helps that the Indios are healthy and rested. Olympic Stadium is hosting the border's first home game of the new season. The chances of an Indios victory are about as high as they'll ever be.

I watch the game at a friend's apartment in Miami Beach, two blocks from the ocean. I'm wearing shorts and a T-shirt. A soft breeze rustles palm fronds outside open windows. Tuning in to Televisa Azteca on a small set, I'm jarred to see how cold it still is in Juárez. The same sun warming Miami is shining on Juárez, too, but the colors of the border are muted, whites and blacks and dark grays that almost aren't colors at all. Fans shiver in puffy parkas, knit hats stretching over ears. The cold slows down the run of play, as if the ball were covered in frost. No score through halftime. Marco is in the game, looking fine.

Midway into the second half, a Santos player commits a hard foul that draws a red card; the referee sends the offender to the locker room. Santos must play a man down the rest of the game. Television cameras pan the bleachers, where El Kartel bounces in excitement. What an opportunity! The Indios are at home. They have a man advantage. Plenty of minutes remain on the clock. "Now is the time for the Indios!" the announcer bellows. Yet the Indios never put the ball in the net. They don't even come close. The final score, 0–0, feels like a loss. The next Sunday, down in Mexico City, the Indios lose outright to the Eagles of Club América, a team regarded in Mexico the way Americans regard the Dallas Cowboys. The final score is 1–0. It's the Indios' third-straight game without a goal. Club América wins despite missing its star striker. Six days before the game, in a Mexico City nightclub called Bar Bar, someone shot the player in the head. He fell into a coma. The gunman got away. Because Juárez was coming to town, national journalists speculated the shooting may have been a cartel-related hit.

CHAPTER 4

The Game

IT TAKES THREE DAYS TO DRIVE back to Juárez. My hatchback is crammed so full I can't see out my rearview mirror. I'm bringing to the border every single thing I own in the world. All my clothes—jeans, socks, T-shirts, dress shirts, suits I never wear, winter coats, a raincoat, every shoe, everything. I've got books, a portable safe protecting my tax records and birth certificate, essential pots and pans, decent computer speakers, cell-phone cables, and my Memory Hole, a small box containing photos and cards and scrap-paper reminders of who I am and what I've been through. I feel whole once again, a man reunited with his possessions.

The road trip starts early on a Sunday morning, a week before the Super Bowl. The game will be played in Miami. Ocean Drive's pink sidewalks already overflow with fans of the New Orleans Saints, a team making its first-ever appearance in the championship game. The sports punditry contends the Saints' success is the best thing to happen to New Orleans in the four and a half years since the destruction of Hurricane Katrina. They're probably right. All the Saints banners and bumper stickers and flags I see on the road make an impression. Fans declare themselves at the gas stations and fast-food restaurants where I refuel. When I cross into Louisiana, cries of "Who dat?" pour from every station on the radio. Every station: gospel, jazz, public, Cajun, hard rock. A city and a state are excited, united. It's rousing, evidence that a sports team really can lift the mood of a depressed city. I find myself authentically pumped up by the time I stop for the night in Baton Rouge. In my roadside hotel room, I fall into bed and turn on the news, primed to enjoy a few minutes of proudly biased Saints hype. I find instead the worst story out of Juárez yet.

Just before midnight on Saturday night, seven SUVs sealed off a street in the working-class neighborhood of Salvarcar, not far from the Indios' practice facility. More than a dozen gunmen stormed out of the trucks, showering bullets on a house where teenagers were celebrating a sports victory by their high school team. At least fourteen people were killed. The youngest victim to be identified so far was only thirteen years old. In images flashing across the television screen, blood drips down walls and pools on the house's concrete floor. Neighbors had called the police, but no officers or soldiers arrived until well after the shooting had stopped and the killers had driven off. These neighbors believe the shooting was a mistake of some kind. The victims, they insist, were good and responsible kids. Mexican president Felipe Calderón disagrees. The man who made Juárez the key battleground in his declared war on cartels states that the massacre must have been "a settling of accounts" between drug dealers, an insensitive and inaccurate remark for which he soon offers his "most heartfelt apology."

Massacres happen in Juárez. It's only been a few months since gunmen shot up a drug rehabilitation clinic in El Centro, killing seventeen. Two weeks after that massacre, shooters outside yet another drug rehabilitation clinic slaughtered ten more. Those mass murders, as horrible as they were—surely some innocents were gunned down—could be written off as cartel thugs killing cartel thugs, the social cleansing Calderón reflexively invoked with the students. But the details of this latest massacre are so horrific, and the victims so universally believed to be blameless, that the slaughter rises above the *ruido blanco* of ten anonymous murders a day. President Calderón eventually declares the massacre a national tragedy. "Ciudad Juárez," says an anchor on a Spanish-language network I flip to in my Louisiana hotel room, the anchor shaking his head and biting his lip at the end of his broadcast.

I reach Texas the next morning. My overloaded car shoots through Hill Country on my way to the flat and endless western half of the state. I drive all day and into the night, but I only reach Ozona, still three hundred miles from El Paso. I pull into a highway motel, my phone vibrating with text messages and phone calls from friends and worried family members. Black humor abounds: "Stay away from high school parties!" jokes a colleague. "I hear Juárez is nice this time of year," writes a college friend who'd reconnected on Facebook and who thought my announced return to Mexico meant Acapulco or Puerto Vallarta. I reach El Paso the next day, not long after lunch, scared once again. It's the same generalized fear I felt when I first crossed the bridge in December. What in the world am I getting into? I haven't forgotten that Juárez, day to day, can seem mundane, like any other city. But part of me somewhere in my subconscious expects to be shot as soon as I cross the border.

I am not shot. When I cross, nothing happens at all. I drive over the Bridge of the Americas, otherwise known as the Free Bridge because there are no tolls. My car, visibly overloaded with all my possessions, is not stopped for inspection, not even for guns. No one checks my passport. I'm well into Mexico before I know it. I pass the statue of Abraham Lincoln, a supporter of city namesake Benito Juárez. A roadside vendor hands me a copy of *PM* I shoot down López Mateos to the Rio Grande Mall and then finally to my apartment. My car is unloaded at great speed—perhaps a bit too quickly, in my paranoia. When I'm done I lock the car in the gated lot that was a big reason why I signed a lease in this complex. I lock myself inside my apartment. I start to arrange my stuff. It's good to be home?

I MISS MIAMI immediately. When I step out of my car at the Grupo Yvasa complex the next morning, a puff of white exhaust forms in front of my face. It's cold—early February. I've voluntarily traded the warm breezes of Florida for the Indios' gray and icy practice facility. The two fields where the team trains have been wedged onto a large construction yard. Marco cycles through a passing drill before a backdrop of conveyor belts, water towers, and a herd of aboveground gas tanks. Dump trucks and bulldozers grind among enormous piles of sand and rocks of different muted colors. When the wind blows from the gravel toward the fields, as it is doing today, the air tastes acidic, like the prongs of a nine-volt battery.

Thick stone walls barricading the yard remind me of a colonial fortress. The walls stand some fifteen feet high and are topped with

an extra few yards of chain-link fence and two strings of concertina
wire snagged with plastic grocery bags. I scaled the walls once just
to see what was behind them. I found a maze of houses the size of
jail cells, rebar sticking out of their roofs and laundry strung across
plots of dirt that pass for front yards. It's a humble subdivision very
much like Villas de Salvarcar, where the students were killed. Alongside the houses sit two auto-body graveyards crammed with row
after row of dead cars and pickup trucks, many having been shot
into submission by up to seventy bullets each.

Old and sun-bleached plastic banners hang on the fortress walls,
facing the playing fields. Two banners shout the single word HUE-
VOS! The word literally means "eggs," which in this context means
"balls," in the genital sense, which means, essentially, *Play tough*.
There's a banner paid for by the city government and another banner advertising Grupo Yvasa. This last banner features a slogan the
company uses to advertise the houses it builds: WHERE DO YOU
WANT TO LIVE? How many would say Juárez? Ramón in the media
office laughs at me when I check in, as if he can't believe I actually
came back. Wendy, a woman who works in sales, kisses me on the
cheek and declares my return *un milagro*, a miracle.

I watch Marco run through strength and endurance drills, trying to sprint across the field while anchored to a weighted sled. The
exercises progress at a rapid clip: A juggling contest. More sprints.
Now shots on net. I'm a bit surprised by the efficiency of the drills.
After poor results in the last two games, I expected to witness a lazy
workout, but that's not the case. The coaches still command respect.
The players continue to work hard. Pepe Treviño blows a whistle to
start a half-field scrimmage. The *futbolistas* left out of the lineups
jog laps around the pitch. I walk over to greet the usual scrum of
reporters.

"You heard about the students, yes?" asks a reporter from *El
Mexicano*, one of the daily papers covering the team. We still don't
know the reason for the massacre. *El Diario*—the best newspaper
in town—speculated in print that one of the murdered students
had witnessed a shooting, and so had become a target. This theory
has not yet been confirmed, and is not generally believed. The government claims the ringleader of the massacre has been killed in a
firefight. Another suspect, paraded before television cameras, con-
fesses his involvement. He helpfully admits that the shooters acci-

dentally targeted the wrong house—a comforting closure only if anyone, anywhere, really thought the suspect was involved.

"No way," chuckles a newspaper reporter. We all laugh, as if it's funny. The ringleader killed? Too convenient. This guy confessing his involvement? Then why is there still a million-peso reward offered for the killers? Mistaken identity remains our best guess, though. We think the killers shot up the wrong house.

"I live in Salvarcar," says a photographer, referring to the neighborhood where the massacre went down. That's not a choice address. These reporters don't make much money covering the team. Few of them are even journalists in the traditional sense. Only the beat writer from *El Diario* shows consistent initiative and an independent voice. The rest of the guys, for the most part, type up the story released each day by the Indios' press office, sometimes simply reprinting the release in their papers. One photographer has told me he needs no more than ten minutes to capture his pictures for the day. For the remaining three hours of practice, he's just hanging out on the grass, talking to his colleagues and watching young men run around. Even if it's freezing cold, even if the air tastes like battery acid, it's still better behind these stone walls than it is out in the city. Or even inside his own home.

When practice ends, I congratulate Marco on his return to the starting lineup. "Anything happen in my absence?" I ask. He recaps the last two games. The Indios played much better, he insists. It was simply unlucky that the goalies for both Santos and Club América had happened to rise to a world-class level. He does not mention the Student Massacre or President Calderón, who is so chagrined by his own comments in the wake of the massacre that he's flying up to the border to apologize to the families in person. Marco has bragged to me that he never reads the newspapers and has not once watched the local news on bloody Channel 44. He remains in his soccer bubble, willfully ignorant of the game being played around him, outside the walls.

ATOP FRANKLIN MOUNTAIN, looking down from the bleacher seats, it's one big pitch. One giant brown field stretching on and on until the horizon dissipates in the haze. Shoebox-shaped factories. Little tan *casas* with gray-shingled roofs. Scrawny trees that, from on high, look like tumbleweeds. There's the BIBLE IS REAL, READ IT! sign that's definitely in Juárez. Closer are the tall buildings of downtown El Paso, banks mostly, the house collecting vigorish off every bet. One has to really strain to make out the line. It's down there, beyond the interstate, past the railroad tracks. A denuded slash, all sand and concrete. The chalky marker where the playing field begins.

El Paso is the sidelines. A safe zone, out of bounds. Team captains—*importers/exporters, ha-ha*—cruise to their West Side mansions in the Hummers and BMWs that have been banned from the field of play. The linesmen—DEA, FBI, Border Patrol, Secret Service, CIA, National Guard, Army—keep their flags down, never calling offsides, since no one brings the game over the bridge. El Paso is for rest, for safety. "It's much easier for them to commit their crimes in Juárez and get away with it," El Paso County sheriff Richard Wiles said when asked why his city is so secure. More than fifty thousand wealthy Mexicans have moved to El Paso in the past three years. These are the elite. Even Juárez mayor Reyes Ferriz lives here, quietly socializing with the clubhouse attendants, the pillars of El Paso and Juárez, "honest" businessmen who pocket the spare change found when washing the laundry of the home team, or the visitors, or both if they can somehow pull it off.

It's crowded in the press box. That's in El Paso, too. Reporters prefer to fly into an American airport and sleep in an American hotel, close to the excitement but protected by all those linesmen and their flags spangled with stars. El Paso has hosted the international press for a hundred years, ever since Pancho Villa raided Juárez in part to impress John Reed, an American war correspondent watching the Mexican Revolution from a sideline seat. Even Armando Cabada broadcasts from El Paso. He's the anchor of the morbid Channel 44 news that Marco refuses to watch. Cabada is prominent and respected. It's not a stretch to call him the Walter Cronkite of Juárez. I prefer to think of him as the Crypt Keeper, because (1) he looks kind of sinister and (2) his newscast is one dead body after another. Cabada decries all the blood. Since the Student Massacre, he's been downright livid. Yet, just as the killings drive readers to the popular *PM* tabloid, there's no denying the dead bodies are great for Channel 44. Cabada calls the play-by-play from his remote studio in El Paso, where he lives and where he's safe.

We've established the teams already. La Línea is in maroon, the home side. The Juárez Cartel. A dynasty playing the game for decades. "You know why they're called La Línea, right?" the Indios' team masseur asked me one afternoon as we shared a lunch. "If you stay on the line you'll be fine, nothing will happen to you. The only people in Juárez who have anything to worry about are those who step off the line." The Juárez Cartel formed in the 1970s, really coming into its own in the 1990s, when its former head coach, Amado Carrillo, chartered jumbo jets to fly his cocaine from Colombia to the border. It helped that Mexico's drug czar was on his payroll. The apparent blessing of Mexico's president helped even more. Carlos Salinas, who held office from 1988 to 1994, has always denied protecting the Juárez Cartel, but there's no doubt his close brother Raúl, a cabinet minister, amassed more than $100 million in cartel protection money. La Línea is still understood to control most local politicians in Juárez. City Hall, the municipal police. The Chihuahua state attorney won't call fouls on its players. When a riot broke out at the Juárez city jail, she ordered surveillance cameras to film only the insurgents that played for the visiting team.

That would be the Sinaloa Cartel. Picture them in uniforms the same navy blue as the federal police, who are believed to be under their control. (Alternate uniforms: green, for the army, which they control, too.) The Sinaloans are dominant upstarts. Their star player is Joaquín "El Chapo" Guzmán, the most wanted man in the world. A drug trafficker hunted everywhere but, it seems, in Mexico. El Chapo bribed his way out of a maximum-security federal prison in 2001, escaping in a laundry cart. Officially, the Mexican government wants him back in jail. There's a five-million-dollar bounty on his head. Yet El Chapo has been seen riding around the state of Chihuahua in caravans protected by the Mexican army. His Sinaloa Cartel has captured lucrative drug routes on the Pacific coast, on the Gulf coast, and in the populous heart of the country. The Sinaloans are said to control eight seaports. Chapo's cartel has even occupied its own hangar at Mexico City's international airport.

It helps that the current president is on Chapo's side. Or seems to be, at the very least. Felipe Calderón is the league commissioner, the man responsible for a level playing field. He won the presidency in 2006 by the very slimmest of margins; some two million protesters insisted the election had been rigged. To show strength, and perhaps to placate the angry masses, Calderon took office promising war on an agreed evil, the cartels. He sent troops to Baja to cripple the Tijuana Cartel. He ordered the army to take down the Beltrán-Leyva Cartel. He won some battles. In almost every victory, the Sinaloans, whom he insists he is also at war with, ended up moving into the coveted territories, growing their cartel ever larger.

"This isn't to say that the president of Mexico has deliberately made a deal with Chapo Guzman," UTEP anthropologist Howard Campbell tells me. "But people below him may have, and the outcome may be about the same."

When Calderón declared his war on cartels, Chapo Guzman stepped up his pursuit of Juárez, the World Cup trophy of drug routes. Juárez has been a smuggling corridor for as long as there's been a border. Even with all the military attention shining on the city, and even with $3.4 billion from the United States government to fight importation, Juárez remains an ideal place to move drugs up to Dallas and Denver and Chicago and Manhattan. La Línea has been vulnerable ever since Amado Carrillo died during plastic surgery, in 1997. (The bodies of the Colombian surgeons who botched the operation were found encased in concrete.) Guzman wants Juárez. The home team refuses to give it up. Last man standing. That's what the fight is. That's the sport being played.

El Chapo's game plan is scorched earth. Kill, burn, behead. Destroy anything in his path. Since the Sinaloans invaded Juárez, some ten thousand stores and restaurants have burned down or been otherwise extorted out of business. An entire roster of La Línea players have been executed or tortured or both. The home team matches this aggression with a spirited counterattack. La Línea foot soldiers shoot Sinaloans and decapitate turncoats who jump like grasshoppers to the other team. The rise in violence is in itself a victory for the visitors. If La Línea can no longer guarantee stability, then there's no reason for the city to tolerate its historically murderous presence. Just give us a winner, the people demand. We just want to get back to work.

The game has raged for three years now. There are no signs it's about to stop, and no shortage of bodies waiting on the benches of both teams. The cartels remain stocked with moonlighting police whose day jobs give them guns and badges but not enough money to live on. These cops fight alongside migrants unable to find honest work in a city with a recession-hammered unemployment rate that has climbed in five years from less than zero—there were more jobs in Juárez than there were people to fill them—to over 20 percent. Even those "lucky" enough to find work in the maquiladoras can earn less than one hundred dollars for six days of labor. It's cheaper to live in Juárez than in El Paso, but not by *that* much. You need to eat. Your kids need to eat. You do what you have to do.

The league commissioner flies up to Juárez on the Thursday after the massacre. I leave practice early to try and catch him, but my car is blocked by traffic when they shut down the Carreterra Panamericana, the main road to the airport. All I can do is watch as Felipe Calderón rolls past in a caravan of Chevrolet Suburbans with heavily tinted windows, long radio antennas, and Mexican tricolors for license plates. First stop, I will later watch on the news, is the Villas de Salvarcar, where the massacre occurred. The president meets with the families of "Los Estudiantes," as the dead have come to be called. "They were good students and good kids," he says. "I'm sorry." Protesters respond with signs stating CALDERON DOESN'T SERVE YOU and CALDERON: FUCK YOUR SYSTEM.

At a convention center near his hotel, the commissioner outlines a new social program, Todos Somos Juárez—"We Are All Juárez"—named so that residents of Monterrey and Toluca feel connected to the border violence. He vows to expand his efforts beyond the military. There will be sports centers for youth, more social programs, and subsidized health care for 25,000 families. He says he'll improve 066, the Mexican version of 911. Free English classes will be taught. The specificity of his promises amazes me. At one point, he vows to start up an orchestra. But even while protesters chant that the soldiers are part of the problem, Calderón also announces he is flying four more military helicopters to the border, to aid his ongoing cartel war. At least 435 additional federal police will join the thousands of soldiers and federal police already patrolling Juárez—troops and police widely believed to be serving the visiting team from Sinaloa. Several women in the convention-center audience stand up and turn their backs.

"As far as I'm concerned, you are not welcome here," a mother of two boys slain in the Student Massacre shouts at Calderón, dramatically standing right in front of him, maybe four feet from his face. "If somebody killed your child, you'd be looking for his murderer."

The audience claps when the mother finishes chewing out their nation's president. Calderón stays quiet in his seat behind a conference table. Functionaries flank his shoulders. Whatever his intentions, whatever his alliances, Calderón is the commissioner of a game with one of the ugliest scoreboards of all time: more than nineteen thousand Mexicans slaughtered since he launched his war. In Juárez, in January alone, 217 fresh kills. Among the dead: fourteen "good students and good kids."

THE SUNDAY OF the game against Monarcas Morelia is the nicest day in Juárez since I've moved here. A bright sun lifts the winter chill. It's still sweater weather—most of the players will take the field for warm-ups in long-sleeved jerseys—yet the air is exceptionally soft for the first week of February, fresh in a way that carries the promise of spring. It feels good to be alive, even to be right here at this particular spot on the map. No clouds blot the bright sky. The trash and broken windows I pass on my walk to the stadium don't seem so ugly. The paint peeling off abandoned houses gives off a shabby-chic sort of vibe, reminiscent of the old palazzos in Venice. Sort of. A little bit.

I watch the game with Gil Cantú. He usually sits in the stands just below the press box, one section over from where Francisco Ibarra sits with his family. Gil's knee twitches during the Mexican national anthem, which always precedes kickoff. "I was up all night worrying about the game," he shares. "If you don't worry, that means you don't care anymore." The Indios come out energized. Edwin and King Kong and Maleno Frías launch sustained attacks on the Monarcas goal. The Indios hold on to the ball for so long, waiting for a defensive mistake, that they seem to be toying with the visitors. It's a cocky performance. Whenever Monarcas do manage to touch the ball, Marco—he's started his third game in a row—calmly squelches their attacks, distributing the ball back to Edwin for another offensive push. TV cameras pan the bleachers where El Kartel waves its flags. My learned pessimism has vanished. The Indios definitely belong in the Primera. Then, seconds before halftime, a Monarcas forward somehow slips an impossible, low-percentage shot past goalie Christian Martínez. That's all they need. That ends up being the final score: 1–0. Another loss.

"They're all on the take," Gil spits, venting to me about the refs. "Bad calls cost us seven points last season. They cost us at least one point today. Probably three! I know for a fact the refs don't want to travel anymore to Ciudad Juárez. No one in the league wants to come to Ciudad Juárez anymore."

The refs? Aren't the Indios losing because they can't score? The players don't appear to have the skills. They *want* to do the right thing. They work hard, in my opinion. I know they practice hard. With Marco on the field, the defense has really tightened up, letting in a total of only two goals in the past three games. But who's stepping up on offense? King Alain N'Kong? No goals. He's grown so predictable I know what he's going to do the moment he touches the ball. Edwin Santibáñez? "Edwin is a fighter," Gil whispered to me before the start of the season. "He deserves to be in the first division, but between you and me he doesn't have the talent." I'm expecting little from this new Guatemalan striker Gil found, whose go-to move is to flop to the ground whenever he's challenged, hoping for a penalty shot. Even favorite son Maleno Frías disappoints. He hasn't scored, either. Nobody has scored.

"I told the ref at halftime, What do we gotta do—buy a TV station?" Gil continues, still arguing for a conspiracy. Monarcas are owned by TV Azteca. "They hate us. We're this city in the desert, the forgotten city in the desert. They take a lot of our tax money and use it to fund the Metro in Mexico City. Government fails us. Police fail us. The [Mexican Football] Federation fails us, too. It's not easy to play this game, but it's even harder when the refs conspire against you. It's us against twelve. It's corrupt to the core."

Gil complains for so long I start to tune him out. Everyone gets bad calls, sir. The Indios could not have streaked to twenty-three games without a win because one corrupt guy on the field carries red and yellow cards in his pocket. If you don't want to lose by one goal, then put two goals in the other net. Score more often than the other team. Play better. "The Federation came up here last season. I told them, 'You cost us four games,'" Gil continues. "Four games the Federation cost us!"

He goes on, drones on. Gil is whining, showing me an unattractive side of his personality. It doesn't matter if I pay attention. I scan the field instead, watching the groundskeepers rip down the goal nets. I look up above the opposing seats to see the towering Mexican tricolor flying on this gorgeous day. It's huge, a *megabandera*, 50 meters long and 28.6 meters wide. It's also a good reminder: I'm not in the United States. I'm in a country where the former president and the drug czar were in the pocket of La Línea. I'm in a country where the current president, wittingly or not, is helping the Sinaloa Cartel take over this strategically valuable city. Mexico is where Chapo Guzmán, the most wanted man in the world, can escape from a maximum security prison with the laundry, and where he can live in relative freedom despite a five-million-dollar bounty on his head. Why wouldn't Gil believe there was a conspiracy? Is his reasoning really so irrational?

"Conspiracy?" laughs Sofia, Ken-tokey's girlfriend. "The players just don't want it bad enough. They don't give their all out there." Sofia's standing with the rest of El Kartel in the parking lot on the west side of the stadium, along the fence protecting the team bus and the small pen where reporters interview the players after the game. I've left Gil to enter the pen. Marco took a tumble in the second half that was so serious he had to rest on the sideline for a few minutes. He returned to the pitch, but I still want to see if he's okay. While I wait, El Kartel grows more animated. They are chanting for Pepe Treviño's head. My sobriety after watching the game with Gil—he was on the job, and he doesn't drink anyway—allows me to notice how wasted El Kartel has gotten. Ken-tokey and Kinkin and several others rattle the fence. The chain links shake with enough violence that a soldier standing near me grabs what looks like a sawed-off shotgun and pulls the trigger. A canister the size of a twelve-ounce beer arcs over the fence.

Hey, that must be tear gas, I think as the canister falls onto the parking lot. A Kartelero picks up the can and tosses it back over the fence, into the pen where I'm standing. The white trail that follows the can reminds me of a comet, or an Independence Day smoke bomb. It's kind of pretty.

Tear gas paralyzes lungs, making it impossible to breathe. "Irritates" is too mild a word for what the gas does to my eyes. It's so painful, so quickly, I find myself mad at the officer who first released it. I run from the press pen, striving not to trample a toddler in my blind animal instinct to get as far away from the gas as possible. I join a mob of fans and reporters and even police clawing back inside the stadium. Security wisely opens up the field. There's nowhere else for us to go; a toxic cloud hovers in the sheltered air over the seats where Gil and I had watched the game. The gas seeps into the owner's box, too, and then down into the players' dressing rooms. It will take hours to defumigate the motor coach that had been waiting to drive the Indios away. All around the field, men and women and quite a few children hack and spit, breathing through jackets and shirtsleeves to filter the poison. The sprinklers have started up near the southern goal, pushing us all onto the north half of the field. Close to where I'm standing, a very young boy kneels on the ground, soon dropping to all fours like a dog. Warm sunlight shines on the stream of vomit falling from his mouth.

CHAPTER 5

EK

My eyes still sting as I cross Chamizal Park, heading to a nightclub located near the Free Bridge. Liverpool Bar is El Kartel's regular postgame hangout. Pregame, too. It's also where everyone parties most Friday nights. A Kartelero owns the place, which he has named after his favorite English soccer team. The big main room is painted Merseyside red and white, a color scheme that extends to clusters of vinyl couches and to a long plywood bar that looks as if it were constructed in a high school shop class. It's a big space, crowded with the whole gang. Everyone enjoyed the tear gas experience, which doesn't surprise me. I think all that these guys really want is some attention. The Super Bowl plays out on TV, back in Miami. I accept a beer. Before I've finished it, my bad feelings from the loss and its ugly aftermath dissipate. I fall into friendly conversation.

What do I think of the Who, the halftime entertainment at the football game? Someone buys me a watermelon-and-vodka shot. *"Vamos Indios!"* he cheers. Another guy tells me there's no reason to use Facebook since he's already on MySpace. His e-mail address ends in @hotmail.com. He also shows me his brand-new phone, a model of BlackBerry I grew out of five years ago. Mexico really *is* behind the times. Do I like the music of Rush? I'm asked. The band from Canada? No, not really. People still listen to Rush? They do in Juárez.

"There's a saying in Mexico," a man at the bar tells me. "Only a rat jumps off the ship. I am not a rat." He's a systems analyst at the huge Delphi maquiladora. He moved here from Chihuahua, which is like moving to Chicago from Springfield, Illinois. He loves the Indios because he loves Juárez. This city gave him an opportunity, he says, feeding me the universal line. Day to day, life isn't dangerous, he insists. He claims to have never seen a body. He works, he comes home to his house and his family. Nothing more. As for the slaughtered innocents, they kind of deserve it. "If you know your friend is mixed up in something, that's it—end it," he tells me. "If you hang around a bad friend, you will be killed. That's just street smarts."

Someone asks where in Juárez I live. That gives me a chance to bitch about my apartment. The place isn't working out. It's too dark, and it's also too hot; the heat I'd freeze to death without comes in only one strength: full blast. A recurring sewage backup in my building sometimes makes my place smell like a Porta-Potty. I'd rented the apartment impulsively, for a number of good reasons. It's in a better neighborhood, it's affordable, it's furnished, and it comes with a locked lot where I can park my too new car. I suspect that on some level I was also attracted to my unit's thick concrete walls and to the way my building hides at an angle off the street. A sister building stands just seventeen feet across a narrow walkway. Unless they start minting bullets that curve, there's no way a stray shot can find me as I sit on the couch watching television. That's good. That's how paranoid I was when I first got here. But the fact that my apartment looks directly into another apartment means I must cover my windows with thick blankets for privacy. A staircase up to the second-floor units blocks all sun from ever reaching the windows anyway. It's totally dark inside, twenty-four hours a day. Pitch-black dark, like a cruise ship's inner cabin. I've started calling the place Alaska, the land of the noonday moon. I'm pretty sure I'm developing seasonal affective disorder.

"You should come live in the El Kartel office," suggests Mike, the Kartel capo. He's overheard my complaints. "There's an open room."

I laugh, at least initially. Seriously? Live with you hooligans?

THE EL KARTEL office is a three-bedroom apartment near the university. Don't picture a Cape Cod bungalow on a leafy street in Ann Arbor. The campus itself isn't so bad: tan cinder blocks stacked into language arts centers and halls of science, each building fitted

with windows so small and narrow they remind me of bunker gun-
sights. Like all good property in Juárez, the university cowers behind high concrete walls ringed with barbed wire. A particularly
ugly neighborhood festers outside the walls. Empty gravel lots collect mounds of garbage. Black bunting hangs from the roof of a burrito restaurant, a signal that someone there has been murdered. The
neighborhood isn't a slum; all the houses and apartment buildings
are constructed of concrete. It's just that the buildings are particularly uninviting. The office occupies the ground level of a four-
story unit where even the windows on the second floor need the
protection of iron bars.

I often end up at the office after the postgame action at Liverpool
Bar dies down. I'll buy a hamburger from Don Roberto, an El Kartel
co-founder who tells me he earns his living catering the after-
parties. I'll sit atop one of the many cars spilling from the front yard
into the street, talking soccer with as many as fifty other Karteleros. Indios players have stopped by a few times, including Maleno
Frías. When I've had enough talk and Tecate Light for one night, I'll
throw out fist bumps, holler *buenas noches,* and start the long walk
back to my home. Mike, the other founding capo, doesn't need to
walk. He lives at the office. Until recently, so did Kinkin, the guy
who hazed me on the bus to Monterrey. Kinkin's decided to move
into the apartment of his serious girlfriend, an American who is
also in El Kartel and whom I consider to be a friend. Kinkin's become my friend, too; surviving a road trip was all it took to earn
his respect. His decision to decamp from the office has opened up
one of the bedrooms. Mike says I can have it for only a thousand
pesos a month, or about eighty dollars. I won't even have to chip in
for electric, water, or (most attractively) to pay off the *ladrones* at
Gas Natural de Juárez, an evil monopoly that handed me a first-
month heating bill so high I thought it was a misprint.

The office's small living room—*la sala de estar*—is painted with
the Indios' soccer-ball logo and with the gunsight logo of El Kartel.
A Mexican flag hangs over a computer where Mike designs fliers
and posters for upcoming road trips. Furniture consists of four
office chairs of varying stability and, surprisingly, a live ficus tree.
One wall is blank save for a hook rug of the Indios logo, clearly
homemade. Someone's also knitted an El Kartel scarf, which has
been taped to an air duct along with a small painting of Che Gue-

vara. Che makes a second appearance on a red flag near the kitchen, along with the words HASTA LA VICTORIA SIEMPRE. There's also a Cuban flag, which I recognize from Miami.

The three bedrooms are minimalist. Each tiny square features a worn mattress without sheets. Kinkin's clothes remain piled on the floor of the room he occupied, along with a bass drum and a stack of empty aluminum cans. I poke my head in Mike's bedroom to find it similarly distressed. One room always remains open, I'm told. The office is not only where everyone in El Kartel comes to paint banners and sew flags before games; it's also a great place to ingest drugs and screw girlfriends. I don't think this could be a permanent living situation. But for a few months, at least, it might be a good experience. The price is definitely right, and how much worse can it possibly be than Alaska, the black hole where I currently live? I check the stove and microwave in the kitchen. They work. So does a refrigerator stocked with eggs, Coca-Cola, and Don Roberto's hamburger meat. We're so close to the border my American cell phone picks up a signal. I'm tempted.

"Don't do it," an Indio warns me at the next practice. Keep your nose down. Stay on the line. "Do not move in there. Even if you think of these guys as your friends, you don't know who they might be messed up with."

It is with some reluctance that I tell Mike thanks, but no thanks. I'm going to persevere in the Last Frontier. If I'd accepted his offer, I almost certainly would have been there, in the office, when the gunmen broke in.

MIKE IS HOME alone, sketching out a new El Kartel T-shirt. The executive committee sells the shirts outside Olympic Stadium before every home game. A new design every two weeks. Some in El Kartel grumble that their *barra brava* seems to be devolving into an arts-and-crafts club. I've heard whispers that the capos, Mike and Don Roberto, are channeling their energies away from team support and into mining as many pesos as possible off the membership. The grumbling is pretty low-level. The shirts remain popular. I've bought a few myself, and have requested that they reprint an old design I've seen: the words EL KARTEL DE JUÁREZ ringing a silkscreened image of a man wearing a black ski mask over his head, like the *sicarios* do. I think the shirt looks badass. Mike's working on his current design at the computer in the living room. Suddenly, four men burst through the front door. Maybe there's as many as six of them. All the men are armed with automatic rifles. That they are concealing their identities behind ski masks is an ironic detail Mike doesn't have time to contemplate. One of the men grabs El Kartel's captain by the hair and drags him into the street, out where we eat our hamburgers.

"Where are the drugs?!"

More forcefully: "Where are the drugs! Who's selling the drugs?" A gun barrel pokes Mike's stomach. Other gun barrels circle his face.

"Pinche puta!" Where the fuck are the drugs, faggot? Mike is sure—Mike knows without a doubt—he is about to die. "We know someone in El Kartel is moving cocaine. Who is it? Where is he? Where are the drugs?"

Mike sells insurance. He makes pretty good money for Juárez, or at least for a member of El Kartel. He's thirty-one, though the puffy skin around his eyes makes him look at least ten years older, perhaps even on the cusp of fifty. He's the father of two young daughters, both living in El Paso with their mother, a woman who left Mike some years ago. Soccer split them apart. Even before Francisco Ibarra started up the Indios, Mike followed Juárez's semi-pro and amateur teams. The Astros. Los Soles. When the Indios arrived, he fell hard, immediately. He hasn't been able to explain to me the sudden and intense love he felt for La Frontera's new team. "It was a diversion," he offers. "It was fun." He began attending all the games. With Roberto he formed El Kartel so he could think about the Indios all week long. His wife eventually laid down an ultimatum: me or that stupid soccer team. Indios it was. Indios it remains. She took the kids and moved to Texas. Mike stayed in Juárez with El Kartel.

Don Roberto handles the social side, recruiting new members. Who knows how many Karteleros there actually are? Members of the 915s, the El Paso subgroup, get angry when they pull up to Chico's Tacos to find an unfamiliar car with the El Kartel logo displayed in its rear window. A splinter group of kids living in Juárez near the new U.S. consulate calls itself Los Fabulosos Muertos, with *muertos* basically meaning "dead bodies." The stickers these guys display in the windows of their trucks feature three menacing skulls. Another subgroup calls itself Los Sicarios. El Kartel's Internet chat room keeps all these subgroups in the loop. Dues are voluntary. There's no secret swearing-in ceremony. To become a member in full, all you really need to do, I've discovered, is survive a road trip to Monterrey.

Mike certainly doesn't monitor membership. He handles logistics. He books the road-trip buses and the hotel rooms. He signed the lease on the El Kartel office. He does not know where the drugs are. He does not know who is selling the drugs. Lying on the pavement, his eyes clenched shut in expectation, Mike thinks of his mother, who died recently. They were very close. He'll miss his daughters, but he'll see them again someday. While he waits for them, he and his mother will be together again, together forever.

It's taking too long. He's still breathing. When Mike opens his eyes, he sees the gunmen running off. He does not know why. He's still on the street, on his back. He clutches his ribs, which are bruised from boot kicks. He does not think to call the police. There's a very good chance those *were* the police. He knows only one thing for sure: The El Kartel name, which was *una broma*, a joke, a spin on the border's negative image, is no longer funny.

"You've got to come to the meeting," Ken-tokey shouts when he reaches me on my Mexican cell phone. Everyone is gathering at Liverpool Bar. "They're changing the name of El Kartel!"

By the time I arrive, the meeting is already under way. Mike stands on a platform where young *rock en Español* bands sometimes play. He lays out his case, speaking with passion and force. His words carry the weight of his acknowledged leadership. Still, no one wants to change the name except him. "We're a different type of cartel!" counters Ken-tokey. Someone points out that when Francisco Ibarra once offered to pay their traveling expenses for a season if they'd rename themselves after the indigenous Tarahumara Indians, El Kartel turned the owner down. To placate the malcontents, Mike offers a compromise that carries the day. From now on the *barra brava* will be known only as EK.

Everyone breaks for beers. Big Weecho the *luchador* finds some blue electrical tape, which he uses to cover the "l" and "artel" on the T-shirt hugging his mammoth frame. Mike will surrender the lease on the office. He'll cross the bridge to El Paso, an application for permanent residency in his hands. Immigration rules bar most people seeking residency from returning to Mexico for at least six months. Mike, the man whose love for the Indios is so strong it broke up his marriage, can't attend the team's games. He can't set foot anywhere in Juárez. As if that's even something he might want to do anymore.

I start walking back to my dark apartment well before the emergency meeting breaks up. I need to pack for an extended road trip I'll be taking with Marco and the team. On the way home, I buy an *El Diario*. I flip the newspaper open to see that Francisco Ibarra has bought a full-page ad. The tear gas fired after the loss to Morelia shouldn't sour anyone on the Indios or the team's noble mission, he writes. Yes, the play on the field has been poor. Yes, it will take a true miracle to avoid relegation to the minor leagues. But whatever happens, the Indios aren't going anywhere. The club will not fold. His commitment to "this social experiment" is strong and in his heart. It can be difficult to stand with a team as it struggles, Ibarra admits. Be patient. Be brave.

The owner concludes with a line cribbed from Mike, of all people. The El Kartel captain has printed the phrase on those T-shirts he sells outside the stadium before every home game: ESTE AMOR NO ES PARA COBARDES. The line is El Kartel's rallying cry, a testament to the strength of their bond with the Indios. It's Francisco Ibarra's rallying cry now, too, a statement that clearly speaks to a struggle that has nothing to do with soccer, and to a commitment to more than just a sports team.

CHAPTER 6

Faith

When you are at your highest, when you are rich and successful and you have everything, you don't need God.
—JOE GRAJEDA, INDIOS TEAM PRIEST

FIRST, WHISKY UNFOLDS THE TAPESTRY, affixing it to a concrete wall. It's a bolt of silk two feet wide and three feet high, held at the corners with strips of white athletic tape. La Virgen de Guadalupe hovers in the clouds, the sun and the moon at her feet. Her head bows to the left, eyes drowsy but still open, hands raised and clasped in prayer. She is the symbol of all Catholic Mexicans. Gold robes cover her dark skin. Gold stars pretty her indigo shawl. Light radiates from her body, signaling holiness with blond rays as sharp and spiky as the spines of the maguey agave. She has faded after years of locker room consecration. Her colors are muted now, her fibers thin.

Whisky, the Indios' equipment manager, drags an orange plastic Gatorade tub beneath her. He places two candles atop the tub's white lid. One candle is a wide, round wheel of red wax, bent from previous burns. The other candle sits inside a tall glass jar embossed with a second image of the Virgin, the sort of thing S-Mart sells for about a dollar. Whisky lights the candles. Alain N'Kong, back in tonight's starting lineup at striker, hits Play on a boom box. Def Leppard opens the set.

Players snake their way to lockers set up with tonight's uniforms of long-sleeved white jerseys, white shorts, and white socks.

One of the corner lockers, prime real estate, is commandeered by starting goalkeeper Christian Martínez, probably the Indios' best player. He tears off two strips of athletic tape, overlapping them to form a cross on his locker's back wall, "JHS 16" markered onto the crown. He dangles two rosaries from the handle of a toiletry cabinet. On top of his yellow padded bench, Christian opens a Bible, saving his page with a small and silver third rosary. Four tiny pictures of Jesus Christ flank the Bible. A candle embossed with Jesus's face won't be lit until just before kickoff, so that it can burn throughout the game. Also on the bench: a pair of padded white goalie gloves.

New music, still cheesy. The Black Eyed Peas ricochet off the walls, popping up to a concrete ceiling that slopes like the bleachers the locker room hides beneath. Fluorescent bulbs glow the X-ray aura of a basement bomb shelter. Trainers unfold two padded tables in an anteroom between the lockers and the urinals. An official from the Mexican Football Federation steps forward. Yes, the Indios are dressing in all white, as mandated. Good. He pulls aside Gabino, the traveling secretary. The two men synchronize watches to ensure Juárez will take the field at the proper time for warm-ups, and then for the game itself. *Tonight's going to be a good night.*

Warm-ups. Those already dressed jog out to the field for stretching and light wind sprints. Waves of yellow and blue plastic seats wait for fans to arrive, about an hour from now. Billboards advertise Banorte bank, Mexicana airlines, and Voit soccer balls, a brand I didn't know still existed. When an Indios defenseman from Mexico City emerges onto the field, he pauses at the goal line to pick up a tuft of grass, cross himself, and then point his index fingers skyward. He's left his own small shrine back in the locker room. There's a photo of his beautiful wife taken at a street carnival and another photo of his wife with their three kids. In front of the pictures, atop an open Bible, the defensemen has placed two small crucifixes, his personal picture of the Virgin of Guadalupe, and a list of the three Bible verses he studied in his hotel room before the game.

It's a Saturday-night away game in San Luis Potosí. The Gladiators are a bad team, which is good news for the Indios. Every game is a must-win at this point, but this game especially so. This whole week is crucial. On Wednesday the Indios will play their third game in eight days, against Atlas in Guadalajara. Rather than fly back from San Luis on Sunday just to fly south again on Tuesday, the team will spend two nights at a mountain resort in the state of Jalisco. A nice break, actually. A fun trip, though also a business trip. The realistic, attainable—and very necessary—goal is two wins, six points in the standings.

After a short practice on Friday morning, back in Juárez, players dressed in identical black business suits with Indios soccer-ball logos sewn onto the breast pockets. The team looked like a professional outfit, which I sometimes forget they are. A quick meal in the clubhouse commissary, then a shuttle to Aeropuerto Internacional Abraham González. It floors me that Ciudad Juárez has its own airport. Not that it's too small to justify one; it's just that El Paso's own international airfield receives and dispatches planes only fifteen miles away. Such duplication is common along La Frontera. There are two city halls with two different mayors (though both mayors actually live in El Paso), different local news channels covering the same stories, and different state universities employing, in several cases, the same professors. The reasons for the duplication are sometimes less than obvious. When Amado Carrillo ruled the Juárez Cartel in the 1990s, his jumbo jets of Colombian cocaine unloaded at the Juárez airport without incident, something he probably couldn't have gotten away with in El Paso.

It was a two-and-a-half-hour flight to Mexico City, an hour layover, and then a thirty-minute hop to this mountain mining town. The players sat in coach, three to a row. Headphones delivered music. Suit jackets dangled off the backs of seats. When the plane's wheels lifted off the ground, every player crossed himself. Every one of them.

JUÁREZ, LIKE MOST of Mexico, is Catholic. Seeds of faith planted by Spanish missionaries still bloom, full and lush. CIUDAD JUÁREZ: THE BIBLE IS REAL. READ IT was painted without permission onto a mountain face visible everywhere in the valley. Juárez officials have let the message stay up for years, claiming no one really disagrees with it. The Juárez Cathedral defines El Centro. A second big church, San Lorenzo's, is an Indios landmark. Two years ago, prior to the team's huge championship game against León, fans placed Indios jerseys and candles at San Lorenzo's door. It's the same

church that hosted the victory party after the win over León elevated the Indios into the big leagues.

It's a coincidence the Indios name can be parsed to "In dios,"
with *Dios* being the Spanish word for "God." *In God. In God we
trust.* Back when he bought the minor league Pachuca Juniors and
relocated them to Ciudad Juárez, Francisco Ibarra held a rename-
the-team contest. "Indios" won in a landslide, as expected. Every
team in Ciudad Juárez is named the Indios. A professional baseball
team that plays to only a few dozen fans calls itself the Indios. The
volleyball, basketball, and track teams at the university are the Indios. That's just what teams are called in Juárez. While the name is
a mandate from the people, the link to God pleases Ibarra im-
mensely. He's set up a shrine to the Virgin of Guadalupe in the
foyer of his El Paso house. A painting of the Virgin has been baked
onto tile and set into a wall of the Indios' home locker room. Olympic Stadium billboards advise fans to GO WITH GOD TODAY. On the
rare occasions when the Indios score a goal—I've only see it happen
in the preseason—Ibarra rises from his padded club seat, points to
the sky, and offers up *gracias a Dios.* In a promotional video assembled by Ibarra's radio station employees, the "In Dios" connota-
tion is spelled out plain as day, flashed repeatedly on the screen: IN
then DIOS, IN then DIOS. His club is on a crusade.

"God bless you, my brother," Gil Cantú tells me every time we
shake hands. An assistant coach wears one of those WHAT WOULD
JESUS DO wristbands. Whenever Marco Vidal steps onto the pitch,
even for practice, he does that same pulling-up-a-tuft-of-grass
thing, crossing himself and then pointing two index fingers to the
heavens. Riding around Juárez with Marco in his beat-up Mercury,
I've noticed him make the sign of the cross when we pass a church.
He does this even though he doesn't sit for mass nearly as often
as his wife would like, and when I once asked if he ever attends
Easter services, he replied that he attends only when Easter happens to fall on a Sunday.

"God has a plan for this city," Gil has told me. "God has a plan
for the Indios, too."

GAME DAYS INVOLVE as little activity as possible. Players do almost
nothing besides eat and rest. In the room they always share on the

road, Marco and Maleno Frías watch Primera games on television. Like everyone else on the team, they allot plenty of time for shut-eye.

"I'm a champion napper," Marco has boasted. "I really like to sleep."

The team hotel—a generic Courtyard by Marriott—sits on the strip-mall fringe of San Luis. While the players rested up, I hailed a cab into the Colonia city center, which is a much nicer area. The Mexican Revolution started in San Luis, in 1910. One million Mexicans subsequently lost their lives (out of a population of only fifteen million). Two million more Mexicans fled to the United States, setting up migration trails that remain to this day. The city twice served as the national capital. On the short connecting flight from the current capital, head coach Pepe Treviño told me that in addition to the Revolution and also the silver mines advertised on the city seal, San Luis is most famous for its tuna. Tuna? I thought he might have been pulling my leg, or testing the limits of my Spanish. San Luis is landlocked. While walking around the city's many plazas, I didn't see any fishmongers. But what I did find were slices of sweet cactus fruit grown on San Luis's semiarid hills. Gringos would call this cactus the prickly pear. For centuries, Potosinos have enjoyed such desserts as *tuna* honey and *queso de tuna*, or cactus cheese. The soccer team's nickname, before it was switched to the more manly Gladiators, was the Tuneros, or cactus growers.

Plaza de Armas is the main square in San Luis. I sat for a while on one of the square's green park benches, taking in everything. A married couple amused a toddler. A very attractive woman in a white sweater kissed her *novio*—boyfriend—between shared spoons of soft ice cream. A young girl carried a silver balloon shaped like a crescent moon. Her sister carried a balloon of a monkey wearing boxer shorts, both girls' father trailing with a camera stuck to his face. *Tap, tap, tap*—a drummer tested his snare in advance of a free rock concert scheduled to start in half an hour. The scene fascinated me. It kind of overwhelmed me. So many people outside, recreating, living. Away from the border, Mexico seems like a pretty sweet country.

The plaza fronts an enormous orange cathedral with twin spires and baroque flourishes paid for with mining money. Shops fan out along tight streets tiled with limestone and open only to pedestrians. I walked the streets, inhaling vapors of tamales and of roasted corn slathered in mayonnaise and dusted with chile pepper. I stumbled onto the Calzada de Guadalupe, a long pedestrian path lined with green trees. Stepping off the path at one point, I explored the old penitentiary where imprisoned politician Francisco Madero drafted his plan for revolution. Seven barracks inside the jail have been retrofitted into loft-like schools for different artistic disciplines. I watched ballerinas stretch in the dance wing. In the music hall, a woman flipped through a composition fanned across her desk. I could hear a full opera company belting out Italian lyrics. Space in the complex serves sculptors and painters and photographers. There's also a literature wing with quiet writing rooms, which got me to daydreaming. As in Monterrey, I again felt a powerful attraction. I could live here, happily.

I loitered inside the penitentiary for more than an hour before stepping back onto the pedestrian path. The path had started at the main cathedral, in the center of town. When I reached the end of the trail, about a mile later, I found myself at the foot of yet another impressive cathedral, this one built specifically to honor the Virgin of Guadalupe. Once a year, every year, pilgrims crawl to the cathedral on their knees, offering penitence before the same painting of the Virgin reproduced on a silk cloth and taped to the Indios' locker room wall. San Luis Potosí was built on faith, too.

MARCO FEELS THAT he can't be touched in Juárez, that he's not in particular danger. "First, I'm not in the drug business," he tells me. "Second, I'm a soccer player in the Primera. If they killed me it would really bring the heat, and they know it." I feel untouchable, too. I'm a tall, pale gringo, an American. I'm a journalist, the writer of a couple stories for the *New York Times* (even if I wrote those stories years ago). If I were killed, President Obama might get involved. The State Department would really bring the heat.

At least that's what I tell myself. Actually, several Americans have been murdered in Juárez this year, and Obama has yet to show up. Still, I choose to feel protected, as if I float inside a bulletproof force field. I'm not in the drug business. I never honk my horn. I stay on the line. Juárez would completely shut down without these kinds of rationalizations. Marco and I believe what we must to feel secure. So does everyone else in the city. For most people, the sense of protection is faith-based.

"We prayed. Maybe you cannot believe that, but we prayed," said Sandra Rodríguez Nieto, a friend of mine who reports for *El Diario*. She was scared after a newspaper colleague was shot to death in the parking lot of the shopping mall near my apartment.

Monica Ortega crosses over to El Paso almost every day to work as a nurse. She's also a member of El Kartel, the only one I've met who refuses to drink alcohol or take drugs, which, as I understand it, goes against the very purpose of El Kartel. I sat next to her for several hours on the long bus ride to Monterrey.

"I feel a connection with the Virgin of Guadalupe," she told me. "I feel like she watches over me, and has always watched over me."

I MADE IT back to the hotel right after the team's pre-game meal. Marco, energized by the cold shower he always takes before games, joined his teammates in Salon Azteca Dos for a video study session. Everyone in the room wore black Indios sweatsuits. Like Catholic schoolgirls forced into uniforms, the players personalized their outfits with accessories: Ed Hardy baseball hats worn backwards or white running shoes with red laces or perhaps a bulky block of a wristwatch. Marco carried a white Armani Exchange satchel that he defensively calls a toilet kit. The murse worn by the guy next to him was sewn from Burberry plaid.

A video projector hummed atop a small table covered in a white cloth that made the table resemble a magician's stand. The video flashing onto a white screen, to my surprise, was from the Monarcas game a week ago. They hadn't gone over that yet?

"Normally we'd show it no later than two days after the game," an assistant coach told me, "but with this team we've learned we need motivation more than information. Some teams, you tell them something and they've got it—snap. But with this team, we have to be . . ." He searched for the right word. "Encouraging," he finally said.

Pepe Treviño wielded a laser pointer. As game footage flickered on-screen, he drew circles around what he called the Indios' "defensive recovery zone." Who should sprint forward on the attack?

Where should everyone stand when the play shifts back to the Indios' end of the field?

"That was a very good conversion," he said, referring to a sudden
counterattack from defense to offense. *"Muy bien. Excelente.* But
Edwin, cut straight to the goal next time." Individual responsibility, people. Teamwork, too. Jair Garcia will take the corner kicks.
Listo, Jair? Ready? Edwin will start as always. King Kong is our
striker. Marco will start, too. He's locked down his spot supporting
Edwin in the midfield.

"La vida es lo que hacemos," Treviño declared. Life is what we
make of it. He dipped his head slightly, a signal for an assistant
working the video projector to hit a button.

Twenty killed in one day. A child orphaned after his parents are
gunned down at a traffic light. The projector illuminates scenes of
violence in Juárez. Newspaper headlines about teenagers shot to
death outside their schools, about assassinated police, about an
ever-growing body count in the most murderous city on the planet.
It's gruesome footage, morbid stuff I'd pretty much forgotten about
during my pleasant afternoon in San Luis. *What other team shows
videos like these?* The video horror show segued into snippets from
the movie *Invincible.* Mark Wahlberg anchored the true story of an
unemployed teacher invited to walk on with his hometown Philadelphia Eagles, *un equipo de fútbol Americano.* The movie was in
English with Spanish subtitles.

"Man can only take so much failure," Wahlberg said, in character as Vince Papale. The key scene took place in a locker room. Eagles
in green uniforms huddled before kickoff, eager to play the first
game of a new season. Greg Kinnear stepped forward in his role as
former Eagles head coach Dick Vermeil.

"Starting today, we are on a path towards winning," the coach
told his team. A list of old Eagle greats followed, from a heyday the
current team wants to recapture. "Those players weren't just out
playing for themselves, they were playing for a city. The people of
Philadelphia have suffered. You are what they turn to at times like
these. You are what give them hope. Let's win one for them. Let's
win one for us!"

Police escorted the Indios to the stadium.

★ ★ ★

"JESUS HAS A purpose for me," Sergio Bueno once told me. He's the father of Adir Bueno, from the Indios' media department. Sergio's a dentist. I've paid him to fill a couple cavities I'd been living with longer than I should have. Until I moved to Mexico, I could never afford to fill them. Dentistry is cheap in Juárez, much cheaper than in the United States. So cheap I also asked Sergio to install a crown, which he did for $2,500 less than I paid—even with dental insurance—for a similar crown in Boulder. And Sergio did a better job.

Dental tourism was, until recently, a huge borderland business. The university prepared scores of oral surgeons and root canal specialists to meet foreign demand. Then Americans stopped crossing over. With the violence spiking in Juárez, once-crowded clinics directly across the bridges have been abandoned. Practices have also closed near my apartment, deeper into the city, often after the dentists fled—or were murdered—in the wake of extortion attempts. An office complex across López Mateos that once housed several dentists sits as empty as the shuttered Italian restaurant up the block and the Chinese buffet down the street—the one with the banner still advertising live music—that closed after gunmen shot those five patrons dead.

It's not just dentists (or restaurateurs). A plastic surgeon I met at an Indios game said the drop in medical tourism has thrown her practice onto life support. An emergency room doctor told me he was busy when the violence first escalated, in 2007. Back then, he'd regularly treat patients wheeled in with five bullet holes in their legs or perhaps in a shoulder or a buttock. Work for even him has dried up.

"They've gotten much more professional," he says of the *sicarios* who had kept him busy. "Now they'll shoot thirty or more bullets to the chest. They make sure they've killed him off."

Sergio and his wife, also a dentist, had at one time owned and operated a chain of three clinics in Juárez. Their son Adir, before falling in love with the Indios and changing careers, had inspected and repaired bicuspids, too. Adir got out at the right time. Business has fallen off so severely that Sergio has pondered relocation to El Paso or farther into Texas. He wants to move someplace safer, a city where "Am I going to get shot today?" is not a top-of-mind question. His research discouraged him. The relicensing process in Texas—in a foreign country—is long and expensive. Sergio's too old to start fresh, but also much too young to retire. So he stays. He feels he has no choice. He stays in Juárez as a working dentist even though *ladrones* recently burst into one of his clinics demanding the wallets, purses, and car keys of everyone in the building.

No one was killed when the *ladrones* broke in. No one in the office was even hurt, at least physically. That Sergio and everyone else escaped with their lives is proof, he proceeded to tell me, that Jesus won't let him be killed. Sergio is protected.

AFTER WARM-UPS, THE Indios file back into the locker room. Whisky hands out tape to secure shin guards. Eminem's relentless "Lose Yourself" on the boom box now, loud, a mash-up with Survivor's "Eye of the Tiger." Orange Gatorade slides into green cups. Jair climbs onto a massage table that has been draped in white towels decorated with Gatorade logos. A trainer rubs Jair's calves, hamstrings, and thighs, liniment radiating a proper locker room smell. The referee and his two linesmen duck inside with wishes of good luck.

Pepe Treviño sits on the bench in front of an empty locker, his elbows on his thighs. His assistants aim the video projector at a white dry-erase board, which has been scrubbed clean. The plays Pepe covered back at the hotel slide onto the board, sliding off every fifteen seconds. In his corner locker, Christian, the goalie, cuts holes in the toes of his game socks so he can pull them over his knees. Whisky hands plastic insoles to Coco, to be slipped into his spikes. Marco laces up a pair of Adidas, which the shoe company pays him a small amount of money to do. King Kong unboxes new Pumas: red, white, and black, in a design intentionally evoking the superhero Spider-Man. A slow song comes on, inappropriately. Kong hops over to the boom box and presses a button, advancing the set list to Guns N' Roses: "Sweet Child of Mine." Still kind of slow, but turn it up. Raise the energy in the room. *We can win this game!* Kong hops on the balls of his feet. Gabino, the traveling secretary, claps his hands. Slash segues into a guitar solo.

Outside the locker room, fans find their seats. Bass and snare drums from San Luis's arriving *barra brava* snap and thump. In a tunnel leading to the field, schoolgirl cheerleaders wave pom-poms. Little boys in white uniforms and cleats wait to march onto the field holding hands with the players, one of soccer's nicer traditions. Inside the locker room, more Guns N' Roses. "Knockin' on Heaven's Door," another slow song, but still, Guns N' Roses, man. The energy is up! Edwin kicks his legs high in the air like a Rockette, rotating at the hips on the descent to stretch his flexors. The whole team joins him, loosening, limbering up. Old man Coco finishes a black pot of hot herbal tea, his youth potion. Pepe Treviño claps his hands together, which wins everyone's attention. It's time for the big speech. Yet Pepe merely looks over to an assistant, who presses the Play button on the overhead projector. It's the same pep talk from the movie *Invincible*, shown back at the hotel, Greg Kinnear as Dick Vermeil again pumping up his troops.

"Pepe's not the *rah-rah* type of coach," an assistant confides to me. "He's just not that type of coach."

When the movie clip wraps up—*win one for Philadelphia!*—a circle forms in the open space in the middle of the room. Arms hang over shoulders, hands fall to the small of each other's backs. A prayer is offered. Crosses are signed. All hands join in the center for a cheer.

"Indios! Indios! Indios!"

Running out of the locker room, Christian the goalie pauses to touch the tapestry of the Virgin of Guadalupe. So do players named Danilo and Alejandro. Jair touches her as well. Marco touches her, too.

"THEY HAD GUNS, but they weren't real guns," Sergio Bueno told me. I'd stopped by for a routine cleaning at his current office on the seventh floor of Hospital Angeles. It's a new, private hospital at the entrance to Campestre, an upscale neighborhood fronted, to my amusement, by a full-scale replica of the Arc de Triomphe. *Classy!* Like Campestre, like all of the better parts of Juárez these days, the hospital is mostly empty, a gleaming ghost town operating on a skeleton crew. American soft rock music played on Sergio's laptop when I arrived. Perhaps listening to Mister Mister and John Waite helps him improve his English. Or maybe all dentists simply like that kind of music.

"One of the men fired his gun, and as soon as he did I felt relief. It was obviously a—how do you say it?—a starter gun? A starter gun, like in track and field. I could see my daughter over in another room, curled under a cubicle desk. I had been worrying about her, but right then I relaxed. It wasn't a real gun, so I knew nobody was going to get hurt."

Sergio and his grown daughter were working at their clinic near the Zaragoza Bridge, a location convenient for bargain-hunting Americans. It was not yet lunchtime when the *ladrones* stormed in. They moved with a military precision. Had they been police in the past? Were they policemen still? They took Sergio's car keys and also his wallet. They also took the keys and cash from every other person they could find, which was everyone save Sergio's daughter. She had dashed into that other room, curling up under that cubicle desk.

"I remember thinking, *Just don't go in there*," Sergio recalled, referring to the side office where his daughter hid. "*Don't harm her. Don't scare her. And don't scare anyone else in the office, either, of course.*"

When one of the cops—er, robbers—fired his gun, apparently in an attempt to command attention, Sergio relaxed. *He's firing blanks. Nothing to worry about. They just want our cars and money. Nothing truly important.* Sergio surrendered everything they asked for. So did everyone else.

After the men fled, Sergio darted around the office, checking to see if his patients and staff were okay. His daughter threw her arms around him; she had been worried Sergio would be kidnapped. Sergio called 066 as a formality, out of a sense of routine. The police showed up to record the narrative and to write down victim names. That was it. No one is ever going to be arrested for the break-in, which Sergio already knew. The incident wasn't even mentioned the next day in the crime briefings of any of Juárez's several daily newspapers.

That next day, Sergio returned to work. He needed a ride to the clinic, but he still made it there at the usual time. He was alone after he was dropped off, and he spent a few minutes scoping out the reception area. Nothing particularly amiss. He walked back to his office desk, which was where the men had confronted him with their guns. It was all quiet, morning, the beginning of a new day. Sergio stepped over to his chair and sat down. He just sat there for a while. At one point he dropped his head. He stared at his feet. He stared at the ground.

"And that's when I saw it, right under my chair."

A bullet. The guns had been real after all. At least one *ladrón* had fired a live round that ricocheted around the room, settling on the floor beneath Sergio's office chair.

"At that moment, when I saw that bullet, I was overcome with the calmest calm I have ever felt," Sergio told me. "I knew with certainty that God does not want me to die. God does not want me to leave my family or to leave my city. I felt closer to God than ever."

NO MUSIC PLAYS in the locker room after the game. It's somber, like at a funeral. Pepe Treviño and his assistants talk quietly, lamenting the fading health of their team. Heads nod. Pepe fingers his mustache. The players, as they undress, stare straight ahead. Christian ices a knee. Marco and Maleno linger at their lockers, in their underwear, saying nothing. Jair walks over to a massage table to have a trainer slap lactic acid out of his thighs. The flame on the Virgin of Guadalupe candle flickers as he passes it.

It was going to be a good night. For a while it *was* a good night. Guadalupe delivered the first Indios goal of the regular season, and it mattered little that no one on the Indios had actually scored it—a San Luis player accidentally kicked the ball into his own net. Unfortunately, the 1–0 lead Juárez carried into the second half came attached to two red cards. It's very hard to play high-level soccer even one man down. With two Indios players ejected for rough tackles, it was only a matter of time before San Luis equalized. The tie arrived with fifteen minutes left in the game. Plain luck prevented San Luis from scoring more: Twice the Gladiators hit the crossbar on open nets. A tie is worth a point in the standings, and a point is usually better than nothing. But the Indios absolutely needed all three of the points that would have come with a win. This was a bad game, a blown opportunity. Pepe Treviño slumps onto the bench of a vacant locker. I watch him scribble in a pocket notebook.

Balls of grass-stained athletic tape roll across the floor. Players dry off after showering. Kong dresses silently; the Cameroonian showed nothing on the field, as usual. A functionary from the Federation pokes his head into the locker room, catching Pepe's eye. The man is very young, practically a boy. He has been assigned to the least important game in tonight's national schedule. His blue

blazer with the Federation's tricolored crest on the pocket is too big
for his body, and he swims inside it while Pepe hits him with the
usual conspiracy theories. It's always the Indios getting called for
penalties. Two red cards in one game? Come on. The Federation
doesn't want Juárez in the Primera anymore. The refs are afraid to
travel to La Frontera, and so are the teams. The whole world would
rather pretend Juárez doesn't exist.

The players, dried off and dressed, make their way to the bus,
their egos shielded by bulky stereo headphones. Whisky flies
around the emptying room. He stuffs muddy leather cleats into one
bag, plastic shower flip-flops into another. Voit soccer balls bulge
inside a red cotton travel bag adorned with the logos of a team that
has now gone twenty-two straight games without a win; lose or tie
their next game and they'll be the worst team in the history of Mexico's top division. The balls and a stack of orange plastic cones are
tossed into the storage hold of the bus, along with the watercoolers
and the massage tables and a duffel bag ripe with dirty uniforms.

One last check of the locker room. Whisky climbs onto a bench
to see if anything hides on a top shelf. A stray watercooler is spotted in a far corner. Whisky drags it into the showers, where he over-
turns it to pour melting ice cubes down a drain. Whisky flips the
cooler upright, carries it to the bus and then returns for a truly final inspection. That appears to be it. Everything is accounted for.

Save one last detail. The Indios' equipment manager pulls four
tape strips off the concrete wall, freeing the Virgin of Guadalupe.
He folds her tapestry down to a small square, which he tucks into
a travel bag. During the game, the wax in the tall glass melted from
white to clear. The glass's embossed image of the Virgin glows orange and blue and gold, translucent, incandescent. Whisky leans
over. Quickly, without ceremony, he blows out the candle.

CHAPTER 7

Fear

AFTER THE GAME, THE INDIOS SIT for a late meal back at the Court-yard by Marriott. I join them, warily, feeling uncomfortable the whole time. Nobody talks. Nobody at all, about anything. Hotel management, experienced in the rhythms of traveling soccer teams, has prepared spaghetti and chicken cordon bleu, two soup options, cottage cheese, raw eggs, raw vegetables, and salad with ranch dressing. It's already after midnight, but players stow apples and individual-serving boxes of Frosted Flakes in the pockets of their suits in case hunger strikes before down. I sit at a round table with the coaches, Pepe Treviño on my right. I want to express some support, but I sense it's best not to break the silence. *Nobody* says a word. I twirl spaghetti onto my fork, spearing a small hot pepper off my plate before putting it all in my mouth. The Indios needed a win, could have earned that win—should have earned that win—and have just plain failed. These boys are doomed. The end is neigh. "If we go down, we'll be stained as players," Marco told me before the season started. He sits at a table not far from me, among seven of his teammates. All of them stare at their plates, their brows furrowed as if contemplating stain-removal strategies. After only fifteen minutes I stand up, say my first words, *"Buen provecho,"* and race back to my room.

I run six miles the next morning along a strip of Wal-Marts, Mc-Donald's, Kentucky Fried Chickens, and American car dealerships. Where is this Mexico I've heard so much about? When I return to the hotel, the team has started its own training. Pepe Treviño and his staff have elected to squeeze in a workout in the hotel's modest fitness center. Coco Giménez grinds his old bones into a treadmill sprint. Edwin and goalkeeper Christian navigate a Universal apparatus. A platoon of six Indios crunches out sit-ups, alternating with push-ups and jumping jacks. Marco climbs out of a bent semicircle of a pool not much bigger than an actual kidney. In the back parking lot, near where the team bus idles, everyone else circles lap after lap.

By breakfast the Indios feel better. The San Luis disaster is behind them, even if only by half a day. The Indios have not yet been eliminated. The next opponent, Atlas, doesn't look too imposing. And before they play Atlas, the schedule calls for two days of training at a hilltop resort outside Guadalajara. Sunshine, no distractions, no other obligations. Should be a good time. Before the bus drives off, we stock up on sodas and snack foods at an OXXO convenience store, looking much like El Kartel on the road to Monterrey, minus the shoplifting and the alcohol. Gabino, the traveling secretary, offers me a chocolate chip cookie when I take a seat next to him on the bus.

We roll through 190 miles of sunbaked central Mexico. Farmers' fields stretch from the interstate to brown mountains off in the distance. Tufts of green grass mix with shocks of wild wheat. The occasional cactus breaks things up, along with ramshackle roadside cantinas and ranchers stepping their potbellies into pickup trucks. I count skinny cows. Gabino fiddles with the antenna on a portable television replaying yesterday's biggest game, Cruz Azul losing to América at Estadio Azteca. We're trapped on the bus long enough to screen three and a half feature films: *Slumdog Millionaire*, *The Bank Job*, half of *The Curious Case of Benjamin Button* (which is interrupted because nobody likes it), and all of the Will Smith vehicle *I Am Legend*, an apocalyptic film about a virus that turns the residents of New York City into zombie vampires.

Jair Garcia sits a few rows behind me on the bus. He last played for Atlas, traded to Juárez when the Indios rose to the Primera. He hasn't exactly enjoyed the change of cities. I've heard him moan about dust from sandstorms blowing into his house; lifting up a glass reveals a clear ring on a table covered with brown grit. Jair is the father of three kids. He's married to a woman so tall and striking it's a bit unsettling to stand near her. On the flight down from Ciudad Juárez to Mexico City, I watched Jair slowly flip through the front section of the newspaper *El Sol de México*. No one else on the team read the front pages. Most passed around only the sports sections of the better papers out of Mexico City. King Alain N'Kong controlled Wayne Rooney on his PlayStation portable. Music pumped through Marco's noise-canceling headphones. Yet Jair read an article about President Felipe Calderón, who had again visited Juárez to apologize one more time to the mothers of the students massacred at that high school party. Jair lingered on the Calderón article for several minutes before turning to the next story, a roundup of every murder in Juárez from the day before.

In the movie *I Am Legend*, Will Smith's wristwatch beeps just before sundown. It reminds him to get off the streets immediately. Blood-hungry zombies come out at night. When his watch beeps, Smith hurries home, bolting every door and window in his house, and waits out the darkness curled in his bathtub with his dog and a high-powered rifle. Night is when bad things happen in his city.

"That's exactly the way it is in Juárez," Jair tells me after we step off the bus. "You stay off the street at night. You're home with family."

I know to stay in at night. I've learned. Yet I still get caught out sometimes. Running errands with a friend one afternoon takes so long that the sun has set before we've checked everything off our list. When we finally finish, I spring for dinner at a taqueria on Oscar Flores Boulevard. The restaurant isn't crowded, but it isn't empty, either. A family takes up the table next to us: two young girls in puffy pink coats, a mother and a father, and a small boy more interested in a crumpled ball of paper than in the food cooling in front of him. This isn't so bad, I tell my friend. There are still families eating out at restaurants, at night.

"No, Robert," my friend says. "There was a shooting here less than a year ago."

It never ends. Everywhere in Juárez knows violence. My reporter friend at *El Diario*, looking for a place to eat after finishing a story, couldn't find a restaurant where there hadn't been a slaughter. This burrito stand over here? Seven killed in October. That seafood place? Two killed last month. The low-rent steakhouse down the block? Two more killed only a week ago. She ended up driving back to her house, where she cooked her own food in the only place she felt safe.

I drive home from the restaurant on eight lanes of traffic slicing between endless strips of convenience stores, shopping malls, and other restaurants, many of which are closed. A truck of *federales* zooms up behind me, blinking headlights. *Get out of the way!* But there is nowhere I can go; I'm boxed in on both sides. *Blink. Honk-honk. Get the fuck out of the way.* Shit. Okay. I must swerve to my right, into the maybe fifteen feet of space between a car and a school-bus-like *rutera*. I go for it, wedging myself in there and downshifting because the car now in front of me isn't going as fast. I pray the bus won't crumple my back bumper. The *federales* pull even with me. One cop aims his assault rifle at my window, at my head. These guys shot a student in the back at a peace rally near the university. In the back. At a peace rally. And they got away with it. The *federales* have complete immunity. They wear navy blue uniforms and carry weapons and zoom around in fleets of hulking GMC trucks doing whatever they want. They no doubt noticed my Colorado plates. Am I now on their radar? *They'll hunt you like a deer, brother.* Have I won their attention because I didn't get the fuck out of the way at a time when getting out of the way wasn't possible? They terrorize, these cops.

I exit onto Avenida de la Raza, another main street. I stick to the major arteries on purpose. My dim lights catch a flash of human leg. The leg belongs to one of two men darting into traffic. I slam my brakes to save their lives. The driver of a small white car behind me slams on his brakes, too. I brace for an impact, but the white car manages to stop in time. I recall something Marco Vidal told me: that while auto insurance is mandatory in Mexico, if you get in an accident there's nobody to call. There's nothing you can do. I start up, I stop. I start up again, I slam on my brakes again. Eventually I arrive at the intersection of López Mateos. I want to turn left, so I flip on my blinker. The turn signal is red, though the go-straight light remains green. I'm stopped, very scared some car behind me might want to go straight. (Street signs and traffic lights are as relevant in Juárez as the No Smoking signs in bars.) Here comes a big SUV. The driver lays on his horn. Oh, no. *Please brake. Please don't hit me.* Fuck. Another conflict. I have again drawn attention to myself, though I'm doing nothing wrong. I weigh my options. Before the light even changes, I turn, taking my chances, hoping I can successfully split the cross-traffic, which I do.

López Mateos is congested tonight. I get into the right lane, preparing to exit onto my side street, which is coming up quick. A car falls in behind me. To avoid pissing him off, I drive too fast over a monstrous pothole. *Thunk!* There goes my alignment. I barely slow down to turn onto my street, not illuminated tonight with working lights. I drive in the dark to my apartment building, where I lock my car in the lot. I'm sweating. I'm rattled. Some nights I want only to barricade myself behind my security door.

Other nights, I can't stay in. I break curfew in Juárez more often than I should. My apartment is stuffy and dark and at times can smell like sewage. There are only so many evenings in a row I can lie alone on my couch watching the Channel 44 news or, to work on my language skills, watching a telenovela in Spanish with Spanish subtitles. I'll walk around my neighborhood, critically grading the security measures of each house. Is that wall tall enough? Are three lines of barbed wire overkill? Is that fence electrified? I pause at each of the many For Sale signs. Most of the houses for sale remain dark at all times, their occupants not waiting for an offer before moving somewhere else, most likely to El Paso. I listen to ambulances and police sirens wind closer and then fade in intensity as they rush farther away. A yellow haze of air pollution gives the few streetlights that still work a cinematic glow. The air is thin in Juárez, but there's no shortage of atmosphere.

Sometimes the military stops me. They patrol the neighborhoods at night, slowly cruising the side streets in their trucks. The soldiers wear body armor and helmets and carry automatic rifles like the *federales*. But they are not *federales*. They wear green instead of blue. Their big trucks are painted green, too. They see that I am alone. I am walking at night, which nobody does in Juárez. A flashlight shines in my eyes. All the soldiers in the truck—there's maybe a dozen of them—aim their guns at my chest. Four of them leap out to confront me. I raise my hands over my head. When instructed, I move my hands onto the hood of the truck. I spread my legs and am frisked. I do whatever is asked. A soldier rifles through my wallet. Another soldier finds my passport and pulls it from my jacket pocket.

"What the fuck are you doing in Juárez, gringo?" he asks. I live here, I say. This is my home. He doesn't buy it. It makes no sense, me being here. What am I doing outside at night? I'm just going to a bar to watch a boxing match, I reply. The great Manny Pacquiao is fighting. The match is taking place in Dallas. Marco had planned to watch it in person. He bought tickets for both a flight and the fight. Yet he's too embarrassed by the Indios' record to show his face in his hometown. He canceled the trip, opting to watch the match while barricaded in his house. I want to watch it with other boxing fans, which the soldiers can understand. They admire Pacquiao. They wish they could watch the fight, too. I'm handed back my passport. They keep a beam of light trained on me as I walk off, making sure I head in the right direction.

That would be north on López Mateos, toward the border. I pass a crowded Blockbuster Video. A chain that's obsolete in the States survives in Juárez because entertaining at home remains the option almost everyone chooses. "This has really brought my family closer together," a maquiladora owner told me, arguing that there's an upside to the violence. Indios media assistant Adir Bueno celebrated his birthday by renting a karaoke machine and singing songs in the salon of his father's big house. I don't have a house, or a family. Staying home alone gets old. So I continue walking, passing the Poker strip club, a seedy joint where you can order shockingly attractive women out of a catalog they keep behind the bar. Wherever in the world the woman is—Quito, São Paulo, a seaside resort in Uruguay—they'll ship her up. Poker is where young, jittery men will tip away two thousand dollars in a night, money they've just been paid for their first professional kill—something they tried because it seemed easy, because it seemed exciting. They pulled off the job, no problem—it *was* easy—only to find their sinful wages unbearable, hot in their hands. They can't touch it, the money. They can't shake the backseat screams from the victim as they drove him out to the desert. They can't believe the line they've just crossed.

I continue past the Rio Grande Mall and the offices of *El Diario* and an incongruously bright Chevrolet dealership. I pass a couple of heavily fortified hotels. About a mile from my apartment, just beyond the General Hospital where they bring shooting victims the other hospitals refuse, I enter the Pronaf District. It's a once-hopping nightclub zone. Marco used to party here when he was single, before the owner of his favorite club was shot in the head. Only a few bars remain, but it's amazing how crowded they are. It's strictly locals, hundreds of young Juarenses who, like me, have to get out of the house, absolutely need to be around other people. Marco, with a wife and a name to protect, parties only at home nowadays. If he's not watching a fight, he's usually playing poker with Maleno Frías, Edwin, Jair, and other friends on the team.

I choose randomly between two pool halls: Pockets, which is larger and looks crowded, and Club Oxido, which seems newer. I choose Oxido, for no real reason. I watch the fight. I drink a few beers, too, walking home afterwards without incident. It's not so bad in Juárez, I conclude. I'm glad I went out. In the morning I flip on the news to see technicians lugging heavy black plastic bags. The bags look like garbage, but inside them there are the bodies of four people murdered while watching the fight—at Pockets.

I should stay in. I keep going out. I hit the Liverpool Bar on Friday nights with El Kartel, drinking with Ken-tokey and Mike late into the night, usually ending up back in the Pronaf District for cigarettes, *cerveza*, and ska—*ska!*—at Fred's Bar, home of a disco dance floor straight out of John Travolta's youth. When Ken-tokey's girlfriend, Sofia, turns twenty-one, she throws a party at San Martin, a still-popular cantina near the Free Bridge, very close to the statue of Lincoln. The cantina is a landmark of sorts, historically popular with the tourists who no longer visit. It's my first time in the club, and I'm pleased to see it remains crowded. Mariachis roam a hall grand enough for an Oktoberfest. Good music pumps out of the stereo system. We drink a lot and have a lot of fun, and I again conclude it's not so bad in Juárez. Two weeks after the party, eight people are shot in the cantina. Three of the victims die. One week after that, the cantina opens again for business.

I don't go back. I try not to be bonehead stupid. I never visit this one hopping bar in El Centro called Nuevo Sinaloa. As in the Sinaloa Cartel. I have walked around El Centro at night, though. I sometimes order beers in the bars that lack an obvious cartel association. El Centro's safe, I once assured a friend. My friend showed me a fresh bruise on his head. He'd been mugged in El Centro just one night earlier. Maybe I don't get touched because I'm a gringo. Maybe I'm doing a good job keeping my head down, walking the line. More likely, I've just gotten lucky. I know that the best place to be, the safest place, is in my apartment, behind the iron bars protecting my windows and the four locks that fortify my front door. I know this. I've learned.

VILLA PRIMAVERA IS a resort hotel operated by the University of Guadalajara. It sits on a mountain thirty-five minutes outside the city, a world away from urban congestion. Seventy-five acres of rolling forest rise and dip until they fall in with other mountains on the horizon. Patches of spring flowers color wide fields of green grass. Cool, thin air carries notes of pine and dandelion. The view is best from the swimming pool, a cinematic platform ringed by long and thin evergreen trees that remind me of fountain pens. When we first pulled in, I jokingly called this place the Eagle's Nest. Now, as I start my morning with a glass of fruit juice in the restaurant that overlooks the pool, as I take in the forest and distant farmers' fields and the mountain view accurately advertised as "tranquil" and "beautiful," it might be more fair to say I'm in Mexico's version of Tuscany.

We've got two nights here, and altogether two full days. The hotel operates in partnership with a high-end sports club, located within walking distance down a winding road. The sports club features an Olympic swimming pool complete with a high-dive platform. There are basketball courts and squash courts and tennis courts, including a tennis stadium for championship matches, should Rafael Nadal ever stop by. Inside a clubhouse, rows of free weights gleam alongside their attendant apparatus. Hardwood studios serve dance classes and yoga poses. The Indios are training among the six regulation soccer fields carved like terraces into the mountain slope. The fields are green and manicured and are not located anywhere near a working cement plant. They do not smell or taste like the battery acid the Indios are used to. I think we've landed in soccer heaven.

The morning workout is already under way. I finish up at the restaurant, then walk over to the sports club. I take a seat on a grassy hill and watch the team progress through the usual warm-up drills. Soccer volleyball is played without hands and with a net only waist-high. In passing triangles, three players keep the ball away from an unlucky fourth player trapped in the middle. I watch a circle of forwards juggle the ball in yet another drill. They are loose, laughing, trying on purpose to keep the ball afloat with minimal physical effort. No one lunges for the ball until the very last second. No one exerts more than a quick foot flick or head snap or shoulder twitch. It's amazing how skilled these guys are. Here at practice, away from the harsh grades of competition, their athletic gifts are obvious—and dazzling. Even old man Coco looks graceful. They all keep the ball in the air for a very long while.

The drills continue for more than an hour before Pepe Treviño blows a whistle. The head coach divides the players into two teams of roughly equal talent. Gabino, the traveling secretary who used to play professionally for the Juárez Cobras, launches into laps around the field, his usual endurance workout. I'm so seduced by the setting that I decide to run, too. I opt to hit the country roads around the resort complex. I jog about five miles up and down rolling hills, cutting through farmers' fields and passing vacation homes both modest and opulent, many of them for sale; the global economic recession has hit Guadalajara, too. By the time I make it back to the resort, the whole team is swimming in the Olympic pool. All the players who lost the scrimmage have been ordered to jump off the high dive. It towers ten meters above the water—three stories, way up there. I've never been on a high dive before, so I take off my shirt and running shoes and climb to the top just to check out the view. My knees start shaking when I walk to the edge. High diving looks fairly easy on television. Actually standing on the top platform is something else. Mistime my entry and I could rupture a spleen. My health insurance plan isn't exactly comprehensive, if it even covers me in Mexico. I turn to walk back down.

"Salto! Salto!" *Jump, gringo!* An entire professional soccer team razzes me. My manhood is questioned. I realize I'm trapped. I walk back to the edge of the platform. I gaze down at the water. My knees again buckle, and I must grab a railing to stay upright.

"Salto!" *Jump!* I retreat once more. I can't help it. I can't possibly drop from this height. A young midfielder from a line of Indios backing up on the platform loses his patience. He runs forward, leaping off like an Acapulco cliff diver, somersaulting a full revolution before untucking into the water with barely a splash. Yet another reminder that these guys, for all their struggles on the field, really are fantastic athletes. I have no choice. I've got to jump, too. I plug my nose with one hand, not even aware that I'm doing it—"That

jump was *feo*, gringo. Ugly!"—and step off with a prayer for simple
survival. I survive. Nothing breaks. Better still, I emerge from the
water fully accepted by the team.

"You're our hero, man," an assistant coach tells me at lunch.
Not one of the coaches had jumped off even the lowest platform.
After lunch everyone will hang out by the hotel pool, watch television in their rooms, or maybe surf the Web on the Wi-Fi floating
over the grounds. Tomorrow the team will put in a light workout,
then we'll drive down to Guadalajara proper. It's all great fun, even
lunch. We share fajitas and pasta Alfredo and salad and fruit and,
for dessert, flan or Jell-O if we want it. Pitchers full of fruit juice
rotate around the tables. Who looked better yesterday in Champions League action: AC Milan or Real Madrid? Alain N'Kong cracks
jokes, funnier because Spanish is the least his three languages.
Pepe Treviño jokes along with him, pulling out his wallet at one
point to bet pesos that, contrary to King Kong's claims, there's no
eighteen-year-old fashion model wife waiting for the striker back in
Cameroon. We're all kids at summer camp. Marco hanging with
his best friend Maleno Frías. Everyone playing the sport they love,
and for money. Juárez feels very far away.

"This is our life," the assistant coach says as we linger at the
table for another hour. I understand more than ever why they don't
want it to end.

The next afternoon, we take the bus down to the city. A WEL-
COME INDIOS banner hangs in the lobby of our hotel. We're still in
the big leagues, a team worth celebrating. Three clubs in the Primera are based in Guadalajara, and this hotel is where the Indios
bunk down every visit. The restaurant staff, which knows the
Indios' schedule by now, has a meal waiting. After dinner, everyone
marches up to their rooms to watch movies and catch some sleep.
We're all exhausted. I'm tired, too, which is surprising. I went for
another run this morning, but aside from that I haven't really done
anything. I never realized the physical toll road trips take on professional athletes. It seems like no big deal—flight, bus ride, rest—
but traveling as a team can be a grind.

The schedule on Wednesday gives me only a couple hours to tour
Guadalajara. That's not enough time. Some five million people live
in a dense urban area that stretches across the state of Jalisco down
to Puerto Vallarta, on the Pacific coast, more than a hundred miles

away. There's supposed to be a good zoo in Guadalajara. They distill Jose Cuervo, appropriately, in the nearby town of Tequila. I'm told the murals of Hospicio Cabañas are a must-see. I don't have time to see them. I have only time for a surgical strike. After lunch, when I ask a taxi driver to take me to the heart of the city, he drops me off at the Guadalajara Cathedral. It's a really big church, the burial place of three cardinals, including one shot fourteen times at the airport in 1993. Officially, the cardinal got caught in a shootout between rival cocaine cartels. But maybe he was specifically targeted because of his opposition to cartel violence. Or perhaps his assassination was ordered by members of the government of La Línea–friendly president Carlos Salinas. There have been several investigations over the years, with conflicting conclusions. The U.S. Department of Justice has pinned the cardinal's murder on a leader of the Tijuana Cartel. Nobody really knows for sure.

By the time I step out of the church it's started to rain. There's little time to travel anywhere else, so I duck into a coffee shop to read the local papers. An English-language newspaper serves forty thousand Canadian retirees clustered in the suburb of Lake Chapala. I know Canada lacks a tropical province, but why retire to a foreign country just to hang around people from the homeland? I switch to the Spanish-language press to read up on tonight's game. Atlas is the least of the three Primera teams in town. Chivas is far more popular, locally and throughout Mexico. Atlas stays afloat by developing good young talent, then selling this talent to the richer clubs. The Atlas game against the Indios is acknowledged in the papers, but most stories look ahead to more exciting matches on the schedule. I find myself a bit annoyed. The Indios aren't *that* bad. Their defeat is *not* guaranteed. Atlas remains one of the two or three other teams in danger of relegation, should the Indios get their act together. I've just seen up close how good the Indios players can look. I'm excited for the game. When I glance at the clock on my cell phone, I realize I need to get going if I want to watch the game in person. I taxi back to the hotel just in time to catch the team bus to the stadium.

Estadio Jalisco, which is one of Mexico's soccer temples, is surprisingly run-down. Constructed in 1952 during a public-works building boom, and the venue for two World Cup semifinals, the place isn't half as fancy as I'd expected. It's an aged concrete bowl lined with bleachers of dented steel. The stadium's primary tenant, Chivas, will move into a new palace next season. I'm guessing they've stopped paying their maintenance fees on this dump. Even the playing field is a disgrace. With Atlas, Chivas, and two minor league teams all hosting games here, Indios players run pregame sprints across what can be described as slop. No grass remains in one entire corner of the pitch. They've actually sprayed green paint over the mud to make this embarrassment look better on television. I'll never insult Juárez's Olympic Stadium again.

It's Ash Wednesday, which I hadn't realized even when I toured the cathedral. A priest working a small chapel in the stadium's bowels smears black soot on the forehead of Pepe Treviño and other coaches and players. Treviño's ash mark remains visible even after everyone has warmed up and dressed and pumped up on bad heavy metal music. The head coach calls everyone into the center of the locker room. Marco quickly ties special cleats with long metal spikes appropriate for a muddy pitch. A boom box playing the Scorpions is flipped off. It's time once again for Pepe to motivate his men. It's not that hard a task. I'm even willing to write him a proper speech—"Atlas isn't very good. We've played ourselves into a hole, but it's not too late to turn things around. We've all had fun over the past couple of days. Let's have fun out here tonight."—but Pepe really and truly isn't the kind of coach to seize the moment. He asks an assistant to play a clip from a movie starring Al Pacino.

Gil Cantú recognizes the need for something more. Gil wasn't with us in San Luis, or at the mountain hideout. He flew down today just for this game. When the movie clip concludes, he steps forward to address the team. Gil turned his life over to Jesus Christ two decades ago. Whenever he talks, about almost anything, he usually finds a way to weave in his faith.

"There are five churches in El Paso praying for you tonight," he tells the team. "One lady said she won't pray just for the Indios, because God might want the other team to win, so she just prayed for you to fight hard and do your best."

That'll have to do. The players gather in a circle, say a prayer, count to three, and shout the word "Indios!" Everyone touches the tapestry of the Virgin of Guadalupe, then runs onto the field. My cell phone vibrates with a text message from Ken-tokey's girlfriend, Sofia, back in El Paso. El Kartel is watching, she says, and is confident of a victory. Gil and I sprint up to the visiting team's skybox, hustling so we can make it there before kickoff. We find something less than a luxury suite. The small room we enter looks more like a concrete bunker built by the French to repel the Nazis. The view is obstructed. Whenever the ball crosses midfield, I'm going to have to turn to the television to see the rest of the play. Still, there's a buffet of chips and sodas and even beers, though I'm not going to drink alone, and Gil gave up alcohol during his religious conversion. I take a seat just as the referee blows his whistle to start the game. I'm flipping open my notebook when Atlas scores.

This is a record. In a bad way. Not even thirty seconds have ticked off the clock. I turn to the television for a replay. The kickoff soared over to King Kong. Instead of clearing it forward, he headed it backwards and onto the feet of an Atlas striker. A quick pass, a quick shot, and a one-goal deficit for the Indios to climb out of. The television shows Edwin throwing up his hands in disgust. Gil and I are still digesting this disaster when Atlas scores again. Not much later, Atlas scores a third goal. Christian, the Indios' regular starting keeper, strained a hamstring in the game against San Luis. His backup got the start tonight. I've never seen worse play at any position at any level of the game.

"This goalie stinks," Gil spits. "We've known it for four or five years, but Treviño likes him." A more talented backup goalie quit the team last year, fleeing Juárez with his family after receiving an extortion attempt.

Reserve players who did not dress step into the skybox. They'd gotten lost, and they haven't seen any of the action on the field. The score shocks them. There's a momentary lift when Jair nets the first intentional Indios goal of the season, off a corner kick: 3–1. That's the way it stays for only nine minutes, until Atlas scores yet again, off a very stoppable shot. The home team somehow adds one more after that to make it an amazing 5–1 at halftime. God wants Atlas to win. This is far worse than the Monterrey beat-down. And there's still forty-five minutes left. Gil runs down to address the team in the locker room. I stay up in the box, smart enough not to step into that scene. I prepare for the postgame by flipping through my Spanish dictionary for the word "condolences." *Condolencias.* Gil comes back, the second half starts, and Atlas scores again. I open a beer. Fuck it.

Will the Indios win? That narrative died at kickoff. Now the question is just how bad it's going to be. Can Juárez stop the bleeding? Can the Indios retain some dignity, perhaps net a few more shots to make the margin less embarrassing? The referee calls a foul on our number 3, Juan de la Barrera, a central defender and the Indios' team captain. The foul is harsh enough to merit the formal warning of a yellow card. The call also wins Atlas a penalty kick, a gimme they easily convert to make the score 7–1. The crowd starts chanting *"Ocho!"* I open another beer. The carnage stops only with the final whistle. It's the worst defeat in Indios history. It's the worst loss for any team in the Primera this season. Stretching back to last season, the Indios have now gone twenty-three straight games without a win. That's a record, too. Again in a bad way. The Indios are officially the most pathetic team in the history of the Mexican major league.

"The Indios have fallen within a foot of the second division," declares one Guadalajara-based sportswriter as he waits for Atlas players to sit for interviews. Another writer suggests maybe the Indios should skip the second division and drop straight down to the third. The insults stop only when the Atlas players emerge from their locker room. They address the reporters, then drive off with their girlfriends or wives and in some cases also their small children. Marco and the visitors stay in their locker room for another hour and a half. I wait outside with the Indios' goalkeeper coach, who has reason to feel ashamed. We sit silently, listening to accusations from player to player, from player to coach, from coach back at player. The venom bleeds through the closed door, the message easy to translate: It's over. Not technically—the Indios remain statistically alive. But for all practical purposes, the locker room confrontation is a heated progression through all five stages of grief. The Indios needed two wins this road trip. They got none. Atlas's record is almost as sad as the Indios', yet Atlas just pasted Juárez by an embarrassingly high score. Seven goals! When the players and coaches finally emerge, nobody has anything left to say. Treviño still wears that black smudge on his forehead.

On the bus back to the hotel, there is no music. Just throat clearing, heavy sighs, and the bump of tires on an unforgiving road. The only thing to look forward to is a return flight to the most dangerous city in the world.

CHAPTER 8

The Devil

THERE'S A WOMAN IN JUÁREZ WHO has turned her house into an Indios shrine. She started outside, painting the team logo across her front facade. The image stretches from one side of the house to the other, INDIOS and the soccer ball with the red bandanna covering the wall and the front door and climbing up onto the roof. Her tribute continues inside. Posters and newspaper clippings and team scarves blanket the interior. Every itineration of the team jersey is on display. There's the uniform from back when the team's main sponsor was a cement company. There are last year's Joma-branded uniforms and also this year's jerseys, which look similar but are sewn by the Italian sportswear company Kappa. She reads *Vamos Indios*, the monthly Indios fan magazine, while sitting in a custom-made Indios reclining chair. She sleeps under an Indios bedspread colored red, white, and black. Her head rests on pillows shaped like soccer balls. Logo carpets pad her tile floor, and red Indios curtains drape her windows.

Players visit the house to pay their respects. The woman asks each player to sign one of her interior walls with a black permanent marker, leaving space for a friend of hers to airbrush in the player's portrait. Edwin, Marco, former star striker Sebastián Maz—they're all up on her wall. Maleno Frías is up there, of course. Francisco Ibarra's up there, too.

"I just love this city and this team," the woman says. "I can't really explain it."

I've begun assembling my own shrine inside my new apartment. I moved into a better unit in my complex. It's on the second and top floor. From the front door I can now see El Paso's Franklin Mountain.

A small porch in the back overlooks a cement courtyard. Air whooshes through my living room and kitchen when I open the windows. Sun flows through those windows all day long, immediately curing my seasonal affective disorder. At no time does the apartment smell like sewage. I'm papering one wall of my new place with all the team paraphernalia I've collected so far. My press passes from the away games against San Luis and Atlas. Gil Cantú's red business card. The Kappa tag from a jersey I bought, and the jersey itself, which I also tacked up on the wall. There's a photo of Marco hoisting the trophy in León after the Indios won their way into the Primera. That snapshot cozies up to the cover of a game program from the last home match against Morelia. I've got the season schedule taped up, too. I planned to highlight every win with a yellow marker. Six games have been played so far, one-third of the season. I haven't used the marker yet.

Some of the blank spots on my Indios wall have been filled in with pictures clipped out of newspaper sports sections. Mostly fan shots of El Kartel. There's Juvie from Las Cruces, who got arrested in Monterrey. And capos Mike and Don Roberto showing off their Indios tattoos. The biggest clip on the wall is of a guy in El Kartel named Arson Loskush. There's no special reason his photo takes up so much space. The newspaper happened to have printed the photo large, most likely because it's a pretty sweet shot. Arson's at a game, crying out in support. His round scalp is shaved smooth. He looks a little menacing, to be honest. Like it's a good thing he's rooting for our guys and not for the other team.

Arson Loskush isn't his real name. Loskush is slang, a form of "Fuck you" in border Spanish. His self-selected first name is English, and it means what you think it does. He's twenty-seven years old. He fathered his first child when he was seventeen. He lives with his mother, who dotes on him, and he works intermittently at his stepfather's factory in El Paso. He's a big Indios fan. Really big. The team occupies the very center of Arson's life. Yet he didn't ride the bus with us to the season opener in Monterrey. He hasn't attended any Indios home games since the season started in January. I've only met him once in person, and then only briefly. His absence is excused by the rest of El Kartel. They know the guy's been through a lot.

★　★　★

THE INDIOS RESUME practice at the Yvasa complex. Head coach
Pepe Treviño finds himself on a death watch; he may be fired at
any moment. Mexican authorities arrest a drug lord nicknamed
"La Barbie." They make a big show of it, parading him before television cameras in his Ralph Lauren polo shirt. La Barbie is a young
guy, light-skinned, an American born in Laredo who rose to the
top of Mexico's Beltrán-Leyva Cartel. He doesn't look too upset
about his arrest, at least not on television. He smiles throughout
his perp walk, as if he's in on some joke. In interviews, he claims
to know who shot Club América's star striker six days before the
game against the Indios. When asked, he helpfully breaks down the
current cartel alliances. The Zetas, a collective of rogue soldiers
who work the Gulf of Mexico, are "unspeakably sadistic." The
trouble between the Sinaloa Cartel and the cartel in Juárez started,
La Barbie claims, when an agreement allowing the Sinaloans to
work the border was broken by a man named Juan Pablo Ledesma.
I know about this guy, Ledesma. He's one of La Línea's top men.
People in Juárez call him J. L., pronounced, in Spanish, *"ho-ta el-
lay."* He's also known as Dos Letres. Another of his nicknames: the
Beast.

Away from the border, La Línea is usually described as the Juárez
Cartel's enforcement arm. That is indeed how La Línea started out:
as disgruntled policemen recruited to help the cartel crush its ene-
mies. Yet that's no longer how things stand. Now people in Juárez
refer to the cartel itself as La Línea, because the enforcement arm
has overtaken the operation. When cartel kingpin Amando Carrillo died during plastic surgery in 1997, control fell to his brother,
Vicente, a guy so hands-off, or maybe simply so ineffectual, there is
speculation he might have retired. La Línea stepped into the leadership void. The names Pedro Sánchez and Chalo González are
bandied about in print, but I don't know who these guys are. J. L. is
the name I recognize. He's usually described as La Línea's number
two, I guess after Vicente. He's a strategist, the leader ordering as-
sassinations and drafting the narcomanta warnings dropped around
town to scare the visiting Sinaloans. When he kills someone himself, he always fires one .38-caliber bullet in the head, his signature
move. The *New York Times* calls J. L. La Línea's "point man in
Juárez," "the local crime boss," and a man trying "to establish himself as a gangster in the U.S. tradition, controlling extortion rackets,

prostitution, gambling as well as cocaine traffic." J. L. is omnipresent in the city, even if I haven't yet knowingly seen him.

"He's this big guy, super fat. Super fucking fat," says Saul Luna, one of my better friends in El Kartel. Saul is twenty-five. He played soccer at a small college in New Mexico but dropped out to be closer to his mother, who has breast cancer. He's asked me to wear a pink wristband in her honor, which I've paired with a red-and-black nylon bracelet from El Kartel. Saul has reenrolled in college at New Mexico State, in nearby Las Cruces, where he's majoring in bilingual education. He works nights at a Lowe's. He's growing out his hair so he can donate it to Locks of Love. Saul knows what J. L. looks like because there was a time when the local crime boss partied with El Kartel.

"Arson's brother Charlie is the one who brought him in," Saul tells me. "When we first won the championship over there in León, we came back and started throwing these parties at a bar owned by a friend of ours. Every Friday El Kartel would have our meetings there. Someone would speak for like thirty minutes on what we're going to do for the next season, blah blah blah, and after the meetings we'd just party. This one night we were all there when Charlie shows up. He had a friend with him, Charlie did. I'm like, 'Man, this guy is, like, fat. Like daredevil-fat-guy fat.' And he's sweating. And he's dressed as a cowboy. He's got the boots, got the belt. He's bald. And he's sweating like a motherfucker. I saw him and my first impression was 'Wow, this guy's really fat,' you know? I didn't think anything else.

" 'You guys want a beer?' he asked. Sure, dude. Get us a beer. We drank, like, half our beers with him, then he and Charlie kind of went away. Later on that night, driving back to El Paso, Arson asked, 'What do you think of that guy?' I said, 'Whatever. I didn't even catch his name.' Arson tells me.

" 'J. L.?! Are you fucking serious? We could have been targets!' "

I often hang with Saul when I cross into El Paso, which I've started to do now that I've got my car. We'll lunch at Chico's Tacos or we'll go to his sister's apartment to play FIFA on an Xbox. I'll be Barcelona, the best team in the world. Saul will play as Indios, the worst team in the international soccer hinterland of Mexico. He'll always win. One time when he defeated me, the computer skipped over Lionel Messi to name Marco Vidal the player of the match, which was surreal. I'd heard that Charlie, Arson's brother, ran with La Línea. And that he was murdered last September. I ask Saul to tell me the story.

"It was Arson who was into the Indios first. We all went to El Paso High—the Lady on the Hill—and we used to party in Juárez all the time. Charlie started showing up just because he wanted to hang out with Arson. Charlie had been living in Juárez for like two years, because he'd been deported. He'd been arrested in El Paso for breaking and entering. He couldn't cross anymore, yet he was still really close to his brother. One day Arson told him he was going to be going to an Indios game, so Charlie asked if Arson could maybe get him a ticket. At first the stadium was more of a place where they could see each other, but after a while Charlie just fell in love with the Indios, like everybody else.

"Charlie was involved with the wrong people. After he got deported, his way of making money was selling. He was so involved in selling drugs that he got to work with J. L., who was the main leader of La Línea. They were pretty much in Juárez on their own, La Línea was. There was no Juárez Cartel. There was no Cártel de Sinaloa or Cártel del Pacifico. These guys were kind of like *the* guys who decided who could sell and who did what. Charlie was working with J. L. for La Línea probably for like six months. He stopped working with him maybe nine months before he got shot.

"He saw a murder, is what happened. Two guys from where he worked took two other guys out. They were shot at an OXXO, one of those convenience stores, and Charlie saw the whole thing. He told Arson what he had seen and said he had to get out. He changed. He got a job. It was at some warehouse in Juárez. He still couldn't cross, so he had to stay in Juárez. Charlie realized he had gotten in too deep. He was showing up at games so drugged out. So he just stopped. He quit all that stuff, said 'Enough is enough.' He tried to break from La Línea. He wanted a normal life.

"It's not that easy to get out. The guy who lived in front of Charlie, Fernando, was a really big pusher. He would show up at Charlie's house to party. It was a constant party. They were doing drugs and shit, partying for three days and shit like that. Once Charlie decided to get out, he tried to avoid Fernando. Charlie would pretend to not be home. He tried to stay friends with everybody, but he was pushing the bad people away.

"One day Fernando says to Charlie, 'Go with me to distribute this, and then we're going to pick up some money.' Charlie had to go with him on some occasions. Fernando was a tough guy. If you would look at him bad, or if he got the impression you didn't want to talk to him, he'd tell you straight out. He was just kind of a maniac. Even Arson was scared of him. Fernando beat Arson's ass a couple times to set him straight. To be pretty powerful, you have to do pretty bad stuff. Once you start growing, you're a target, you're a threat to everybody else now.

"The day he got killed, Charlie was at this club called Coco Bongo. He and a friend were drinking some beers and apparently these four men walked in and they asked, by name, for two guys: Charlie and this other guy.

"'What the fuck do you want?' Charlie asked. 'Who the fuck do you think you are?'

"One of the four men says, 'Hey man, we were just asking,' and then they walked out. Charlie and his friend kept on drinking. Ten or fifteen minutes later the four men came back in. They didn't say a word, they just shot 'em. That's it. The other guy died, too. I don't know who he was. I'm guessing he was one of Charlie's friends who was involved in the whole drug scene. That had to be, or why else would he be a target?

"They had a funeral service even though Arson and his family are not Catholic. They're Christian. They cremated Charlie and they brought the ashes to El Paso. He finally got to cross back. They did a little service that we went to. I went over to Arson and we hugged and we both just broke down.

"J. L. got to be *the guy* by doing bad stuff. He made it known that if you come at him he'll kill you. Yet Chapo came in and was killing all of J. L.'s people. That's the main thing that this whole drug war is: Chapo started wanting J. L.'s territory. They're going toe to toe. But Chapo has too many people on his side. Chapo's gaining control. Pretty much everybody in La Línea is getting killed. J. L. is recruiting kids now, because he doesn't want to give up the power yet. But it's true, like, that Chapo has this territory now. It's basic greed with El Chapo. If you're capable of grabbing more territory, you do it. All mankind works that way. *Lord of the Flies* is how I see it.

"Two weeks after we first saw J. L., he came by again. Everyone in El Kartel was at this club in the Pronaf District, those bars off

Lincoln Avenue. The club is not open anymore; somebody torched it. But back then you would walk in and it looked like a black-and-white theme party. After you got past this little entry foyer, you were in a huge room with black couches and white banners. There was a bar to the left, and to the right was a DJ booth. There was another room in the back where they had pool tables. It used to be a gay bar at first. Then it went with the black-and-white theme. It looked upscale. J. L. just showed up that night, again with Charlie.

"I already knew who he was. Call me crazy, but I just went to say, 'Hi.' He and I and Arson and Charlie were drinking when all of a sudden Charlie's like 'I gotta go, guys.' We didn't ask any questions. Before he left, Charlie told Arson that J. L. wanted some El Kartel shirts. He wanted to wear them. Arson asked me if we could make him a shirt. I said, 'Dude, first, I don't think we can *make* a shirt that fucking big. And two, I really don't think you want him wearing our shirt. What if he's seen?' All these years we've been fighting the drug cartels in Juárez. Everyone thinks El Kartel and the cartels are linked together. We don't want to give people a reason. So it was like 'No, dude.'

" 'But he wants one,' Arson said. He had a point. You can't say no to somebody like J. L. When he didn't show up again, we were all just relieved.

"There's these stories from Durango, where my mom comes from. There were parties at the ranches. The Devil would show up at the party. He would appear as a handsome guy and take the girls out to dance. Only when he would leave did the women notice that his feet were the hooves of a goat. My mom tells old stories like that. It was kind of the same thing with J. L. You see this guy and he's nice to you, but when he leaves you can't believe he was there. We were exposed to so much danger. It's crazy nerve-wracking."

THE INDIOS' GREATEST win ever came against a team called Cruz Azul. Blue Cross. A traditional power stocked with stars from the Mexican national team. If the Indios' 2007 victory over León elevated them into the Primera, beating Cruz Azul a year later allowed them to remain in the top league, an achievement nobody expected. The Indios had played so poorly in their first season that a quick relegation back to the minors appeared inevitable. The slim calculus of survival required the Indios to make the playoffs in their second season, then advance to at least the semifinals, the final four. Unlikely. Highly improbable. That they strung together enough wins to qualify for the last of eight playoff spots was considered a miracle in itself. Their reward was a home-and-home series against Cruz Azul, the winningest team in the league that season.

No goals were scored in the first game, played in Juárez. No fans watched the second game, at least not in person. Swine flu hysteria. The health ministry, fearing the spread of the infectious airborne disease, barred the public from entering the sunken blue bowl where Cruz Azul plays on a field below street level. Indios players wore white masks over their mouths on the flight to Mexico City, and then on the bus to the stadium. The absence of fans gave the match a spooky aura, as if the Indios and Cruz Azul were the only survivors of a nuclear war. Quietly, the Indios won, 1–0. When the final whistle echoed around the empty bleachers, Indios piled atop their goalie, as if they'd just won a championship—which in a way they had. They got to stay in the major league. Francisco Ibarra divided among the players some two million dollars in bonuses.

Although a win in today's home game against Cruz Azul is just as necessary, interest in the game isn't as high. At practice all week, television reporters showed up only to grab five minutes of footage before taking off again, no longer able to convince their producers they need to soak up sunshine for the full three hours. A national soccer magazine discontinued its "Relegation Watch" feature, stating, "We all know it's going to be the Indios." Even Gil Cantú acknowledges the inevitable. "Yeah, that's probably true," he admits when I tell him about the magazine insult. The game is being played on Marco's twenty-fourth birthday. His parents are here to help him celebrate, and are sitting in Olympic Stadium alongside several other Texas relatives. When Marco runs onto the field for the pregame national anthem, his young nephew from Dallas runs alongside him, which makes two women sitting near me squeal at the cuteness. Head coach Pepe Treviño runs out for the anthem to a shower of boos.

The Indios play their best game yet. What is it with this team, always bouncing back whenever I abandon hope? Early in the first half, Gil's conspiracy theories are fed when one of our defenders is red-carded out of the game, leaving the Indios shorthanded. But even down a man, the Indios outwork a top team. Marco and the rest of the defense coalesce into an elite unit, an impregnable wall. Cruz Azul forwards sulk in frustration, as if they can't believe the lowly Indios are shutting them down. At one point, Christian, the number-one goalie, back from his injury, snuffs a Cruz Azul break-away to preserve the shutout and earn himself Primera player of the week, a major honor. (The goalie who'd started against Atlas wasn't even allowed to dress in a uniform for this game, a major punishment.) The score is still 0–0 late in the match when Marco somehow finds himself with the ball just outside the Cruz Azul penalty box, unmarked and in shooting range.

"As I kicked it, I thought to myself, *Please give me a birthday gift!*" Marco will tell me after the game. His slow shot dribbles wide of the net, not even close; the guy's a defender for a reason. The game ends soon afterwards, a scoreless tie. Angry Cruz Azul players walk off the pitch shouting insults at their hosts. *Enjoy the minor leagues, chumps.* The tie gives Juárez only a single point in the standings, but I'm happy with the moral victory. It's inspiring to watch these underdogs play with such heart, and at such a high level. El Kartel, never content, chants in Spanish that Pepe Treviño is not a head coach—he's a nightclub whore.

The front door of Marco's house is wide-open a couple hours af-ter the game, when I drop by for his party. Little things like this give me hope. How dangerous can it be in Juárez, really? Marco's extended family, including young kids, have driven down here, by choice. No one would bring kids to a real war zone, right? A host of Dany's Juárez relatives cram into the house, too, overflowing into the backyard, where a flat-screen TV broadcasts a game in the Ger-man Bundesliga. I find a seat at one of ten round tables set up in the garage. Dany carves up a spongy soccer ball frosted with the word CONGRATULATIONS, probably the same cake Marco's been getting since he turned three. He was physically exhausted when he took his shot on goal, he tells me with a sheepish smile. After the mas-sacre at Atlas, it was satisfying to tie a top team, especially short-handed, and even if the Indios really needed an outright win. He tousles the hair of a nephew as he shares this postgame breakdown. Marco tells me he can't wait to have kids of his own.

"We'll find out tomorrow," he says when I ask if Pepe Treviño is going to be fired, as seems certain.

CHAPTER 9

Fussion

THE PLAYERS ON THE INDIOS ARE in great physical shape. Not a lot of other people in Juárez are. I blame the food. Every day in Juárez I enjoy lunches and dinners that, if I were back in Miami, would register as my best meals of the month. I often go with Marco to Los Bichis, a Sinaloan seafood chain. We watch the Champions League as I tuck into the garlic shrimp and yellow rice I always order. Ramón, in the Indios' media department, has turned me on to an even better Sinaloan place, nothing but a small roadside shack out near the airport. The specialty there is aguachile: diced onions, raw shrimp, cilantro, cucumbers, and mounds of other stuff dumped into a spicy and cold Clamato base, splashed with lime and served in these huge black lava-rock bowls. When I'm the mood for pure grease, I go for gorditas and carnitas at El Puerco Loco, "the simple taste of the North." The restaurant's logo is a smiling pig, an accurate representation of how I feel after swallowing pockets of deep-fried pork that I'm compelled to cut with a bottle or two of sugary Mexican Coca-Cola. Chihuahua is known for the quality of its beef. I love the tender arrachera I get at this small restaurant in El Centro decorated with memorabilia from the bullfights city officials have suspended while the cartels duke it out. If I'm drinking with El Kartel in the Pronaf District, I'll usually stop on the way home for tacos grilled by this old guy I've gotten to know pretty well. Nothing better than Juárez street tacos.

To keep from turning into el gringo gordo, I jog. Long-distance running is a bad habit I picked up in Colorado and haven't been able to shake. I'm pretty good at sticking to a schedule. After trying out a few routes near my apartment, and after once getting hopelessly lost in my own neighborhood, I've started running along the river. I drive up to Olympic Stadium, where I park within eyesight of the groundskeepers, who watch over my car. I duck through a hole in a chain-link fence and cross the four lanes of the new and largely unused Pope John Paul II highway. The path I run on is dusty gravel that follows the curve of the river's concrete canal. There are usually a few other joggers out there with me, though mainly I see horses and wild dogs and occasional packs of off-duty *federales* riding expensive mountain bikes. (*Federales*, with their college degrees and better salaries, are considered the yuppies of Mexican law enforcement.) I once ran stride for stride with a jogger visible on the other side of the fence, in Texas. I ran on the American side myself my first full day on the border, when I was staying at that El Paso hotel. Union Pacific Railroad linesmen yelled when I ran past. They thought I was a Mexican who had just snuck across.

Border Patrol helicopters zoom overhead, following the concrete canal so closely they remind me of airborne bobsleds. I duck under the Stanton Street and Santa Fe bridges, continuing past the Puente Negro, a black steel railroad bridge commercially linking the two countries. Bass-heavy horns blast from the engines of trains stacked up on the El Paso side. I'm always startled by the sonic chain reaction when two cars crash together with an energy that reverberates all the way down the line. If I run beyond the point where the concrete canal ends, the path transitions into long and wild grass. I usually turn back at a riverfront shack where a pack of wild Chihuahuas once attacked me, initially to my amusement, then to my dread. The first gangster Chihuahua seemed mostly adorable. What are you going to do, *perrito*, nibble my ankle? But soon I was surrounded by five, then seven tiny dogs. They circled around me, yipping like mad, waiting for me to trip and fall so they could tear at my flesh. I envisioned the most embarrassing human death ever. "American Killed in Juárez," wouldn't be a shocking headline. The subhead, though, would slot my demise in the News of the Weird: "Face ripped off by pack of supercute Taco Bell lapdogs."

The return leg of my regular run passes a drainage canal always clogged with garbage. The first time I ran past it, I thought to myself that it would be an ideal place to dump a body, that thought perhaps a sign I'm becoming Juarense. (I was right, too. Within the

month I read about a dead body found right there.) When I return to
the main concrete canal, and if it's dry, I like to run down inside it.
The actual international border lies in the middle of the viaduct. I
once jogged over the line, just to do it. Although I immediately
darted back to the Mexican side, the U.S. Border Patrol dispatched
a trio of officers on green ATVs to follow me the rest of the way.
One early morning down in the canal, under the Puente Negro
bridge, I leaped over a puddle of blood. *I bet someone was killed
there*, I thought to myself, casually noting to pick up the paper on
the drive home.

Someone *had* been killed there. A Border Patrol officer had shot
a Mexican boy. The kid had being trying to slip through the fence
into El Paso. When the Border Patrol showed up, the boy abandoned
his mission, darting back to the Mexican side, to that spot I ran
past. U.S. officials say the boy was lobbing rocks at an officer who'd
arrived on a mountain bike, on the American side. So the officer
shot the boy in the head. Across the international border. Reading
the story in *El Diario*, I could tell the shooting would be big news
on both sides of the river.

BIG WEECHO CLIMBS until he's standing on the third and top rope.
To simply balance up there without falling seems like a challenge.
A row of three-year-olds in lawn chairs taunt him, boo him, and
wish him great bodily harm in high-pitched little voices. He turns
his mask to the left to showcase the fiery curlicues of Muñeco In-
fernal, his first wrestling alter ego. He turns his head to the right
and now his black mask appears to be marked only with the simple
white piping of Blackfish, a second character he played, until a
knee injury knocked him out of the game for a while. Like the district attorney in a Batman comic, Weecho's united the two *luchadores*
into one, particularly imposing, new wrestler. His opponent, Punisher, lies in the center of the outdoor ring, illuminated by a single
shop light, the kind you might hook to the hood of a car while
changing the air filter. He's on his back, Punisher is, rolling left
and right, clearly drained but trying to muster the strength to stand
and rip Weecho down from the ropes, which is what the kids want
him to do.

The loudest shrieks come from a tiny girl wearing blue jeans, a flowery pink top, and a pair of sneakers that flash pink lights every time she takes a step. It's her party. She had been asked how she wanted to celebrate her third birthday. Would she like a bounce house? A pony to ride for a few hours with her friends? *"Lucha libre!"* she shouted, to the great pleasure of her father, a professional *luchador* who fights under the name Rey Escorpion and who happens to be Weecho's cousin. Even without family connections, finding *luchadores* to work a backyard birthday party in El Paso is an easy request to fill. A Justice League of masked wrestlers roam the border, fighting up to three times a week in venues from the Poliforo Juan Gabriel, in Juárez, to the nightclubs of downtown El Paso. Weecho invited me to the little girl's birthday party even though *luchador* law forbids him from acknowledging his masked alter ego. He brought me because he wants to show why he must don a mask to reveal his true identity.

When Weecho picked me up on the Texas side of the Free Bridge, he looked like the same giant Kartelero I've come to know. Big round face. Full lips. Ears perched unusually high on his head, his eyebrows so thick and wide they appear to have been finger-painted on. His meaty hands connect to strong arms that are in turn welded onto a barrel chest. The impact of his physique is softened by an ever-present smile. The first time I met Weecho, on the bus to Monterrey, I wrote in my notebook that he was a teddy bear, a big softy. Nothing I've seen since has changed my impression. He's a super-nice guy. Almost everyone on the border is warm and generous— *"Mi casa es tu casa,"* Marco Vidal said to me only two minutes after we first met—but Weecho seems kind at the very core of his gargantuan frame. And he is gargantuan. I once asked him if *luchadores* take steroids to blow up their bodies. "You do what you have to do to get big," he replied. "It is what it is."

Weecho was born into a wrestling family so serious about the sport they've set up a regulation octagon in the backyard of their El Paso house. *Lucha libre* has taken his brother to fights in Paris and London and currently in New York City, where he's trying to develop a *luchador* television series. In the show, Weecho's brother hopes to adjudicate disputes—and also grocery shop and care for his TV kids and share meals with his TV wife—all while wearing his wrestling mask. It really is a violation of the *luchador* code to be seen without the mask. Weecho had to show up at the backyard birthday party long before any of the invited guests. When the kids arrived, I ate chicken and cake with them out in the backyard while Weecho waited in a bedroom with the other wrestlers. He wouldn't step outside until he was fully outfitted and it was time to fight.

I appraise his figure in the ring. Weecho's not exactly in top shape at the moment. He blew out his knee about a year ago while moonlighting as a nightclub bouncer, an injury that left him unable to fight but free, apparently, to smoke weed, drink beer, and down bag after bag of potato chips. He's carrying a gut. Soft skin hides the musculature of his arms. His legs aren't even visible. I thought all professional wrestlers were required to wear tights and a tank, but Weecho's sporting baggy black leather pants embellished with green lightning bolts. Still up there on the ropes, he continues to goad the kids heckling him from their front-row lawn chairs. Will Punisher rise off the mat? Will Weecho get his comeuppance, his punishment? Suddenly, Weecho leaps skyward, flipping heels over head to land chest-first atop his opponent, pinning Punisher with every one of his 340 pounds and I can't even calculate how many extra Gs of force. *Wham!* The mat shakes with a sonic boom. The kids—the adults, too—shriek in shock. When our brains catch up to the spectacle our eyes just witnessed, when we see the ref slap the mat three times and we realize Weecho has just won in the most spectacular way imaginable, our shock gives way to awe. That might have been the greatest physical feat I've seen in my life. Axl Rose takes over the stereo system. Weecho ducks under the ropes, exiting to a shower of hosannas. He stops to pose for a picture with a baby a woman thrusts into his arms. A dozen little kids scamper into the ring. Several of the boys and even a few of the girls sport *luchador* masks of their own. They climb on the ropes and flop onto the thinly padded ring, taunting and preening like the superhero they just watched.

"I did that just for you, man!" Weecho says after he changes back into his civilian clothes, after he slips out of the house unseen by the kids and as he drives me back to the Free Bridge. Adrenaline continues to flow through his veins. (Mine, too; that backflip was awesome.) "I wanted to show you something you'd never forget! I just want you to see the good side of us. I fucking hate stereotypes, man. We're not all gangbangers."

Weecho's right forearm is a canvas for a giant black tattoo in honor of the California metal band Tool, whom he worships. A second tattoo higher up the arm features a stylized eagle's mask, a logo I've seen on T-shirts in Juárez and on food packaging at the S-Mart grocery store I frequent. HECHO EN MEXICO. He was born in Juárez, though he was raised and still lives in El Paso.

"I'm all about roots," he tells me. "I love my Mexican roots. Mexico pretty much made me who I am, you know? Just the whole culture. We wear masks in the ring because the Aztec warriors, when they went into battle, they wore masks, too. Morally, personality-wise, everything I am is Mexican."

I'm often struck by the fluidity of the border. Radio signals flow freely in both directions. If I'm driving around Juárez at midday, I'm in the jungle with Jim Rome. In the mornings and late afternoons I'm usually following Washington politics on NPR. Often, even when I'm in El Paso, I like to listen to Orbita radio out of Juárez, the most eclectic radio station in the world, home to a playlist that bounces from a French torch singer to Ozzy Osbourne to an Appalachian folk song. Juarenses ask for "sodas" when they order a soft drink, using the English word although everyone else in Mexico says "refresco."

Yet the border is so concrete. The woman who cuts my hair in Juárez has never set foot in El Paso despite living along La Frontera for thirty-six years, her entire life. When I'm surfing the Web at the burrito stand near my apartment, I can't watch clips of *The Daily Show* over the Internet, because they are available only to people physically inside the United States. Ken-tokey is unable to visit his girlfriend, Sofia, at her house in El Paso. To him and to hundreds of thousands of other Juarenses, the border is as impregnable as the Indios' defense against Cruz Azul. How impregnable? The U.S. government will kill to secure it.

After the Border Patrol shot that boy, I heard Buzz Adams, El Paso's best-known radio personality, talk about the incident. Adams worried about the Border Patrol officer. "I really hope they don't throw the guy under the bus," he said. Under the bus? How about throwing him in jail? I think the shooter is a murderer, straight up. Killing a fourteen-year-old? (That's what was initially reported. The boy turned out to have been fifteen, which to me is no different.) Because he was throwing rocks? I don't care if the kid chipped the officer's tooth, which he didn't; there's no evidence the officer was struck by so much as a pebble. That's no reason to take a boy's life, I believe, an opinion not popular on the American side. Listening to El Paso radio, or especially reading the hateful comments posted after articles in the *El Paso Times*, I think the entire city of Juárez comes across as irredeemable, Juarenses as subhuman scum. Of course the border must be fortified! *We don't want any of* them *coming over here.*

"They call us *frontchis*," says Saul Luna. Saul was born in El Paso, to a Mexican family. "I wanted to stay in Juárez, but my parents were caught up in the American Dream and all that. I'm really proud that I can speak two languages, but when I was young I was embarrassed about it." Weecho tells me that when he was in high school—not that long ago—one of his teachers told him that, as a Mexican, he shouldn't want a Starbucks to open in his barrio.

"I'm like, Fuck that, man," he told me. "I love coffee every day, man."

Weecho is an American who literally fights to promote his Mexican heritage. When he talks, his words slip from English to Spanish, probably without his even realizing it. He loves premium American coffee and he also follows a Mexican soccer team with a losing record. His feet straddle two cultures, like so many people living along the border. Cultures that are often violently divided. Which is why I love the intentionally misspelled name he currently wrestles under: Fussion.

THEY BURY THE boy in a cemetery up in the Juárez hills. On the television news, red and white ribbons flutter on wooden crosses marking dozens of other fresh graves. I watch his parents sob in grief. A glass window cut into the lid of the coffin reveals the boy to be wearing a soccer jersey. His friends wear T-shirts that state, in English, IN MEMORY OF KEKO. A couple days before the funeral, the boy's aunt walked down to the river with a broom and a pail of soapy water. She washed the bloodstains off the concrete canal where I'd jogged back on that early-morning run. We're calling this dead body *el joven Juarense*, the boy from Juárez. That's a rare honor, to be named. Usually we try to wash the murders from our minds as quickly as possible. Almost seventy more people have been murdered in the week since he was shot by the Border Patrol. The officer who shot him has not been named, much less charged with a crime. (His name has since leaked out in court documents, as has the disquieting fact that he continues to patrol the border.)

Not long after the funeral, I walk over the Free Bridge to watch Weecho wrestle once again. Marco has taught me not to drive across the line if I can avoid it. Instead of waiting up to two hours for my car to clear customs, it's easier—and dirt cheap—to just park in the secure lot near the bridge, walk across, and have the El Kartel shuttle service come pick me up. Usually that's Weecho or Saul Luna or Saul's close friend Angel. Tonight when I reach the narrow parking lot on the Texas side of the bridge, I find a rusty Malibu waiting for me. I see Weecho in the passenger's seat, but I can't tell who is driving. Only when I get right up to the car do I realize it's Arson Loskush behind the wheel. I throw him a fist bump and climb in the backseat. "Big night tonight, Fussion," I say to Weecho.

"Hey man, I'm not supposed to acknowledge that," he responds. Weecho—I mean Fussion—is headlining at the Wild Wild West Ball Room. It's his official public return to the ring after his knee injury, an occasion advertised on fliers posted on both sides of the river. Daddy Yankee thumps on the stereo as Arson steers east past the Ascarate Drive In and the Chevron refinery, continuing until we come upon a squat and square warehouse that is the ballroom. Arson finds a space in the crowded gravel lot. Weecho raises his duffel bag, signaling that he must head over to the back entrance to maintain the *luchador* illusion. The rest of us walk toward the front door, passing a bronze statue of a buffalo before we slip inside.

Sofia's already here, standing next to her sister and her father, Rigo. Mike the Capo, legally trapped in El Paso, hovers nearby in a pack of six or seven other Karteleros. We have to pay to join them, ten dollars each. Any tickets Weecho might comp would come out of his modest purse. I hand over my money happily, proud to support the wrestling arts. I wave to Sofia as I enter the ballroom, blinking my eyes as I adjust to the darkness.

"We've been laughing so hard," Sofia says, kissing me on the cheek. "We were joking that when the *lucha libre* ends, then the *quinceañera* begins."

The Wild Wild West Ball Room has the feel of an underground

fight club. Bare concrete walls, linoleum tiling the floor, a ceiling so low they had to remove the blades on two overhead fans before setting up the ring. Sofia's joke that the wrestling will be followed by a coming-out party for a fifteen-year-old girl is not far off the mark. There will be a wedding reception here tomorrow afternoon. In a dark corner I spy a giant paper heart, arrangements of white plastic flowers, and several folding tables covered in white paper tablecloths, all to be pulled out as soon as the ring is broken down. For now, metal folding chairs fan out on all four sides of the ring, almost every chair occupied. Little girls blow bubbles and tap on tambourines illuminated with glow-stick technology. A man rests his arm on his wife's shoulder as their son shadow-wrestles, aping the moves the pros execute in the ring.

The undercard is under way. A seemingly endless supply of *luchadores* parade forth, fight, and are dispatched back to the dressing room. I watch four *luchadores* dance around a fat referee costumed in the mandatory black-and-white stripes. One wrestler sports leather pants embroidered with the word NASCAR. A small man in a blue mask grapples with an even smaller man in a silver mask decorated with what look like red wings over his eyes. Two female *luchadores* leap over the top ropes and tumble into the ring, the traditional entrance. A trio of bumblebees—wrestlers in black singlets and yellow masks—buzz around the action. There's a sonic, cymbalic crash every time a *luchador* falls to the canvas, wooden boards under the thin mat clanging on a steel framework. The ring is loud by design, each crash intended to rise above screams that are predominantly high-pitched, female, and preadolescent.

Every kid in the ballroom swarms into the ring during the breaks between fights, just like they did after the backyard birthday party. The music rotates from Spanish to English, cumbia to Nirvana, banda to Eminem. A tremendous cheer erupts for a *luchador* in a pink tank top, which makes me suspect all of us in the audience might be friends and family of the many fighters on the card. I'm pleased to see that Mike the Capo has smuggled in an eighteen-pack of Bud Light. He hands me a can just before Weecho enters the ring.

He's the tallest *luchador* by far. The largest, too, though his frame is softer than those of his opponents; he really does need to cut down on the weed. He's wearing the same black leather pants with the green lightning bolts. He's also wearing the same black cape he wore when he entered the ring at the backyard birthday party. There is one change for tonight's show: When Weecho lets his cape fall to the ground, he reveals a chest not covered in tight black spandex, as before. This time he's wearing a red Indios jersey. We go crazy. He turns to let us see the number on the back: 915, the El Paso area code.

"Fussion! Fussion! Fussion!" At the backyard birthday party, Weecho was the heel, the villain reviled until he pulled off his amazing backflip. Tonight he's the hero, the well-known veteran returned to the ring after a long absence. He starts the fight by ricocheting off the ropes, rocketing back across the ring to slam into his opponent, who wears a red mask. *Lucha libre* looks completely scripted. I'd figured Weecho spends hours sketching out his routines. Turns out that's not the case at all. He had never met Punisher before that first backyard fight I saw, not even under any of Weecho's previous wrestling identities. Experienced *luchadores*—the only kind Weecho will wrestle—communicate via subtle signals, telegraphing, and intuition. It's a dance—no one is really being slugged in the head—but the choreography is improvised. And physical. And dangerous.

The crowd screams for blood. A high school teacher who moonlights as Weecho's coach bleats encouragement from a ringside seat. The referee, as integral to the drama as any of the fighters, counts and cautions and separates clutching opponents when necessary. Two more wrestlers waiting in the corners tag into the match. Then, unexpectedly, two more arrive and join the fray. Six wrestlers now clog up the ring, with still more streaming in from the dressing room. Eight wrestlers, then ten. In the chaos, two of the wrestlers tumble under the ropes, continuing their fight in the crowd. They overturn folding chairs as they barrel toward where we're standing. Mike the Capo pulls the Bud Light out of harm's way. Sofia snaps photos. I find myself grinning stupidly. It's so funny.

"Is this a real fight?" someone asks.

"That man just hit a woman," says someone else. "Should we do something?"

Fussion slips out of the ring and runs toward us, picking up a metal folding chair along the way. He uses the chair to slap down the man who had just hit the woman. Okay, that wasn't real domestic violence earlier, just part of the theater. *This is improv to put Second City to shame.* The woman-slapping man scurries back into the ring, as if he were a *luchador,* which he obviously is. Weecho chases after him, catches him, and body-slams him down on the mat, hard. The man wriggles on his back, apparently incapacitated. Weecho climbs the ropes. I know what he's going to do. I'm ready for it this time.

Weecho again pulls off the backflip, to complete pandemonium.

"That may have been the best night of my life," I say at the after-party at Sofia's house. Everybody's still talking about the backflip. "As a life experience, it tops my birth."

Sofia's father, Rigo, has turned his backyard into a nightclub complete with every amenity but a state liquor license. The U2 Bar, he calls it, established in 2005 after a road trip to see Bono and the Edge play Phoenix and San Diego. Posters of Irish arena rockers are augmented with pictures of John Lennon and Jimi Hendrix and more than a few Indios team photos. There's classic bar neon and also a Pink Floyd wall clock. Two TVs, one of them a very big screen, broadcast highlights of a soccer game played earlier. Cases of Bud Light chill in a refrigerator, the blue cans embossed with outlines of the state of Texas. Sofia's mother sets out bowls of tortilla chips, plates of picked jalapeño slices, and a Crock-Pot bubbling with orange melted cheese. Incongruously, at least to my sensibilities, bottles of Perrier sit in ice buckets atop the bar. Also on the bar are a tray of chicken wings and the lemons and Tabasco sauce necessary to make Bud Light palatable. I'm handed a shot of tequila. Arson points to the swimming pool in the backyard. "Get in, Robert! It's not cold." Mike the Capo runs into the house to borrow a pair of swimming trunks.

The pool is the only part of the backyard nightclub that Rigo didn't design and build himself. He's lived in this house for twelve years, though neither he nor his wife nor even Sofia or her sister is an American citizen; all are here on temporary visas. When he was a boy growing up in Juárez, Rigo used to cross on the weekends to mow lawns for five dollars each. His mom crossed too, to clean houses for fifteen dollars a day. He says he might return to Mexico when he's done with the El Paso warehouse he runs. Until he does return, *if* he ever does return, he and his family remain Mexican citizens living fully American lives.

Saul Luna drops by with his girlfriend, a teacher here in El Paso.

When he sees me at the bar, he points to one of the many license plates Rigo has nailed to the walls. The lettering on the bottom of old Chihuahua plates spells out FRONT, for *Fronterizo*, and CHIH, for Chihuahua—the genesis of the derogatory label *"frontchi."* Saul asks for my take on the Border Patrol shooting. I say there was no excuse for the officer to fire his gun. Saul agrees. Weecho has studied criminology and he thinks the officer was totally in the right.

"The kid was throwing rocks," Weecho shouts over to us.

"And for that he was shot in the head?" Saul asks.

"They said he might have been a coyote, too," Weecho adds. Coyotes smuggle Mexicans across the border for a fee.

"And for that he was shot in the head?"

Weecho says someone on the Santa Fe Bridge captured the shooting on a cell phone, and the video has been posted online. "All you have to do is look at the video, man," he insists. Saul and I still doubt him, so Weecho finds a laptop and pulls up the footage on Univision .com. The officer can be seen arriving on his bicycle, on the American side of the river. Several kids who had been trying to cross into El Paso scurry back over the dry riverbed, to what they must have presumed was the safety of the Mexican side. The officer steps off his bike, pulls out his gun, and fires. No rock throwing is visible. If the officer is under any threat whatsoever, it is not apparent.

"Sorry, Weecho," Saul says when the video concludes. "That's disgusting."

I agree. Even Weecho agrees. The evidence is damning. The *luchador* folds up the laptop. I head out to the lawn that circles the pool. I lie on my back and look up at a moon that is waxing. Thin trails of clouds rush across the dark sky. I'm a little drunk, and my head is spinning. Until he saw the shooting video, Weecho—*hecho en Mexico*—had taken the side of the Border Patrol. Saul Luna, born in the United States, living, working, going to school, and dating on the American side of the river, sided with the murdered Mexican.

CHAPTER 10

Immigration

LAST DAY OF FEBRUARY, A SUNDAY. The Indios are scheduled to play down in Toluca against a club called the Red Devils. "It's the hardest place to play," Marco told me before the team left for the airport. "The altitude there is something like nine thousand feet, their fans are intense, and it's a small stadium, so those fans sit right on top of the field." The Red Devils are playing well this season, good enough that they've become my favorite to win the title. Marco says it's going to be hot in Toluca, a mountain town forty minutes southwest of Mexico City. It's far from steamy back in Juárez, where I've stayed behind. The hints of spring that have been floating for a couple weeks have yielded to a last spasm of winter, one of those wet, gray, and all-around nasty days where all you want to do is stay in bed. I've pulled myself up to the river to put in a run before the eleven A.M. kickoff, but I'm having trouble getting started. I linger in my car listening to Morning Edition on the radio. My American cell phone picks up a signal, so I check my e-mail. I send my nephew a text. I read the top stories in the *New York Times*. While I'm procrastinating, a red pickup truck pulls into the stadium parking lot. I flick on my wipers to remove a coat of sleet clouding my view of the El Paso railyard.

Three men step out of the truck. I watch them speed-walk toward a hole in the fence that rings the stadium lot. They're wearing cowboy boots and denim jackets and they move low to the ground in a sort of duckwalk, as if a helicopter were approaching. Instinctively, I realize they're making a run for the border. *They're trying to break into Texas!* This gets me out of my car. I bring my cell phone, which I use to snap a photo of the trio, already on the American side of the canal and leaning against a concrete curb below the first of several fences, presumably out of sight of the Border Patrol. I notice for the first time a series of strike-zone-size patches in the fence, places where migrants must have breached the chain links in the past. I feel conspicuous watching the men—*keep your head down, stay on the line, etc.*—so I scurry back to my car. I'm tucking my phone into the glove compartment when the men come running back toward their truck. They dive into the cab and fire up the engine.

Guess they were spotted.

ILLEGAL IMMIGRATION REMAINS a hot border issue, even more so in the depressed economy. An unemployment rate in Juárez above 20 percent provides a strong incentive to sneak into El Paso, a city almost untouched by the recession, thanks to Fort Bliss and UTEP and all the displaced Mexican investment that El Pasoans quietly praise as a gift from heaven. In regional cities where the downturn is taking a greater toll, Mexicans crossing to "take our jobs" have become a popular scapegoat. Arizona has passed legislation that would require police to check the papers of anyone who seems as though they may, possibly, be in the country illegally. Civil libertarians—and just about anyone with brown skin—are challenging Arizona's activism. DO I LOOK ILLEGAL? asks a T-shirt I've seen in El Paso. Yet the bill has its supporters in Texas, the governor among them. Illegal immigrants are targeted in at least forty bills winding though the state legislature. One of those would require El Paso police to check papers during traffic stops.

"It doesn't make sense to put this burden on local officials who already have plenty of work to do," El Paso County sherriff Richard Wiles protested in an interview with Fox News Latino.

Marco Vidal's father first crossed into the United States illegally, in 1983. The first place he tried to cross was Ciudad Juárez. Both Marco and his father have remarked to me about the similarities of their life stories, as if they're living mirror images of the same journey. Both are soccer obsessed. Marco's father thought he could have played professionally if he hadn't needed to help out his family. When Marco started playing, his father screamed from the sidelines with such intensity that Marco's oldest sister, Claudia, stopped watching games with him. When Marco first washed out at Tigres and moved back to Dallas, his father refused to give up on his son's Primera dreams. He would wait up until Marco got home from work at midnight. They'd jog down to a neighborhood park and together they'd put in a workout under the moonlight. Both men married their wives only months after meeting them, initial couplings that both occurred mere days after they'd broken up with serious longtime girlfriends. Marco moved from Dallas to Juárez for the opportunity the city gave him. His father snuck into Dallas for the same reason.

Marco's father told me his story when I visited him at his house in DeSoto, a Dallas suburb of wide lawns and green public parks.

"I was born in Mexico City in 1958. I have three brothers and two sisters. I was the second oldest. My father, he had a lot of problems. He used to work at a textile company until he had an accident and cut off his hand. That happened right when I was born. So my mom had to work. She used to make clothes in a factory, and sometimes at home. She bought two sewing machines, and she would sew shorts and sell them in the neighborhood. We were poor. It was hard.

"I've been working since I was eight years old. My grandmother had a little store, and I used to help her. She sold candies from a window. She gave me twenty pesos a week and I'd give all the money to my mom. It was the way I helped out. When I was ten, my oldest brother got married and he left the house. So I was the oldest. I understood that I had to work. There was no money to go to school. I worked in the big store like Wal-Mart that we have in Mexico. I was stocking the groceries. I used to start at seven in the morning and I left at eleven at night. I worked the whole day. All the money I brought to my mom.

"My older brother was [an auto] body man and painter. When I was thirteen years old, I went to help him. I learned how to work on cars. That is how I got an opportunity at General Motors. Somebody had recommended me. I started in the kitchen. Really! I was serving all the employees and bringing them sodas. I was washing dishes and cleaning the ovens and the stove. I wanted to work on the cars, so I took a test and I passed. We were making Malibus and Impalas. That was a good job. I had health insurance, vacation, everything. But there was an engineer, a bad person, a very bad person. A bad boss. I was tired of him, so I quit. I used to make big money when I was working there. I quit a good job.

"I thought I was going to drive my own taxi, but that didn't work out. The car I bought was bad. I spent all my time in the shop, in the mechanic's room. My taxi idea was just a bad idea. I had a headache daily because my daughter Claudia, she was two years old, and we just had my second daughter, too. The taxi wasn't a solution. That's when a friend in the neighborhood, he told me, 'Let's go to the United States.'

"He just really wanted to go. And he wanted somebody to go with him. We had all heard stories about the USA. I had some aunts who lived in Los Angeles, and every time they would visit us in Mexico, they always had money. I thought if I come to the United States and I work for one year, I'll get so rich that when I come back I won't have to work in Mexico. I didn't talk about it with my mother, only with my wife. It took me two or three days to decide. When I left, my mom was in bed. She was sick. I left her crying. I left my wife crying, too. It was difficult.

"My friend had another friend, and the three of us went to Ciudad Juárez together. It took all our money just to get to Juárez. We didn't have any more money to cross. So I said, 'Let's go and get jobs in a body shop.' The owner of the shop said he would pay us a thousand pesos a week. He charged us fifteen pesos a week to sleep there and for food. At the end of the first week, he paid us two hundred pesos and said he'd pay us the rest in the future. At the end of the second week he said the same thing. At the end of the month he said he didn't have any of our money, and he didn't have any more work for us. We were trying to save money to cross, but in the end we only had enough money to take a bus back to Mexico City.

"It took a couple weeks before we could try again. This time we went to cross in Piedras Negras. There is a little town next to it called El Moral. At that time we came with a coyote. We were nine peoples. We walked about three hours in Mexico until we finally found the right place on the Rio Bravo. There were stairs on the other side. Sometimes the river is too high, so we had to wait until we could see the bottom stair before we could cross. We stayed for, like, eight hours waiting for the river to drop. I was just watching the coyote. When he said okay, we all took off all our clothes so we wouldn't get them wet. We held them over our heads and we crossed.

All nine of us like that, with our clothes over our head. There was a waterfall on one side. It was *peligroso*, dangerous.

"So we cross and we start walking. We walked the whole night. We walked about three nights more. In the day we hide and in the night we walk. All we had was just our clothes and water and a little *comida*, food. We end up in La Pryor, a little town north of Laredo. If you go driving to La Pryor, it's twenty minutes from El Moral. And we take three days walking! So when we get to La Pryor, the coyote, he calls somebody from Austin. And the guy came to pick us up. He had a big ranch. We paid him with three days of work. Then he brought us to Dallas.

"Soon as I get here I have a job, because of my friends. We arrived at our friends' house at one o'clock in the morning. And at four thirty in the morning they took us to their work, and we were hired *inmediatamente*. So we started working the first day. At that time I used to make $350 a week. Better than at the body shop. I used to work a lot, fourteen to sixteen hours a day, but it was good money for me. I used to send a thousand dollars a month back to Mexico. A thousand dollars a month!

"After a year and a half, I was ready to go back. I missed my family and I thought my wife had saved enough of the money that I could live in Mexico without working. When I came back, I bought a refrigerator and I bought some other things and I didn't work for three months. And that used up all the money! So I told my wife, 'I gotta go back! We all gotta go back.'

"The second time I came to the U.S. was with a passport and a visa. I told my wife to let me go first. Then she and Claudia and Maribel came the same way, with visas. Marco was born in Dallas in 1986. When he was born, my passport was about to expire. So I saw my son alive for one day and then I gotta go to Mexico! I have to renew my passport. I went to Mexico City, but they didn't give me my passport back. They discovered that I never serve in the military. So my family is legally in Dallas and Marco is born in Dallas and I'm stuck in Mexico.

"I talked to my friends. I said, 'Hey, let's go to the United States.' I did what my friend had done to me the first time we ended up in Ciudad Juárez. I convinced them to accompany me. I had to do it illegally again. But this time I was the coyote. I remembered how we did it the first time and I did the same thing. We go to Piedras

Negras again. We waited until we could see the first stair and then we crossed. Soon after I get back to Dallas they pass a law giving everyone amnesty. So I've been legal ever since.

"We all lived together in Dallas, in a Mexican neighborhood. At the time we used to live with two of my brothers and their families—about sixteen people in a little two-bedroom house. I was the first in my family to come to the United States, but all three of my brothers, they follow me. When I came back the second time, I got a job with my oldest brother in a body shop. And then after a year he said, 'Hey, let's open our own shop.' That was in 1987. I never did retire. I still have to work!

"That law in Arizona is racist. It's *mal*, bad. The people who want the law are racist people. The United States was built on immigration. It wasn't easy to leave Mexico and come to a totally different country by myself. But now all the opportunities my children were able to get because of it, I don't regret it one bit. I still feel Mexican, 100 percent, but I don't think I'll return to Mexico. I am an American citizen. My family is here. This is my home.

"And Mexico, it is a dangerous country now."

I LOVE TO read *El Diario* on Fridays. That's when the paper publishes a special section of things to do over the weekend. Notably, the section is entitled Escape. Also notably, the first page of the section recommends movies to rent and watch at home. That's followed by a full page listing the movies to be broadcast on cable. In the nightlife section—The Night Is for Pleasure—only seven bars are suggested as safe places to go for drinks, and all of the bars are located inside major hotels. There *are* cultural events in Juárez. I've been to book readings and to more than one play at the university. A symphony orchestra and a desert opera come around in the summer. Touring musical troupes regularly bring the Disney brand to Juárez toddlers. But more and more of the culture *El Diario* spotlights, I've noticed, is taking place in El Paso. In their attempts to promote leisure activities on the southern side of the river, the paper's editors sometimes must really stretch. The lead story one Friday was headlined "Robert Downey, Jr. Returns to Juárez." What? A Hollywood actor coming to Murder City, and not for the first time? The article turned out to be about Downey's latest movie, which was

opening at the Misiones Mall cineplex; the actor himself would not
be present at the screening. Another week, the featured "nightclub"
was Applebee's. "All week long, Applebee's is the place for friends,
food, and parties—all your enjoyment in one place."

I watch the Toluca game at an Applebee's, just because of the
paper's recommendation, which amused my snobbish sensibilities.
I pick the branch of the restaurant across from the Rio Grande
Mall, opening the door to find it stuffed with Troy Aikman and
NASCAR memorabilia and dozens of fans in Indios jerseys. The
waitresses wear Indios jerseys, too. *Applebee's really is the place.*
Because I was so late starting my run, I've missed most of the first
half. Thirty-five minutes have elapsed, and the Indios are down 1–
0. As I head to the only free seat I see, at the bar, I notice the Indios'
radio crew broadcasting from a corner table, watching the same
satellite feed as the rest of us. I wave hello, turning back just as the
referee calls a penalty on an Indios defender, in the box, which means
an automatic free shot on goal from only twelve yards away. A sure
thing. This'll make the score 2–0 at the half when . . . but wait!
Christian blocks the shot! Our goalie is the best. Marco flies over to
congratulate Christian, pumping his fist while screaming with emotion. It remains only 1–0 at the half, a margin the Indios may be able
to overcome.

If they were anybody but the Indios. Toluca scores late in the second half to make it 2–0. Then they score again to make it 3–0. Another shellacking. The radio color man repeatedly says the words
"muy mal." Applebee's patrons in their Indios kits file out to the
parking lot. Only the broadcast crew and I hold out until the end,
which is bitter. As I put on my coat and as the broadcasters pack up
their microphones and cables, we acknowledge the open secret:
Pepe Treviño is out of a job. This was his last of many strikes. When
the team returns to the Juárez airport tonight, he shouldn't bother
unpacking his bag. I like Pepe, and I feel bad for him, but clearly he
can't coach. What is it now? Twenty-five straight games without a
win? That's not acceptable at any level of sport, or even in any other
profession. I throw fist bumps to the radio crew and head out into
the same ugly sleet from my morning run. I wonder whether those
guys in the red truck launched another assault on the border fence.

They'd peeled out of the Olympic Stadium parking lot immediately after returning to their truck. When they were out of view, I

stepped from my car and slipped through the hole in the stadium fence, the excitement from their attempted breach enough to get me finally running. Three green-and-white Border Patrol Jeeps were parked on the opposite bank, right above the spot where I'd seen the men trying to hide. Farther down the canal, at an open fence gate, a patrol agent swept his eyes up and down the river, looking for more migrants, then looking at me suspiciously as I started to jog. I ran west, my normal route, though at a quicker pace than usual. *An attempted border crossing in broad daylight!* I'd presumed it would be easiest to cross at night, but maybe that's when the Border Patrol is most vigilant? Downtown El Paso seems particularly well policed. Why hadn't the men marched to somewhere more remote, like Marco's father had? I guess it's a risk/reward thing. If you cross right into downtown El Paso, you're immediately home free. How could anyone tell an illegal migrant in El Paso from everybody else? If that immigration bill passes, El Paso police are going to have to spend their time questioning just about everyone.

On the return leg of my run, when I came upon the point where I'd started (and where the men had attempted to cross), the Border Patrol trucks were still there. A fourth truck had joined the pack, a pickup with a tank of acetylene stacked in its bed. I could see an agent with a blowtorch and a welding mask repairing the fence. The other agents waved at me. Did they think I was about to make a break for it? I waved back. As I did, I noticed a lone vehicle on the Juárez side, slowly headed in my direction on the otherwise empty John Paul II Highway. The vehicle crawled closer and I realized it was the same red pickup truck. The three men were still inside. They looked over at the Border Patrol and at the fence, no doubt taking notes for their next attempt.

CHAPTER 11

Paco

"Where are you going?"

"To Albuquerque. Just for the day."

"For the day? Back and forth, that's a ten-hour trip." It's already two in the afternoon. I shrug my shoulders. The U.S. Customs agent takes my passport, issued in Miami, pausing to inspect stamps from multiple visits to Bogotá. She looks me up and down. I'm a single male traveling alone. I haven't shaved in a few days. When she asks where I live, I tell her Juárez. She raises her eyebrows. Yes, it's my permanent address.

"All I'm doing today is making a run. A friend and I are going to drop something off and then we're coming straight back."

Her eyebrows arch higher.

"What's your friend's name?"

"Paco."

She takes her time handing me back my passport, first typing a few notes into her computer and asking her colleague to hand-inspect my backpack. The American government is growing suspicious.

Paco—Francisco Ibarra's twenty-two-year-old son—greets me in the Free Bridge parking lot. I climb into the Jeep his father bought him and we exchange the customary fist bump. A twenty-seven-inch Apple Cinema Display rests in the backseat. That's our mysterious cargo, the package we're delivering to Albuquerque, home of the closest Apple Store. Paco turns up the volume on the Jeep stereo. His favorite band, the Mars Volta, screeches and whines as we pull onto I-10, the starting line of our till-midnight run.

Paco is an aspiring filmmaker. The broken computer monitor

usually serves a Power Mac G5 on which he edits his works in progress. One feature film so far, a couple music videos, and a handful of short mood pieces: a good-looking girl takes off her clothes and swims in a pool. Or, in another film, another good-looking girl removes her shirt and smokes. Each of the shorter movies is four or five minutes of atmosphere, the kind of brief and focused meditation that reminds me of smoking a cigarette, which really is the entire plot of that second film: Topless girl lights up. These unhurried works stand in contrast to Paco the person. He's hyper, sometimes all over the map, the kind of guy who tweets and updates his Facebook status every three minutes: "It's off to the gym!" "I'm hungry for Subway!" "El Paso: *aburrida esta noche!*"

"I'm not the kind of person who can shut up," he admits.

His one full-length movie is strange. The female half of a young couple is cursed with the ability to see the future, a gift that has informed her the world will end in a week. Total destruction, everybody's going to die. She and her boyfriend pass the week sulking through a road trip from El Paso to Ruidoso, a New Mexico ski town where border wealth likes to weekend. First there's some moody brooding in the backyard of the El Paso house where Paco, in the Mexican tradition, still lives with his parents, his sister, and his two younger brothers. Blood drips from the actress's mouth, somewhat biblically. There's the obligatory sex scene. (I knew her shirt was coming off at some point!) There's also a long and languid exchange in a church: stained glass and sunlight and lots of unspoken angst. It's heavy, knowing the world is about to end. She's thinking about killing herself ahead of time, so as not to witness the death of everyone she loves.

"It's not either your fault or mine," her boyfriend counsels. "It's how God wants it."

During the Indios' rise to the Primera, Paco served as team cinematographer. He shot videos of preseason training on the beaches of Cancún. He filmed the bus ride to that spooky and crucial playoff game in Cruz Azul's empty stadium. He has an idea for a new feature film about the team, a complex weaving of the stories of his father trying to bring soccer to the border, of a player like Marco Vidal trying to keep the Indios in the Primera, and of a fan who, in Paco's fictional world, tries to use his love of soccer to keep his brother from running with La Línea. When I met Paco for lunch a few weeks ago at

Tacos El Campeón in Juárez, he was transitioning into self-funded commercial work. He's been thinking it might be cool to open a branch of the Ibarra family restaurant in El Paso. That's certainly the trend. El Taco Tote, Flautas Los Canarios, Aroma: The biggest names in Juárez dining have migrated north of the river, along with the families who run them. A new restaurant will need televised advertising, Paco figures, and that's what really gets him going.

"I've got all these ideas for commercials," he told me as I sampled a simple beef taco garnished with guacamole and spritzed with lime juice. "I want good production values. I'm such a sellout, I know, but I can see a naked woman, just with a taco covering her nipple, barely covering it to where you can almost see it. Then the words 'Want a bite?' I'm such a sellout! I know! But if they're excellent films, like three minutes long and way better than you'd expect for a taco stand, people will be watching them on YouTube. I also see a guy, a douche in a nice suit. We'll have a taco fly at his face, hitting him like a pie in the face of a clown. Then at the end we'll just have the words '*al Campeón.*' This great cinematic film, just for a taco. I can see it. I've got so many ideas."

Paco is not all talk. He has an admirable track record of finishing his projects and accomplishing the goals he sets. Yet I don't expect Paco will ever open a restaurant. Zoning and staffing and construction permits aren't details he's wired to tackle. Stick to movies, kid. He seems to be flirting with the taco business simply because he needs something to do. He's stuck on the border. After graduating from an elite prep school in Juárez, Paco studied film for a couple years in Orlando. He returned to La Frontera upon graduation, intending to stay only briefly before flying off to start his career in Barcelona. But Spain wouldn't let him in.

It was because of the violence in Juárez. Paco was born in El Paso, the first in his family with automatic American citizenship. Though he was raised south of the river, when the killing escalated he became an unplanned anchor baby, the reason why his parents were granted residency in the United States. Paco claimed to miss his mother and father. He said he wanted them in El Paso, where, after Orlando, his parents had propped him up in a house on the upscale West Side. A good enough story for the State Department. But if Paco missed his parents so much, the Spanish government wondered, then why did he immediately apply for a visa to live in

Barcelona? The Iberians told him to wait a few months, maybe even a couple years.

So Paco is marooned here for a while. That's not so bad, he admits. There's a decent film community in El Paso and a great film community in New Mexico. He's also found a serious girlfriend in Juárez, Karina Garcia, a chemist at a maquiladora. She and Paco are the kind of couple who overshare on Facebook about how much "I miss your smell" and "I love it when I wake up next to you" and "I love you, too, baby, mwaaaaah!" Unlike Mike, the El Kartel capo who can't return to Mexico for six months because of his residency application, Paco is free to cross into Juárez and back. Unfortunately, it's no longer safe for Paco to cross the river. His name has appeared on lists of potential kidnapping targets. On the rare occasions he does cross, like when I met him at Tacos El Campeón, he travels with a bodyguard in one of the family's two bulletproof SUVs, then he returns to El Paso as quickly as possible.

"Paco, he's like a woman," says Lorenzo Garcia, Karina's younger brother. "We can't go to the movies with him like everyone else. We can't go to a bar. He's a target."

Kidnapping ranks up there with extortion as an entrepreneurial growth industry, in Juárez and apparently all over Mexico. It's becoming so much a part of the culture that a kidnapping-related commercial airs before and after televised soccer games. The commercial advertises one of the national cell phone companies. A taxi driver in Chiapas witnesses an armed kidnapping. Using his cell phone, he alerts the municipal police and also his taxi-driving friends, who coordinate a blockade that traps the kidnappers. The commercial ends before I can watch the kidnappers gun down the taxi drivers and behead the victim, which is what would happen if anyone tried to pull that stunt in Juárez. Still, it's an amazing selling strategy. Kidnapping tops 4G and "more bars in more places" as a reason to subscribe to a particular cellular service.

Karina's father was kidnapped in Juárez not long after I moved to town, and only about a month after Paco started dating her. I met the father once, when I stopped by the family's house to watch a movie with Lorenzo. Señor Garcia didn't seem like a particularly pugnacious man, but Lorenzo tells me he's always been a fighter. He fought for his education and for his family and for his career. And when he was kidnapped, he successfully fought for his life.

He was abducted outside his fabrication shop, where he mills aluminum and steel fixtures for larger maquiladoras. Three men were waiting for him when he drove up in the morning, and they nabbed him as soon as he stepped out of his car. The men bound Señor Garcia's wrists and ankles with plastic zip ties, covered his eyes, threw him in a car, and brought him to a safehouse still within Juárez city limits, not far from the municipal jail and the Indios' training complex. The kidnappers dialed up the Garcia's home phone, where it fell to Lorenzo to do the negotiating.

"I had to grow up quick," Lorenzo told me. "My sister is three years older than me. She was twenty-six, but she got real young. Like a girl, like a baby. She couldn't handle it. My mom couldn't handle it, either. I was all alone. I just felt all alone."

The kidnappers asked for ridiculous amounts of money, far more than the Garcias are worth. Lorenzo called a lawyer friend for advice. The friend told him to go ahead and call the police. They couldn't think of anything else to do. "It's something you have to deal with in Juárez," Lorenzo said. "You have to work around it."

Back at the safe house, Señor Garcia had no intention of waiting for the police. Two of the three kidnappers had driven off, possibly to pick up food. Quietly, he wriggled out of the ties that bound his feet and hands, pulled off his blindfold, and tiptoed to the front door, where the remaining *ladrón,* a kid no older than eighteen, sat watch. Señor Garcia threw open the door. The kid was so startled he took off running. Karina's father chased after him for a while, out of anger. Eventually, he stopped and asked a woman in the neighborhood to let him use her phone to call home. Lorenzo, who'd expected the call to be from the kidnappers, cried with relief. Karina, snapping out of her stupor, pulled out her cell phone and called her boyfriend. Paco and his bodyguard drove to the neighborhood where Karina's father had said he was hiding. When they got there, Señor Garcia scurried out from behind some bushes and hopped into the SUV.

"And that," Paco says, "is when I met my girlfriend's father for the first time."

THE DRIVE TO Albuquerque doesn't take quite five hours. More like four. We get to the Apple Store right as a power outage shuts down the entire shopping center. Paco's able to leave his monitor at the store, but nobody can fix it until the power is restored, which won't be for a while; he'll have to come back another day to pick it up. We had talked the whole drive up about how we were going to eat dinner at a California Pizza Kitchen. I'm not a particular fan of that restaurant—*what, no Applebee's around here?*—but all our talking really fixed my appetite on a barbecue chicken pizza. Unfortunately, the power is out at the restaurant, too. I joke about this third-world country we've landed in. We don't know where in Albuquerque there's a restaurant untouched by the outage, and we've got a long drive back, so we just pick up some potato chips and sodas at a highway gas station and return to the road.

The drive out from Juárez was eerie. Blond vistas. Tumbleweeds. A town with the strange name of Truth or Consequences. The landscape oddly meshed with the operatic and arrhythmic guitar solos of the Mars Volta, a progressive rock supergroup I'm afraid to tell Paco I'd never heard of before I moved to the border. Our ride back is in the dark. There's nothing to see out the window except the headlights and taillights of other cars on the road. Paco and I fall in and out of easy conversations. He came back from Orlando to find Juárez had changed. He'd been noticing the changes, little by little, when he'd return from film school on short breaks. By the time he came back for good, a year ago, his city was unrecognizable . . . Legalization of drugs won't solve Mexico's problems, he doesn't think. It'll just force the cartels to ramp up their kidnappings and other nefarious moneymaking activities . . . He had this "Macedonian fuck buddy" in Orlando who was insatiable . . . He thinks the planet earth is trying to kill us humans off, to save itself. We just talk, about a lot of stuff.

I find Paco's life story pretty interesting, even if he's young. His grandfather is passionately Mexican, yet we're speaking English in the car, a language Paco says he learned from watching television; his parents don't speak it. He's a Mexican, yet he's also an American, more and more so. He's a young man in both cultures in the Fussion sense, but he's also an unwitting pioneer. The rich and connected of Juárez are all setting up shop in El Paso these days. Even Paco's high school, the most elite prep school in Mexico, is opening its first American branch in El Paso.

"I want to build crazy-ass jails," Paco says, slipping back to our talk of drugs and cartels and crime. "Like awesome super-jails where we could lock people up for the rest of their lives. If their crimes are related to drugs, then they get a lifetime sentence. It would be like getting rid of them. I don't believe the system rehabilitates them. Not at all. I think that most of us are criminals if we are allowed to be. So if they did something once, they'll do it again. I say we have to deny them the chance."

Okay. A conservative, hardcore-on-crime position. Not really how I feel about these things, but that's all right. Paco continues:

"I have this daydream where I'm literally able to do whatever the fuck I want to do. I have, like, powers. Have you seen the X-Men movies? If I somehow could, my mind would be able to know whoever in Juárez is involved in drugs or corruption. I would announce their names on TV, on the radio and other media. I would interrupt the news in Juárez to say that all these people I've named have a week to either get themselves to jail or be punished. They wouldn't report to jail, of course—obviously they'd laugh at my order—but mentally they'd be really afraid. And at the end of the week, late at night, I'd take every criminal who didn't report to jail out to the Rotary Bridge, the one that's rusting. In the morning, the rest of the city would wake up to see all the bodies, and all their severed heads piled up there along with all the drugs they had sold and all the money they stole. There would be a file for every single one of them with proof of their crimes and an explanation of who he was and what he had been doing wrong."

I let that sit for a while. We've been driving back for about three hours so far. There's an hour or maybe two before we'll reenter Texas. It's mostly black out, mostly just white lines shooting underneath the Jeep as we motor south. I think I can see the faint glow of El Paso up in the distance, or perhaps that's just Las Cruces. We drive for some time in a silence that's not awkward, but I can't say it's exactly comfortable. Eventually I shift in my seat, clear my throat.

"That's an awfully violent dream, bro."

"I know," he admits. "I'm fucked up that way. I just hate to see what they've done to my city. Before I went to Orlando, Juárez was a place of freedom. It was one of the best places to be on the planet. People loved it here, just because of the vibe. I could shoot a short film in Juárez, maybe driving real fast on the Camino Real [Highway, which his family won a lucrative city contract to build], actually speeding while also operating a film crane that a friend of mine owns. And we wouldn't need a permit. That's how free it was. You could really live. It wasn't lawless; people had common sense. But even if you were pulled over, the cops would say just to be careful. Stuff like that was amazing. Juárez was positioned to become a new Guadalajara or Monterrey. It could have been better than both of those cities, just from its geographic location.

"At the beginning of the violence, I felt it was people from Juárez actually fucking it up. When I came back from Orlando, a *saltarón*, a mugger, stole my mom's car at gunpoint. I was disappointed in Juárez. I began to wish I could turn my back on it. At one point I told my dad, 'Please, just leave everything, sell the team.' But I still feel so attached to the town. Because, really, it's not fair what's happening in Juárez. I have these dreams because I care about the city. I'm still very, very attached."

GIL CANTÚ, ACTING on Francisco Ibarra's orders, fires Pepe Treviño. No surprise there. Gabino Amparán, the traveling secretary who offered me a chocolate chip cookie on the bus ride to Guadalajara, is promoted to head coach on an interim basis. I'm pretty sure he saw the promotion coming. On the flight back from the Atlas game, as the rest of us blocked out the disaster with music and video games, he was reading a book about the mental tricks a coach can use to motivate a team. (My advice: Don't show any more Mark Wahlberg movie clips.) Other changes in the organization are afoot, most of them cost-cutting. When I stop by the front office after the Toluca loss, I learn that the head of promotions, a guy who's kept a desk in the media office with Ramón and Adir, has been laid off. I often sat next to the guy when checking my e-mail before or after practice. Ramón jokes that if I want to continue using the office, from now on I'll have to pay rent.

The Indios lose their next game, at home to Tigres of Monterrey, Marco's old outfit and the second-lousiest team in the league, the only other club still with a statistical chance to descend to the minors instead of Juárez. Almost impossibly, the game sets a new low point in the Indios' miserable season. After the Atlas disaster, everyone knew this team on La Frontera was bad, the worst team to ever play in the Primera. Nobody could have imagined the Indios might be *this* bad.

The game kicks off on a bright, sunny afternoon, a beautiful day. Cottony clouds float over the border from El Paso. The pregame soundtrack of Bill Haley and the Everly Brothers transports Olympic Stadium back to the 1950s, a brighter time in the city's history. New coach Gabino claps his hands on the sidelines as his players take the field wearing unusually bold colors. Gil Cantú petitioned the league to change from the Indios' normal home whites to the all-red uniforms they sometimes wear on the road, a sartorial switch that Gil tells me signals change and hope and the vitality of oxygenated red blood.

"We're going to win today," he insists as I take a seat next to him. "Gabino's going to coach the team the way we always wanted Pepe to do it. Everything's different now. We'll win. I can feel it. I know it."

I'm willing to believe him, but right from the kickoff, the best things to happen to the Indios are mistakes by the other team. A Tigres player attempts a dangerous tackle, gouging his cleats into the calf of one of our forwards. That earns a red card, giving the Indios a man advantage for the rest of the game. The refs—those nefarious villains supposedly throwing games so they don't have to travel to Juárez anymore—proceed to issue a *second* red card on Tigres, a call that gives the Indios a rare two-man advantage. It is almost impossible for Juárez to lose this game. So when they do, 1–0, the fans turn merciless.

First the Tigres goal: a simple header off a corner kick. Very basic, but a blow to the Indios' fragile collective psyche. Juárez's attempts to equalize prove pointless. Shot after shot misses the net entirely, earning boos and whistles. Edwin completely screws up a free kick, which would normally be a good chance to score. The crowd rewards him with sarcastic chants of "Tigres!" By the end, the team from Monterrey plays keep-away. Tigres—missing two players!—kick the ball among themselves, the Indios unable to intercept, the crowd crying *"Olé!"* after every pass. The inflatable tunnels to the locker room fill with air. The clock ticks closer to the sad and frankly unbelievable end. Francisco Ibarra stands up to leave a little early, as his security detail demands. The crowd turns on him. I hear the word *pendejo,* "asshole." Someone else calls him

una mierda, "a shit." It *is* his fault, to a large degree. It's his team.
He makes the final call on all coaching and personnel decisions.
Paco trails behind his father, hands raised in a sheepish shrug. I can
tell he's embarrassed, and also angry.

When the game finally ends, I slip away from Gil to join Dany
outside the Juárez locker room, where she's waiting for Marco. She's
angry, too. The booing of her husband. The cheers for Tigres. She's
also worried about the future. The Indios are obviously going down.
A return to the minors will stain Marco forever, just like he warned
me before the season started. He might be allowed to languish down
there for only a year or two before washing out of soccer altogether.
"They were calling Ibarra a shit!" Dany cries, twisting the spiked
heel of her left shoe into the dirt. She has always been a big booster
of her hometown. "It's the greatest city in Mexico," she once told
me. "My whole family is here. I want to live here the rest of my life."
Now, as we wait outside the stadium, she throws the evil eye to
every passing fan in a red Indios shirt.

"I hope he gets traded to another team," she says.

Paco doesn't even wait until he gets home to update his Facebook status. In the armored SUV with his father, as their bodyguard maneuvers toward the bridge back to El Paso, Paco whips out
his iPhone. He thumbs out a long screed against the "ungrateful"
and "ugly" citizens of the town where he grew up, where his father
has planted his flower and where his grandfather made the family
fortune. As far as he is concerned, Paco writes, Juárez can "sink in
its own shit."

CHAPTER 12

The Lottery

THE TIGRES LOSS SERIOUSLY DEPRESSES El Kartel. At a postgame drinking session inside Liverpool Bar, Kinkin the hooligan tells me he cried real tears when the final whistle blew. His girlfriend, Briana, cried so hard that mascara smeared down her face. A guy I'll call Oskar and I take our minds off the defeat by discussing his favorite highbrow books. "Roberto Bolaño is my idol," he tells me. The late Bolaño, a Chilean, is best known for writing *The Savage Detectives* and *2666*, the latter novel structured around the infamous and mysterious murders of women in Ciudad Juárez. "I think the man is a genius."

Oskar is studying English literature at UACJ. He's not a fan of the school's program. Too much criticism and appreciation but no actual writing practice. He moved to Juárez from a small town six hours from the border. "I've seen a lot of shit," he once shared. "I could tell you some stories." In addition to taking classes at the university, he also works at a call center, helping the bilingual residents of Florida collect rebates for trading in their old refrigerators for newer, more energy-efficient models. A Bob Marley song comes on the stereo, which makes him perk up a bit; he's such a fan he used to wear his hair in long dreadlocks.

"Robert, I'm going to take a piss," he says. "When I come back, I expect these three beers to still be here, okay? Got it?"

I've been told by at least ten other Karteleros that Oskar subsidizes his call-center income by killing people. For money. I've never believed it. How *can* I believe something like that? If we know he kills people, why don't we turn him in to the police? "That's what my girlfriend asks me," says Saul Luna, my Kartel friend in El Paso. "I tell her that Oskar doesn't kill people in Juárez. He only kills people in other towns. Selling a car is what he calls it. If Oskar tells you he's going to sell a car in Veracruz, what he really means is that he's going there to shoot someone. I tell my girl that he doesn't bring his work around us. To us he's never been anything but a nice guy."

He's always been a nice guy to me, too. He invited me to a birthday party at his house. I went and I enjoyed myself. Most of the guests were literature students or, if they were older, professionals—engineers and maquiladora managers. It was a nice change of pace; El Kartel isn't exactly a book club. Oskar smiled the whole night, topping off drinks and making sure everybody was having a good time. I'll acknowledge there's an intensity about him, a physical presence that makes him seem coiled. But a *sicario*? A guy with the options Oskar has? I haven't seen anything to indicate he has a dark side.

There's a commotion over by the nightclub's big picture windows. I leave Oskar's three beers on the bar and run over to check out what's up. I stand on my toes to look over the crowd. I can see Oskar down on the street, for some reason. He's got a thirty-two-ounce glass beer bottle in his hand. I watch him raise the bottle over his head, then swing it onto the skull of a man wearing a Tigres jersey. The jersey is torn and stretched at the neck and arms.

"Three Tigres fans tried to come in," says a girl standing next to me at the window. "They started yapping their mouths stupidly." Oskar charged at them, defending El Kartel's turf. The beer bottle disintegrates into a liquid firework of *cerveza* and tiny shards of brown glass. Blood sprays out of the Monterrey man's scalp as if from a lawn sprinkler. He crumples to the sidewalk, curling into the fetal position, his hands and arms protecting his head. Oskar continues to kick him in the chest, stomach, and face. Blood pools on the sidewalk, an incredible amount of blood. The Kartelero named Sugar runs outside and grabs at Oskar's arm in an attempt to save the Tigres fan's life, but Oskar continues his assault. He keeps kicking until, finally, some municipal cops arrive. The reflexive cynicism I've developed—*Great, it's the police*—gives way to honest relief. Step in, officers. Please! Oskar darts back inside, running up the stairs to rejoin us on the second floor. I return to my seat at the bar. He reclaims his stool next to mine and takes a deep swig from one of his three beer bottles, as if nothing just happened. He's amped, though, totally torqued. His face is deep red and he's breathing heavily. Drops of blood stain his jeans.

"I'm a natural-born killer!" he shouts. He is not being sarcastic or ironic, nor is he trying in any way to be funny. That's the way he views himself, as someone hardwired to kill. Two police officers enter the club, looking for Oskar. They leave after other Karteleros convince them he isn't here, that he never came back inside. I wasn't going to be the one to give Oskar up—no way I want this guy mad at me. But I feel uncomfortable sitting next to him. I surrender my seat and step back a bit. I need some space.

"What you just saw there was the violence in this city everyone sort of hides inside themselves," says Briana.

I TELL MYSELF Juárez is okay, that it is, for the most part, a normal city. That the violence is overplayed by the press. That people do all the normal things here that everyone else does everywhere in the world. I tell myself this all the time. But it's becoming clear that there's a psychic cost to be paid for all the killing, for all the blood we pretend not to see pooling in the streets.

A SIXTEEN-YEAR-OLD KID sits in his car at a red light. A car pulls up alongside him, on the driver's side. A passenger in the car points an AK-47 straight at him. Then the gunman shakes his head. The car pulls up one more space. *Affirmative. That's him.* The car in front of the boy is sprayed with bullets. The gunmen speed off. The kid doesn't know what to do. He doesn't want to also speed off, lest someone think he was responsible. Nor does he want to stay. He idles for a few frozen moments, then shifts into gear. Slowly he pulls around the bullet-riddled car and drives home.

THE STATE DEPARTMENT sends me an e-mail: "This Warden Message is being issued to warn American citizens that levels of violence and criminal activity continue to increase in the State of Chihuahua and that drug traffickers are targeting individuals who previously were not at particular risk."

THE MORNING PAPER. One absolutely typical day:

A small shop that installs security alarms is raided by men carrying automatic weapons. A fifteen-year-old boy is killed, a seventeen-year old boy is killed, and a twenty-one-year-old man is killed. A fourth person, a customer, is injured.

Two men are shot dead in El Centro, steps from the Santa Fe Bridge. The men were driving in a black Jeep Grand Cherokee with Texas license plates. The car rolled to a stop in front of a barbecue restaurant.

A man driving a white Oldsmobile is shot dead at the intersection of Talamás Camandari and Libramiento Independencia. After the first bullets hit him, the driver loses control of his car, which swerves over a median and crashes into a tractor trailer. The victim is not identified.

Armed men enter a cell-phone shop located at Montes Urales and Blvd. Oscar Flores. César Ponce and César Saucedo, both thirty-two years of age, are ordered to kneel facing a wall. Both are shot dead.

The body of a man missing his head is found on a sidewalk in front of the Catholic Seminary of Ciudad Juárez. "The body was strategically positioned so it could be seen from the windows of nearby houses," reports *El Diario*. The headless man is clothed in blue jeans and a black T-shirt, but no shoes. His hands are bound behind his back. Police remove a message left on the torso. They do not reveal the message's contents. The body is taken to the medical examiner's office for the difficult task of identification.

A man named Ricardo Gonzalez is shot multiple times as he sits on a park bench at the corner of Almendras and Tlalpalpan.

An almost identical list of crimes will appear in the paper tomorrow. And the day after that. And then the day after that. The newspaper stories are remarkable for what they don't say. Published details rarely include more than what is plainly visible in the accompanying pictures. It's not in the paper's interest to point out patterns; solving crimes would almost certainly get its reporters killed. Not two years ago, *El Diario*'s crime reporter *was* killed. Connecting the dots is a job left to the readers.

So the man beheaded and positioned outside the seminary? That's obviously a cartel hit. The two men shot near the Santa Fe Bridge? Probably a drug hit, too. Two men in a Jeep just sounds suspicious, and extortion victims aren't often killed in moving vehicles. Those other two men executed at a cell-phone store? That's trickier. The first impulse is to say extortionists—Pedro Picasso had been shot at his uncle's cell-phone shop after a shakedown attempt. But today's victims were both told to kneel first. That might indicate a drug payback; just because someone's working a straight job doesn't mean they're out of the game. When three young and well-educated men— they'd attended the same elite prep school as Paco—were gunned down at an upscale bar close to Marco Vidal's house, I figured it was bad luck, that the victims had simply been in the wrong place at the wrong time. A friend of mine set me straight. The three were killed because they were dealing.

"You start selling because it's so easy," says my friend, who also attended the prep school. He now works a professional job in El Paso, but for three years he was hooked on cocaine, which he, too, used to sell. He knew the victims. "It's such easy money. It's almost impossible to turn down the money. Then they kill you."

At the other end of the social spectrum from those three dead bodies is my friend Mario, a *parquero* at the Rio Grande Mall. *Parqueros* patrol every parking space in the city, watching over your car as you shop and helping you back up into the crowded lot when you return. For this service they hold out their hands for any one-, two-, five-, or ten-peso coins you might spare. Mario has the lithe physique of someone no older than forty, and the deeply weathered skin of a man in his seventies. He's missing a few teeth. We struck up a friendship when he first saw my Colorado plates. He used to live in Denver. And also in Seattle, Vancouver, Nebraska, Kansas, and Minneapolis, where his wife and two grown kids remain. He's been stuck in Juárez since he was deported, after serving jail time for entering the United States without permission. Or at least that's what he first told me.

Mario works six to seven days a week, all day long in the winter snow and in the spring sandstorms and in the sun that's growing increasingly intense as the summer approaches. He gets depressed on the job, he's told me; he knows it will never get better, that this is his life. After work, in the dark, he rides a bus for forty-five minutes back to the room he rents for sixty dollars a month. He reheats the beans congealing on his electric grill, he eats, he washes his face, and he sleeps on a bare mattress until it's time to wake up for another identical day. On the one or two nights a month when he won't work the next morning, he likes to change into a hand-washed tank top, pull on a red baseball cap, and head to this dive in El Centro where all the bartenders are women and where a thirty-two-ounce bottle of Carta Blanca costs not much more than two dollars. I join him at the bar when I get a chance. We'll sit on stools wrapped in duct tape and he'll show me the pictures of his family that he keeps in his wallet, protected by folds of waxed paper. He'll buy a Nirvana song on the jukebox to remind him of the States, and we'll pour our beers over ice seasoned with salt and flavored with lime. When I pay for a round, he cautions me to ration my money because any of the bartenders I might want to spend time with are available for a price, and a man needs a woman no matter what. One Saturday night, after we were well into our Carta Blanca and after we'd stepped out for burritos and then relocated to a bar by the railroad tracks called the Bermuda Triangle, he let slip that the prison where he'd been incarcerated was Leavenworth. He wasn't merely an illegal immigrant. He'd been caught trafficking cocaine in Nebraska and also in Minnesota.

"I was making five hundred dollars a day, which was more than I made in a week as a roofer," he admitted. "I thought if I told you the truth, you wouldn't want to be my friend anymore."

I've stayed friends with Mario. If I'm in my car around the time he gets off work, I'll swing by and give him a ride home. I figure if he is still connected to the drug trade, he wouldn't be standing in a parking lot every day, all day long. But I can't help but feel a bit paranoid now whenever we're together. It's pretty clear, just from reading the newspapers, that *everyone* who plays the game eventually gets shot. If I had Mario's life, how tempted would I be to get back on the playing field, to purchase a few days of sweetness before the bullet comes?

*   *   *

IN A VIDEO posted on YouTube, a five-year-old Juárez boy fondles a nine-millimeter pistol and announces he's a *sicario*. The gun is almost as big as he is. A young admirer posts a follow-up video in which she calls herself La Niña Sicaria, the girl assassin.

A DOCTOR PRESCRIBES me Xanax. I've been having trouble falling asleep. I visit the doctor at his storefront clinic, connected to the Rio Grande Mall. He keeps a guitar in the corner of his office to help him relax. "Many people in this town have anxiety," he tells me. "Almost half my patients are on this stuff." I take the drug for only two days. It dries out my mouth and makes me feel unusually lonely. I return to the doctor's office on an afternoon when the dust has kicked up, tinting the sky yellow. He gives me a prescription for sleeping pills. He tells me I should look into seeing a shrink.

"What's happening in Juárez is about to happen in other cities," he says. "It's capitalism. Any system, at the extremes, is horrible. Extreme socialism is horrible. Extreme capitalism is, too." He thinks Juárez is the start of what will end up being a second Mexican revolution. *El Diario* reports that the violence has prompted hundreds of psychiatrists in Juárez to cross to El Paso for their own psychological counseling.

MY NEIGHBOR, ANOTHER man in the apartment complex, knocks a gnarly ding in the side of my car. I know which neighbor did it. The gash in my blue car is rimmed with white paint. The truck parked next to my car is white, and the geometry indicates that if I were to open the truck's passenger door too fast, too far, and way too fucking carelessly, it would swing right to the exact spot of the hellacious ding. This infuriates me, in part because I'm so powerless. I can't confront the guy. You can't confront anyone in this town. I have to just suck it up and live with it.

"I could kill him!" I grumble to myself, stopping cold because, when I think about it, I *can* kill him. Easily. No one is supposed to have guns here, but getting my hands on a pistol or a shotgun is no harder than buying a hunk of Chihuahua cheese at the S-Mart up the street. I can shoot my neighbor, let's say, oh, thirty times for every one ding to my car, and there's virtually no chance I would be caught. They *never* catch killers in this town, certainly not the killers of lone men, an execution everyone would presume he'd brought upon himself by trafficking in drugs. I don't have the power to confront an inconsiderate neighbor, but I do have the power to kill him. The knowledge is unsettling. It tastes acidic. It feels disgusting.

MORE THAN 130,000 stray dogs roam the streets of Juárez. I've decided to take one in. My new dog is a tiny blond mix between a terrier and a Chihuahua and maybe, judging from his bushy mane of fur, also a lion. I've been watching him pick through garbage on my block for almost a month. I went and sat outside with him for a while, and he struck me as a good guy down on his luck. So I brought him inside. I cleaned him up and after a couple days took him to a vet for shots and a haircut and for the surgery he doesn't like to talk about. When it became clear he wasn't going to hold his castration against me, I named him Benito Juárez and declared him my new best friend. Every morning and every night now, we walk around a small park one block north of my apartment.

Very late one night, on our regular walk, I'm counting up the vacant homes when somebody sets off a book of firecrackers, maybe one street over. Benito freaks out. All dogs hate fireworks, ha-ha. But it's almost one-thirty in the morning. And it's a Thursday night. The explosions shared the arrhythmic staccato of firecrackers, but they were much louder, much sharper. Benito and I run the rest of the way back to the apartment, the dog wriggling out of his collar and sprinting upstairs ahead of me. Before I can even unlock the door, we hear the sirens wail. They're coming closer. Coming to where the bullets were fired. To where, no doubt, a man lies dead.

I'M SHOPPING IN the Superette grocery store near my apartment. It's a smaller store than S-Mart, but it's easier for me to walk to, and they have a pretty good selection of the basics. I turn down the tortilla aisle to find a woman crying. I recognize the woman as one of my neighbors; she lives in a house not far from my building. Two men I also recognize as neighbors hold the woman in a hug. Both of the men look at me like *Hey, give her some space, okay?* I don't know what's happened, only that something has.

There is a toxic energy in Juárez. It flows underground, vibrating to the surface in scenes like this, scenes I witness in some form almost every day. Living here is like living in that Shirley Jackson short story. We accept that a few of us will be chosen for the daily killing ritual, that the likelihood of being chosen is very small, and that the killing is a cost of residency. We try to wipe the violence from our minds, to "go about living as best we can." But it takes a toll, this game of chance. It flavors every aspect of our lives. A poison leaches into everything.

TWO AMERICANS—a pregnant U.S. Consulate worker and her husband, a guard at the El Paso County jail—are executed in Juárez, in broad daylight, yards from the river. They are murdered soon after leaving a children's birthday party near the consulate. Another man who'd attended the same party with his children, and who was driving a similar white car, is also shot to death. We think the second guy might have been killed by mistake, but we don't know. Nor do we know why the young couple has been targeted. She worked at the consulate, so is it a statement against the U.S. government? Is it because the husband got mixed up in something nasty at the El Paso jail? We don't know, because not one of the ten thousand police and soldiers supposedly patrolling Juárez sees a thing.

The young couple's car is followed from the new consulate to El Centro, a distance of maybe six miles. The high-speed chase—from Juárez's emerging city center to its historic downtown—doesn't attract the attention of any police. The couple apparently wants to cross the Santa Fe Bridge, but they lose control of their car and crash into a light post within sight of the bridge and directly in front of Juárez City Hall. A picture window in Mayor Reyes Ferriz's office overlooks the crash scene. Anyone in his office can watch the assassins exit the trailing car, walk up to the young couple, and shoot them both dead. They can also watch the *sicarios* drive off without being stopped by a single soldier. No cops pursue the killers. And nobody at City Hall admits to seeing a thing. The only confirmed witness is unable to speak. The couple's seven-month-old baby, suddenly orphaned, cries in the car's backseat.

CHAPTER 13

Amor

THERE'S A SMALL SCHOOL NEAR MY apartment where Juarenses can study English. The school has only one teacher: the owner, Francisco Gomez, a man who lost a leg in a car accident a few years ago and who, since the accident, has worked at his school every single day of the year. Christmas, Easter, New Year's Eve. It doesn't matter if there are no students that day. There aren't that many students anyway, holiday or not.

"I get calls where they say they'll come back after the violence," he tells me, rolling his eyes because the killing isn't going to stop anytime soon.

When I first saw the school, I thought it was serendipity that I'd taken an apartment so close by. If Gomez can teach Mexicans how to speak English, I figured he must be able to upgrade my Spanish. I signed on for one-on-one classes. We scheduled to drill four nights a week, but it was obvious from the get-go I wasn't going to learn very much. He'd run through flash cards of the absolute basics: water, meat, milk, ball, woman. I have those down already, *gracias*. Then he'd usually segue into English and a discussion of the National Football League. "Are you aware, Robert, that New York Jets quarterback Mark Sanchez comes from a Mexican family?"

When it became clear that *fútbol Americano* was pretty much all we were going to talk about, I couldn't justify taking more classes. I still visit the school every now and then. I'll bring Gomez a beer and we'll watch an NFL playoff game or maybe just talk for a while about football, or about his son who is studying English literature at UTEP or about how teaching has kept Gomez from sinking into a depression since he lost his leg. He still has a few students, and if there's a class in session he'll ask me to dazzle them with some English sentences. One night Gomez handed over a newspaper article he wanted me to read. An expert in "metaphysics" had been profiled on the front page of *Norte*, the second-best newspaper in town. The expert said the problem with Juárez is negative thinking. Everyone is afraid. Their fear is causing them to elect leaders they don't like. And those bad politicians make everything worse.

I really bristled at that. The problem with Juárez is that people are being shot on the street. And at the mall, at the gas station, and while sitting on park benches at the corner of Almendras and Tlalpalpan. Fear exists because bad things are happening, no? "No," Gomez insisted. He told me that if *la gente* would adopt better attitudes, the violence would disappear. You can't cower in your room. You have to move forward. You have to get out there.

"If you're not positive, you're not growing," he argued. "You're already dead, and the bullet hasn't even found you yet."

That's a solid point. I think most people in Juárez agree with it, actually. While fear may have cost Gomez some students, the majority of Juarenses are optimistic. Take the Indios. There's probably no team on the planet better at shedding negative energy or experiences. Yes, the mood at the first practice after the Tigres loss was darker than I'd ever seen it. I helped a trainer carry orange tubs of Gatorade to the practice field, and when I asked him how he was doing he replied, *"Muy mal,"* the first time anyone in Mexico has ever answered me with something less than *"Bien."* I didn't think the black cloud could possibly lift. But by the next day, Tuesday, the players and coaches weren't as down. By Wednesday hopefulness had somehow returned, as always. "Can't be thinking about the Tigres game, dawg," Marco told me. The Indios aren't dead yet. They believe they can beat a team called Estudiantes down in Guadalajara on Friday night. They believe they can still pull off a miracle.

The Indios lose to Estudiantes, 4–1. The winless streak climbs to twenty-seven. Not long afterwards, bullets find Francisco Gomez's language school. A man runs in from the street, bursting through the school's front door as if he is being followed, which he is. Gomez drops under his desk, his aluminum crutches clanging on the tile floor. He can hear thirty or more bullets fired by an automatic rifle. Then Gomez can hear tires screeching as the assailants speed off in their car.

"It was all over in two minutes," he'll tell me later. "I was not fired on, thank God. Because of my faith in the Almighty I am still here."

FOCUS ON THE positive. Stay upbeat. That is what so many in Juárez try to do. Me included.

I run long the day after the consulate shooting. Ten miles, my big workout for the week. I trot right past City Hall, right past a crime scene already cleaned up, all evidence erased except for the still-dented streetlight the car crashed into. It's a Sunday, warm but not yet summer-hot, a nice day to be outside. The riverbank transforms into a public esplanade, Juárez's dusty version of Havana's Malecón. Families walk over from Chamizal Park to pose on the canal's aluminum guardrail. Kids play soccer down in the dry canal. Teenagers climb the north bank right up to the first fence on the American side, and the Border Patrol lets it slide because they know it's only sightseeing. Just one day after the consulate employees were shot, a girl in the park flies a pink kite. Another rides a pony. I fall in with a fellow jogger, a complete stranger, and we help each other stay on pace for almost four miles, until it's time for me to head back and fetch my wheels. In the Olympic Stadium parking lot, a man teaches his teenage daughter how to drive the family car.

"Sounds like it's getting worse down there," writes my sister. "I'm worried about you."

"I bet you're more vigilant now," texts a friend in Miami.

"It's like you're living in Iraq or Afghanistan but without U.S. protection," says my father in a voice mail.

I go through my messages at a McDonald's, where I stop on my way home. I'm not trying to undermine my workout with fatty food; I mostly want the Wi-Fi. I buy a soda and sit in a booth for a while, reading text messages and e-mails out of sync with what's unfolding around me. "Are you still alive?" asks my friend Glenn in Los Angeles. Alive? I'm watching a team of Little League Pirates enjoy a postgame training table of hamburgers and french fries. A girl in a Snow White costume waddles by. A birthday party screams with contentment over at the indoor playground. The killings might be big news in the United States, but *El Diario* gave them only a small write-up on page 5B of the local section, and then only because the baby found in the car lent herself to a heartbreaking photo. We're not thinking about the consulate murders anymore. We've shaken them off. We're enjoying a nice day.

AMOR POR JUÁREZ. It's a sticker I see everywhere I drive. On car windows, on truck windows, on the windows of school buses and glued onto the rear windows of junker *fronterizas* like Marco's. The stickers were originally distributed by the city government, handed out for free at Indios games. It's a slogan, a take on I♥NY, used in Juárez the way the word "Believe" has been plastered around Baltimore to boost the morale of that also-violent city. *Love for Juárez.* I see it everywhere.

"Why do I love my wife?" Francisco Ibarra asked when I'd inquired about his affection for his hometown. "Why does Paco love his girlfriend? It's inexplicable." He went silent for a while. I could tell he was thinking. *"Es agradecimiento,"* he said finally. It's gratitude.

Sandra Rodríguez Nieto at *El Diario* is an investigative reporter. In Juárez. That's one of the most dangerous jobs on the planet. She's so good at documenting border corruption that a newspaper in Madrid recently awarded her a major honor. The prize, and the significant prize money, was split with one of her *El Diario* colleagues, to her relief. "If I would have won it all, then someone might kidnap me for it," Sandra tells me. She still collects enough euros to escape. Maybe to San Francisco, her favorite American metropolis. Maybe back to Mexico City, where she cut her teeth in journalism. Yet she won't leave. She can't leave. "Juárez is the most beautiful city in the world," she insists. "It's got mountains and great sunsets and the best people anywhere in Mexico." She sinks her share of the prize money into her house. She uses her escape money to pay down her mortgage.

I eat lunch one afternoon at the Yvasa complex commissary with Adir Bueno, from the Indios' media office. I bring up a particularly gruesome killing covered in the morning paper: a man decapitated and strung to a fence in the manner of a crucifixion. "Don't you ever think about leaving?" I ask Adir.

"Moving would feel like quitting," he replies. "I like Juárez. People are very nice, hospitable. I've lived here for twenty-four years, and I love it here."

What I need to do, Adir tells me, is look past the killings. His family has hosted exchange students for several years. One from Finland, one from Switzerland, one each from Germany, Holland, and Slovakia, and at least one more from Japan. "And they all come back to visit, Robert. Why would they come back if they don't love it here?" The student from the Netherlands flew back not six months ago, into the worst of the violence. The killing will end someday, Adir insists. Juárez will revert back to a Mexican resort town, an even better city than before. More fun, more free. "Like Las Vegas but Mexican, so better."

Elizabeth Rojas and Martin Marquez, the mother and father of Marco Vidal's wife, run a bus company that shuttles workers to and from maquiladoras. The buses roll out from a dusty lot near the border at four thirty in the morning, heading to the poorer barrios that are the only places most factory workers can afford to live. All buses in Juárez look like school buses. Private *ruteras* can be painted however the driver/owner likes. I've seen hot-rod racing flames shooting from engines. I've also seen Indios logos drawn on bus back doors and Indios stickers plastered on every window. Any bus that exclusively shuttles workers to border factories is colored the same white with gold-and-green trim. To tell whether the bus is owned by Dany's parents, I have to look closely for three triangles, their corporate symbol.

Their buses are hired by the individual maquiladoras. Cummins is one of the Marquez family clients. The electronics company RCA is another. Hundreds of factories operate in Juárez, enough to support several competitors in the busing business. The maquiladora transportation industry has been pinched by the recession, which has forced client factories to close. The bigger threat is coming from extortionists, who have begun to target the bus companies one by one.

"We left Juárez last February," Elizabeth Marquez tells me. "We went to El Paso. We bought a house. We went because they started calling junkyards and extorting money. Those that didn't pay were killed. Then they started to kill the owners of some businesses like ours, buses. We were afraid. Some people that my husband knew were kidnapped, and they killed them."

We're talking inside her home in Juárez, a large house in an exclusive and gated subdivision of other upscale homes. Five other families in the subdivision have left recently for El Paso. The Marquez family came back. They returned from El Paso after only a month and a half.

"I was bored," Dany's mother says. "The only thing we would do is watch TV and eat and then go to sleep. American people are boring. Mexicans are a very happy people. When we crossed back into Juárez, right away I went back to normal.

"Here most of the families know each other," she continues. "We know what our neighbors have, what they do. When we came back from El Paso, five or six families invited us over for carne asada. We all played in the park together. When you have a problem and you go to a neighbor and ask them for help, they give it."

It doesn't even have to be a neighbor. Before I started running along the river, I would jog through residential neighborhoods near my apartment. One evening, I'd been out for almost an hour, heading in a direction I understood to be due west. My simple plan to turn around and run back home on the same route, due east, didn't work out. I no longer recognized the streets. Was I actually going south? Could I somehow still be going west? I kept expecting to orient myself at the next major street and then, okay, at the street after that. Yet the longer I continued running, the more confused I grew. There were no visual clues, and I simply didn't recognize where I was. Finally, in defeat, I approached an OXXO convenience store to ask for directions. An older man coming out of the store held a twelve-pack of beer, a bag of ice, and the tiny hand of a young boy that turned out to be his grandson. I was nowhere near where I'd thought, he explained. And I was very far from my apartment. He waved me over to a minivan, where three generations of his family sat inside. His wife surrendered the passenger seat and insisted I take it while she crammed in the back with her daughters and their kids. "Have a Tecate! Please!" the man said, handing me a cold red can and firing up the ignition. This could have been where I was kidnapped, but I was never worried. He was never worried I was going to rob his family. He drove me all the way back to Colonia Nogales, he dropped me off, the entire family waved goodbye, and that was the last I ever saw of them.

But neighbors are helpful, too. A woman I met when I was walking Benito introduced me to all the families still living near us. The mansion that dominates our block—it takes up eight plots—is owned by the Zaragozas, who run a gas company. She tells me if I sit on the bench outside the big mansion I'll be in range of their security cameras, which should make me feel safer. A smaller house near the park is owned by a veterinarian. He's willing to take Benito with him to work and back, I was told.

"Anything you need," my neighbor added, "you let me know."

It was a nice day and I wasn't in any particular hurry, so we talked for a while longer. She invited me over for dinner with her family whenever I'm free. She told me the violence is making her crazy, but she can't leave.

"Our young people, they don't watch what they're doing, so we send them to El Paso. But we're all going to stay. We have a mission here. When our mission is up, then we'll go up."

She pointed not north, to Franklin Mountain, but straight up, to the sky. What is her mission?

"To love people. To help people."

EACH WEEK, AS the Indios' demotion grows more certain, the Juárez press comes up with ever more creative ways to describe the worst team in the history of Mexico's Primera division. After the blowout loss to Estudiantes—the team from Guadalajara scored three minutes into the game—a cartoon in *PM* featured an owl (the Estudiantes mascot) pushing an Indian into a fiery pit of flaming skulls.

"You guys are horrible," I tell Marco at the first practice after the team returns to Juárez. "Really, really bad." He'd asked if I'd watched the game, which of course I had. I'd watched it at Applebee's, naturally, along with most of the Indios' front office. Adir from the press department was there, along with the office manager, some men and women from sales, and the youth coach hired to replace Pedro Picasso. Half of those employees have since been laid off. Budget cuts. It's leaked out that even the players haven't been paid in weeks, a rumor Marco confirms for me, sort of. "Weeks? It's been more than a month, dude." Money is so tight the players were afraid there wouldn't be funds to fly back from Guadalajara, that they'd have to chip in and charter a bus.

It's Marco's turn to give the press-pool interview after practice. He tries to stick to soccer. He tells a handful of voice recorders the old line about how the Indios are not yet mathematically eliminated. He says they've got to play hard and fight this Sunday at home against a team from Querétaro. The reporters, suddenly all Roberto Woodwards, ask only about the budget crisis. Has he been paid or what? And if not, what does he think of an organization that's supposedly major league but can't make payroll?

Marco dodges the money questions in the interview, but walking back to the locker room with me, he allows that the problem is so bad the players are talking about striking. They've decided not to only because stories about "the financial disaster in Ciudad Juárez" would further stain reputations already discolored by their disastrous play on the field. He agrees with my assessment of their play. "Horrible" and "really, really bad" sound about right. It's kind of late for a turnaround. The Estudiantes loss pushed the Indios to the brink of a fiery pit. There is no more wiggle room. They must win every single game from here on in, all seven remaining matches on the schedule. No ties. All must be wins, starting with Sunday's game against Querétaro.

Game day is beautiful, a spectacularly nice afternoon for the team funeral we all expect to witness. I walk up to the stadium in shorts and a red Indios polo shirt, my exposed skin absorbing the delicious sun. A silver pickup rolls past, its driver and two passengers wearing Indios jerseys. The driver stops and motions for me to hop into the bed. Ken-tokey remains amazed that I hopped into his SUV back in the preseason, the first time I met him. "You didn't even know us!" he says. Yeah, but I could tell Ken-tokey was a decent guy, just as I can tell today's truck driver and his passengers are *simpático*. For as much danger as there is in this town, there's even more love. The free ride in the truck is the sort of random generosity extended to me every day in this warm and wonderful city.

"*Semillas!* Pistachios! Trident gum!" The vendors are out. The banners are up. El Kartel crowds into the south bleachers. Gil Cantú sits in the owner's box next to Francisco Ibarra, who has shaken off the insults from the Tigres game. (His son Paco, though, is conspicuously absent.) I switch things up and sit in the north bleachers, behind the Querétaro goal, with all six fans of the visiting Gallos Blancos, or White Roosters. Six fans. No more than that were willing to travel a thousand miles to weekend in the most dangerous city in the world. I'm spread out and sunning myself as I watch the Indios play surprisingly good soccer. The players from Querétaro are much taller, and their black-and-blue uniforms fit their physical style of play; one of their forwards shatters the eye socket of our Argentinean defenseman. Yet Los Indios are hanging tough. They're playing well, especially for unpaid amateurs. Christian makes a big save off a free kick and throws the ball to Marco, who calmly distributes it forward. No room to hit Edwin on the right side? No problem. Marco fires a long pass clear across the width of the field, to where Maleno stands in open space. Juárez's favorite son surges forward, the Indios on the attack.

"Far away are those days that Juarense Daniel 'Maleno' Frías looked bold and sassy before trembling enemy defenses," stated *El Diario* after the Tigres loss. "These days, Maleno is only a shadow of the player he was not even a year ago."

Maleno, on the right side of the field, passes the ball to Edwin, who passes it on to a streaking Indios defender named Tomas Campos, who is open on the left side, wide of the goal. Tomas sprints forward with the ball, then lofts it toward midfield. His pass appears to be headed to Querétaro's goalie, but from my seat behind the net I notice Maleno slipping into the penalty box. Before the goalie can catch the ball, Maleno sticks out a cleat to redirect the ball into the goal. The shot is so amazing, the result so unexpected, that I scream out loud, my act suddenly blue: Holy fucking shit. We've scored! Maleno scored. We're winning! I don't have a beer, but I want to throw one in the air, just to do it. We have scored. The Indios have scored.

And the Indios hold on. Seventy minutes played, now eighty. Still 1–0. With only five minutes left, the nylon tunnels to the locker rooms start inflating. I relocate to the owner's box, arriving just as the final whistle blows. The players on the field hug in a pyramid of relief, Marco leaping on top as if summiting a small mountain. Gil shakes Francisco's hand. It's the first win either man has witnessed in more than a year. Their Indios remain alive, still in the Primera, not yet relegated. Positive thinking comes through in the clutch.

"We're playing with fire, brother!" Gil shouts to me as he makes his way down some stairs, heading toward the locker room. I follow him. Players give interviews in the tight and enclosed space between the lockers and the parking lot. "Pachuca, Chivas, Pumas. We have tough teams coming up, but we're not dazzled anymore," Marco says into a bouquet of fuzzy television microphones. None of the reporters ask about the team's emerging financial crisis. No one cares, not right now. Marco showers and dresses quickly, stepping out to the parking lot to sign autographs on posters and jerseys and even, by request, onto the skin of one boy's back.

"We want Maleno!" shouts El Kartel. "We want Maleno!" The local hero, the man of the match, emerges from the locker room a prodigal son, the lost striker who has regained his sassy touch in front of trembling defenses. In the mass of Karteleros seeking Maleno's autograph I spy the grandmother arrested for exposing her breasts at the season opener in Monterrey. "Chicharrón!" I call out. She sees me and smiles. "Oh, *ganamos*!" she cheers. She hoists a can of Coors Light over her head. A cigarette smolders in her other hand. "We won! The whole world is in crisis, Robert, but today the Indios won and I'm just so happy!"

CHAPTER 14

Lost

NOT TEN MINUTES OUTSIDE THE city, Juárez disappears. Did it ever exist? Pale sand dunes dip and rise into gentle peaks, a mocha meringue. Squiggly ridges blown onto the sand are broken by the tracks of a lynx, or maybe a rabbit; I don't know my desert wildlife very well. The only animals I can confidently classify are a pack of *Homo sapiens* in pickup trucks zooming across the dunes as if the Chihuahuan Desert were a giant skateboard park. And also, closer to where I'm sinking into the sand, three more humans. One's a photographer. The others are a young woman in a black dress and, next to her, the well-groomed physique of a seriously metrosexual soccer player. Marco and Dany are posing for their official engagement photos, and I'm serving as a sort of general assistant. I'm holding Marco's flip-flops and Dany's stiletto heels and a bottle of Gatorade that Marco bought on the short ride out here, and which he prefers to drink because, in his words, "I hate water." The photographer is trying to take as many pictures as he can before the sun sets behind the Juárez Mountains, which won't be long now.

"Okay, now Marco, you stand behind Daniela," he says in Spanish. "Okay, good, hands on her arms, the upper arm. Right. Now Dany, you turn back to gaze into his eyes. *Con amor, por favor.*"

Without her heels, in her bare feet, Dany stands half a head shorter than Marco, kind of a perfect fit. They look good together. The other day at the Cielo Vista Mall in El Paso, shopping for this photo shoot, Dany tried on eight dresses, though she has ended up just pulling from her closet a simple and stretchy number as dark as her straight hair. ("I'm terrible with choices," she explains.) Marco's

wearing tight white linen pants and a V-neck T-shirt colored turquoise. No Ed Hardy logos embellish the shirt, to my surprise.
Marco still manages to signify baller status with the appropriate
accessories: two diamond studs in his ears, his bulky white Diesel
watch, Armani sunglasses, and his hair fauxhawked and glistening
with a thick application of styling gel. The photographer commands him to hold Dany's hand and march to the top of a dune
immediately to the east, opposite the waning sun.

"Now Dany, drape your hand over his neck in a way that lets us
see your engagement ring."

Marco and Dany met at the gym. At Total Fitness in Las Misiones Mall, where all the Indios work out for free. Marco had just
finished lifting some weights and had just ended a long relationship with his girl back in Dallas. He found Dany heading for the
elliptical machines, not really going anywhere in particular. Her
classes at UTEP are largely to please her parents, who want her to
get a degree. She cooked food at Disney World for four months,
which she jokes is the only job they let Mexicans do. She agreed to
go out with Marco, the first date went well, and he put the clamps
down after that, right away. No other boys ever again. We're together now and we're going to be together forever. She happily
agreed to his terms. They legally wed in a courthouse in Dallas
only a few months after that first meeting in the gym. Marco feels
certain he has married up. Her family's established in Juárez. He
can see himself transitioning into their maquiladora bus business
when his playing days come to an end.

Ever since their wedding, Dany's been planning their wedding.
Their official wedding, the church ceremony here in Juárez. She
might not be good with choices, but she has a clear vision of how
the day is going to unfold. Marco riding up to the chapel on a horse,
if they can pull it off. Butterflies released during the ceremony. The
reception at her family's house, the one her parents returned to
after El Paso proved too boring. She's going to transform the backyard into a nightclub. White leather couches for lounging, small
round tables for intimate talk, a row of larger tables—"ooh, with
champagne-colored tablecloths"—for dinner and as a safe space for
older relatives to sit witness. A live band, of course. But also mariachis. And one of those chocolate strawberry fountain things. Marco
is paying for much of it, he tells me. During one discussion of

flower arrangements, he made a show of objecting to the price of each bouquet, but it was clearly a show, and he clearly doesn't object. When I asked him how much he was willing to spend on the wedding, he said he didn't care, whatever it costs.

Both of them picked out the photographer. They stumbled onto his shop one afternoon, liked a picture he'd taken of a pregnant woman, and told the photographer to start thinking about sand and sunsets. Dany's vision included portraits on the dunes, even though she's never been out here before. The photographer hasn't been here, either. He's clearly excited by the creative possibilities of this shape-shifting landscape. As the sun sets, the dunes change colors almost instantaneously. One moment they glow with a yellow tint. Not ten seconds later the sand seems to burn a bright pink.

"Okay, Marco, it's time for the sunglasses to go," he says. Marco hands me his Armani frames. "Okay, now guys, lean in for a kiss. Dany, kick up your heel. You know what I mean, right? That's it!"

Dany and Marco are compliant models. They relocate, on command, to a tuft of scrub brush. Marco positions himself behind his wife, both of them facing the light as if looking into their future. Sand stretches out as far as they can see. Those guys in their dune buggies take up only a small patch of a granular ocean, miles and miles of breathtaking dunes. Juárez isn't far away, yet the psychic pressures of the city have lifted. I have to prod myself to remember all that stuff about killing and murder and mayhem. I'm outside of the city. And when I'm out of Juárez, as always, Juárez seems to disappear.

"WHEN I'M NOT in Juárez it feels like a dream," says Manuel Estebane. He's the pastor of a Baptist church located due south of Juárez's Central Park. I first saw his church a few months ago, when Felipe Calderón gave a speech in the park. The church is a big yellow shoebox. With its flat roof and right angles, it looks more like an industrial warehouse than a traditional house of worship. Curiosity— what's a Baptist church doing in Juárez?—compelled me to stop in and introduce myself. Turns out that Manuel's a recreational runner, like me. We've started meeting up now and again for early-morning jogs from the townhouse where he lives with his wife over to the new U.S. Consulate and back.

Manuel is fifty-three years old, a bit full in the face and soft in
the midsection. He started jogging only when his doctor, "one of
those running freaks," told him to sweat his triglycerides down to
a safer elevation. On the mornings we meet up, we start out just
before sunrise and jog slowly along a circuit of sidewalks that ring
his subdivision, which is located close to Las Misiones and the consulate in the emerging city center. I was shocked the first time we
approached the consulate to see maybe three hundred people already lined up for visas. Bodyguards loitered in the parking garage
of an adjacent hospital. Manuel is a Chihuahua native, born in that
tiny apple town where the Indios keep their minor league team.
He's worked in the United States for most of his pastoral career,
primarily at a church outside Kansas City. He returned to Mexico
three years ago because Juárez seemed like it could use some help,
and he felt up to the task. Now he feels like he's in over his head.
People have been kidnapped off the very sidewalks we run together,
at the same *hour* when we run together. Extortionists have phoned
in threats to kill Manuel if he doesn't tithe them a certain percentage of the church's income. Manuel insists he doesn't have any money
to pay out, which I believe is true. I've attended a couple of his all-
day-long Sunday services. His flock is passionate and committed,
but small. If there are enough worshippers for the church to break
even, then they're doing so by the slimmest of margins.

Manuel and I never run terribly fast. Sometimes we'll quit early
and walk a few laps instead, labeling our laziness a therapeutic
"cooldown." We talk about how unsettling Juárez can feel. He tells
me about how the hair rises on his neck when his wife announces
she's going to dash over to the S-Mart for some groceries. Will she
come back? Are extortionists tracking their cars? Juárez has him so
frazzled that his home church in Missouri has ordered him to spend
at least one week every three months away from the city. Just for
his mental health.

"Did that ever happen?" he asks himself when he's out of town.
"I can't believe I ever actually lived in Juárez." I catch the past
tense. He lives here *now*. He has a house, a car, a small congregation
to attend to, and an occasional running partner. It's a tense slip I
identify with. I often slip myself. When I leave the city I forget about
it, too. Like, I can't believe I ever actually lived there.

"Juárez doesn't exist," Paco Ibarra once told me. Now that he lives in Texas, and especially now that his trips into Juárez have become rare and surgical, he feels more than merely disconnected from his hometown. "When I see it from El Paso, it's a different reality, a different place. Now when I drive past it, it feels like it has a dark side."

Juárez may be only a concept, or a rumor. It's an island unto itself. When I was in San Luis Potosí and Guadalajara with the Indios, the people I talked to regarded Juárez (and its problems) much the way El Paso does: as belonging to someone else. It's in Mexico, yes, technically, but it's not *really* in Mexico. The newspaper in San Luis overflowed with stories of mayoral reports and public works, tourism data and sports scores. The big news in Juárez at the time— the Student Massacre—was reduced to a little bullet item buried on the National page. News, but nothing someone in central Mexico need really worry about. In my Guadalajara hotel room, I was startled when Juárez flashed on the TV screen. Univision had sent a reporter to the border to film handguns shattering under the heavy steel roller of a street paver. The police are cracking down on illegal weapons, the reporter said. The "secretary of state for security" or something like that came on-screen to assure viewers that Juárez is under control, that all is well. No need for me or anyone in Guadalajara to engage. I flipped up to a higher channel and a Hollywood movie dubbed in Spanish.

"Juárez doesn't exist," one of the Indios assistant coaches told me before he lost his job in the purge of Pepe Treviño. He was talking about the tribulations of coaching a losing team. The worst part, he said, is when your family reads the negative stories in the papers. I knew that this coach was from Mexico City and that his family had not moved to Juárez with him. Was he saying his wife gets online to read the Juárez papers?

"No, no, no, man. Those guys don't matter," he replied, referring to the reporters at *El Diario*, *El Norte*, and *El Mexicano*. "I meant the Mexico City papers. In Juárez they could write that I've grown a third arm and nobody would ever read it. To the rest of the country, what goes on up here doesn't even happen."

The sheer number of dead bodies makes it hard for anyone outside Juárez to really comprehend the violence. It's almost cartoonish, the amount of blood, like it can't possibly be real. Even the desert climate is a separating factor. In that story I watched while in Guadalajara, armed *federales* shivered in winter coats and face masks while, outside my hotel room, a soft wind rattled a stand of palm trees. It would be hard for anyone in Jalisco to feel connected to the border. How much worse is the separation in Cancún or Acapulco? That phrase President Calderón rolled out, "We Are All Juárez," is a great slogan, I think, a necessary reminder that Juárez is Mexico, too. That Juárez isn't just the national ghost town, its haunted house.

When I'm in Juárez, I feel like myself. I'm living an essentially normal life, going about my business as I would if I were living anywhere else. And when I leave Juárez, I think of a popular American television show winding down to its final episode on the day Marco and Dany and I trek out to the dunes. On the show, survivors of an airplane crash are stranded on a tropical island. Will this ragtag collective make it back to the mainland? Can they learn to work together, to surmount cultural differences and stereotypes? These were the questions when the show first aired, when it seemed as if we were going to get a simple character study. The show soon proved much darker than that. The island has a personality, a life of its own. It moves around in the ocean, and disappears sometimes. It draws the characters back in. An actor might escape, only to be compelled to return to its shores. People get killed on the island all the time. Is it even real? The characters on the island, are they dreaming it all up?

I think of the show when I'm riding around El Paso at night. I might have just gone for Shiner Bocks at the UTEP bar Liquor Dicks. I'll have met up with Weecho and even Arson Loskush and we'll have stayed until last call and then the mandatory run for the bacon Whataburger with cheese Saul Luna demands as payback for his chauffeur service. We'll be in Saul's car, shooting east on I-10. Maybe it's a night when Orbita radio—Rock Sin Fronteras— matches the mood just right by pumping out a hypnotic bass line and Jim Morrison breaking on through. Or maybe it's a night when Orbita makes me smack my forehead by being the last station anywhere to spin "Beth" by Kiss. I'll look outside my passenger-seat window at yellow lights, so close, a dot paper grid rising and gently falling. It won't occur to me that I'm about to march over the Free Bridge, that I'm about to pass Border Patrol agents and then Mexican soldiers sipping coffee while bemoaning their assignment to the graveyard shift. I won't remember my new dog, and how he's waiting for me to give him a walk. Instead, the news of the day will be in my head. Eighteen killed, or perhaps as many as twenty-five killed. What a crazy fucking city. That's it, right, over there? That's Juárez? *I can't believe I ever lived there.* I've actually thought this, momentarily overlooking that I *still* live there, and that I'll be sleeping there that night.

THE SUN HAS set on the Chihuahuan Desert. As it sank lower and lower, the sun flared in ever more intense shades of orange, until at the end it seemed as if Marco and Dany were roasting in a toaster oven. I hand the future groom back his flip-flops and Gatorade. I'm about to give the future bride back her shoes when the photographer sees one more possible shot.

The wedding will be held on the first day of May. That's very revealing. May first is the opening day of the Primera playoffs. For all Marco's talk about "a mathematical chance" and "we're not yet eliminated" and there still being the possibility the Indios will pull off "the miracle of miracles," he and Dany have already booked a church. They don't really think the Indios can pull it off, and haven't for a while. The entire Indios' front office will be invited: Gabino, Francisco and Paco Ibarra, and Gil Cantú, of course, along with every player on the team and all the coaches and support staff down to Whiskey the equipment manager. Marco's clan in Dallas will be invited, naturally. Some of Dany's extended family live in Texas, too. One of Dany's aunts has lived in El Paso for twenty-two years. Her mother's second sister has lived in El Paso for the past decade. When Dany first told these maternal aunts the wedding and reception would be held in Juárez, the women balked. They haven't crossed the river in three years, not even to visit Dany's grandmother. They're not about to cross over with the violence growing worse, not even for their niece's wedding.

The photographer perches Dany and Marco atop a minor dune, the fading light at their backs. In the distance, the jagged Juárez Mountains have been reduced to a silhouette. From this angle, Dany and Marco are silhouettes, too. They're two all-black and human-shaped outlines against a lava-like orange swirl of sky. We'll drive back to the city after this. Soldiers will stop us on our way in, rifle

through our things, ask us what we were doing and where we're going and what we'll do when we get there. "All these soldiers and
police, and yet they never catch anyone," Marco will say. It will be
the first time I'll hear a comment like that from him, a hint that
the wider world is seeping inside his soccer bubble. We'll go back to
Juárez. Back into the thick of it, into a city where bullets are divid-
ing families. The photographer clicks his shutter a few last times.

   "Nice shot," I say. Marco and Dany smile in the gloaming, out
here in the desert. It's a really pretty picture.

CHAPTER 15

Exodus

What you're seeing is an exodus, like in biblical terms. Mexico is collapsing. And any sane person is going to get out, and they are.
—CHARLES BOWDEN

THE MEXICAN GOVERNMENT FINDS the killer, the *sicario* who shot the pregnant woman from the U.S. Consulate. He's a member of the Azteca street gang. In the papers, the Aztecas are usually described as the enforcement arm of La Línea, itself once merely the enforcement arm of the Juárez Cartel. The killer's name is Ricardo Valles de la Rosa, also known as El Chino and as El 29. Police extract from him a full confession. He was going after the prison-guard husband, he says. There had been a dustup in the El Paso jail, and the guard had rubbed someone the wrong way. So, nice work, Mexican police! If only the confession can be believed. "We still maintain that we have no information to indicate that any of the [victims] were specifically targeted," says Andrea Simmons, an FBI spokeswoman. El Paso Country sheriff Richard Wiles, who is emerging as my most trusted law enforcement official, seconds the skepticism.

The Aztecas are easy to finger. There's no doubt they are a force in border crime. I've seen pictures of Aztecas incarcerated in the Juárez jail, their arms, necks, and backs covered with elaborate art. Portraits of masked warriors with feathered headdresses and swords. Battle scenes in black ink. Aztecas are mean-looking dudes, tough and muscular *hombres* exactly like the guy standing next to me on the bus. I'm in Cancún, riding the shuttle that serves the tourist corridor. I'm here in advance of the Indios' next game, against the team called Atlante. Aztec designs darken the upper torso of my fellow commuter, the ink more than peeking out of his wifebeater. A friend riding with him sports the "C" logo of the Chicago Bears on the inside of his left arm. On the friend's right forearm, descending to his fingers, is the word "sin." He's not necessarily Azteca, the friend. The first guy, though: classic. The ink, the shaved head: definitely. I'm surprisingly unthreatened to be straphanging next to him. We're all on spring break here. Our collective energies have been sapped bobbing in beautifully warm turquoise waves. Maybe these two have just finished a drinking session at Señor Frog's, downing tequila shots to forget for a while the game we all left back in Juárez. Even Aztecas need some R & R.

I've come to Cancún earlier than I needed to, three full days in advance of the game. I figured if I'm going to pay for a plane ticket clear across the country, then I should get as much out of this trip as possible. And hotel rooms are cheap right now, hardly an expense. Tourism in Cancún—tourism all across Mexico—is way down. Visits to Acapulco are off 45 percent, according to the latest figures I've seen. Cancún tourism is down by 30 percent. Texas police are warning spring breakers not to visit Mexican border towns. (Which is, like, *duh*.) The State Department has warned Americans about the dangers of traveling *anywhere* in Mexico. Several American universities have shut down their Mexican study-abroad partnerships. A story in the Orange County *Register*: "Spring Break May Be Broken for Mexico Resorts."

I've checked into a hotel off the beach. It's just a motel, really, though they modernized it into a retro-hip kind of place. It's centrally located, there's a pool, they charge next to nothing, and the hotel is still maybe only half occupied. "It's very hot here," says an American down from Los Angeles. It *is* hot, and more humid than Miami, which I didn't think was possible. I picked the motel because I wanted to stay away from the American tourist ghetto. Why go to a foreign country only to spend time with Americans? Yet almost every guest here *is* an American. And the reason they are here is traditional, and immediately obvious: They've flown down for the sun and the possibility of sex and, above all, to legally drink.

"Bro, I got a job offer today. In this recession!" A kid from Brown accepts fist bumps from his Ivy League *hermanos*. He twirls a sugar packet into a tall glass of spiked iced tea and asks if there are any zip lines to ride around here. Spring break may be crippled, but it is not dead. From what I can tell, just from listening to the guests in my hotel, sophomore year sucked, but this year has been great so far, and senior year looks like it'll be amazing. Young men not yet twenty-one down clear bottles of Sol and smoke Cuban cigars and top off their pre-party with shots of vanilla-smooth tequila. "We need some Spanish pickup lines, bro." A sign in the lobby advertises morning jitneys to "the most sexiest beach club," a daylight dance party I can't see myself committing to. I've been wandering around Cancún rather aimlessly, a solo explorer.

I've never been here before. I've never wanted to visit here before. So I never knew the beaches in Cancún are spectacular. It's the warmest seawater I've ever enjoyed, water so clear I stay in it for hours at a time, pulling myself out only to drip dry before repeating the wash cycle again and then once more after that. The beaches counterbalance the disappointing resorts lining the waterfront. They're nothing special to look at, and the guests staying there bore me. I walk up from the sand to check out one resort, passing a pack of students touching each other in a game of *fútbol Americano*. In the shallow end of a giant swimming pool, a kid in an orange Illini hat—he's age nineteen at most—sips from a can of Modelo, shouting out to every girl his age that walks by. There's not much action for him, I'm afraid. It's mostly middle-aged Middle America bulging through the plastic straps of beach chairs, basting in their own beers and reading paperback thrillers.

Fish tacos near the beach cost five times more than they do in the city. Everyone eating is an American tourist, some of the younger ones reporting (with a somewhat forced enthusiasm) that last night's foam party was wild, and tonight promises to be wilder still. It doesn't feel at all like the Mexico I've come to know, but I only have to look up at the *megabandera*—the exact same giant tricolor flag that flies in Juárez—to be reminded that this is indeed the same country. And that the issues that face Juárez affect Cancún, too. Border violence is crippling tourism all the way down here. A pedestrian mall near the waterfront hotels has been abandoned. It's an artificial esplanade designed to look like an Old Mexico village. All the businesses have closed up. Rusting steel gates shield empty storefronts. Graffiti tags the stucco walls. As I walk through the mall, I can't help but think of El Centro in Juárez, which, in the end, makes this ersatz Mexican village more authentic than the developers could have ever envisioned.

Indios and Atlante are playing at night, after the Caribbean sun has set. On the evening of the game, a couple hours before kickoff, the air is still hot (and moist and sticky) as I walk from my hotel to downtown Cancún. I see only one man wearing an Atlante jersey. Cancún doesn't seem to care that it has a team in the Primera. It's like Miami that way, a big-league destination with or without sports. Cancún's indifference is most evident at Atlante's lame stadium. It's just a concrete square, four building blocks of bleachers set down like unconnected Legos. The stands look old and weathered, but when I step into the press area I'm told that that Alain N'Kong, our inept striker, scored the stadium's first-ever goal, back when he played for Atlante, which couldn't have been that long ago. One of the local reporters howls at the mention of Kong's name. He hasn't scored a goal for us all season; it seems he was a fraud when he played for Atlante, too.

The press section isn't an enclosed box or anything, just a roped-off patch of bleachers. The rope seems superfluous. It's not as though anyone's going to take our seats. There's hardly anyone here. I pass maybe thirty-five fans as I walk down to the field to watch the Indios warm up. I find Gabino waiting in the tunnel. The players put in a good week of training, the head coach tells me. He and his assistants have drafted a solid game plan, and everyone's still pumped from last week's win over Querétaro. He expects another win tonight. Marco jogs past us and onto the field, first plucking a tuft of grass and crossing himself. He throws me a wave of acknowledgment, but otherwise he's dialed in, serious. He slaloms around a stack of orange cones, running backwards as instructed. I take a walk around the track that circles the field.

Back when I first met up with El Kartel, before I even rode the bus to Monterrey, I was told to get out my calendar and highlight this game. Ken-tokey promised me it would be El Kartel's best road trip of the year. Three days on the bus just to reach the Yucatán Peninsula, but, in the end—Cancún, man. Big parties. Soccer first, but then an epic night out. Here I am, but where is Ken-tokey? Where is anybody? Not a single Kartelero made the trip. No one thinks the Indios are going to win, so why bother? Atlante is a mid-table team, not the best in the Primera, but good enough to have won a coveted trophy. A banner hanging on a stadium wall identifies the Cancún club as the current champion of CONCACAF, the governing body of soccer in North America and the Caribbean. That's a major title; it comes with a ticket to the FIFA Club World Cup and a chance to knock off Lionel Messi, Gerard Pique, and the other superstars of Barcelona. When I make it back to the press box (press corral?), the reporters expect an easy Atlante win. No one is worried about a possible Indios upset.

ON LEAVING: IT'S estimated that some fifty thousand Juarenses have moved to El Paso in the past three years. Saul Luna's girlfriend, a Juarense, hasn't crossed back to Mexico in more than three years. Neither has an El Paso mechanic I visited when I needed a new set of tires. He and I got to talking, and it turns out he owns a house in my neighborhood, just one block from my apartment, a house he's simply abandoned. Francisco Ibarra postponed his move to El Paso for as long as he could. As the violence ramped up, and as it became clear his family was a target for kidnapping and extortion, he still tried to make it work in Juárez, to adapt somehow. First he bought a bulletproof SUV, then another. He hired a bodyguard to keep his family safe. It wasn't enough. His wife was assaulted. The names of his children appeared on kidnapping lists. He went ahead and set up Paco in El Paso. Immigration lawyers advised Francisco that he was free to join his son, to move the family over. But the residency process, in his case, required a full year on the Texas side. No crossing back to watch Indios games, or even practices. No checking in at his Juárez radio station. None of the schmoozing with politicians he feels is essential to his professional success. He didn't want to cross over. He didn't want to leave his city. He put it off, and he put it off longer still. But, eventually, he knew the time had come.

On his last day in Juárez, he visited the Indios offices down at the Grupo Yvasa complex. He followed that visit by stopping in at his radio station, lingering much longer than he needed to. He thought of his father, who refused to move to El Paso with him. Francisco recognized that if only he'd been born in Texas, as his mother had suggested, then a residency exile wouldn't have been necessary. He waited until the last minute. Finally, he told his driver to take him over. They drove on Colegió Militar, past Chamizal Park, and then past the soccer stadium. Their bridge loomed up ahead, in El Centro, coming into view.

"Stop!" Francisco commanded. He wanted to go for burritos. Immediately. Nothing on earth was more important. He demanded his driver double back, steer deep into the city to his favorite restaurant. It took a while to get there—*qué bueno*—and once there he ordered a full meal. He sat in a booth with his food for an hour, and then a while longer. He couldn't stand the thought of leaving.

"I love Juárez," he tells me. "I just love Juárez."

With their membership in the Primera truly in the balance, the Indios come out with a passion they should have tapped a lot earlier in the season. They look great, right away. Every time there's a fifty-fifty ball, meaning possession is up for grabs, an Indio seems to end up in control. Edwin, always a feisty scrapper, is battling harder than ever. Gabino's game plan, clearly, is to retreat into a shell, to concentrate on defense. Our few chances come on counterattacks. As time runs down on the first half, Kong misses a great opportunity, a breakaway he totally flubs. The reporter next to me in the press box snorts. No score at halftime.

ON LEAVING: AT least 160,000 families have abandoned Juárez in the past three years—if not for El Paso, then for other cities in Mexico. At halftime I talk to a young woman wearing an Indios jersey. She caught my ear with lusty cheers every time an Indios player touched the ball. She's a Juárez native, she tells me. She's been living in Cancún for a couple years, ever since the violence inspired her parents to sell their Juárez properties and sink the proceeds into an oceanfront hotel, which they run.

"Nobody ever thought we'd make the Primera, and still we did!" she says when I bring up the team's likely descent. There's that Frontera optimism I've come to know, that found silver lining. Juárez, she tells me, remains in her heart. She still has lots of family there, including her grandmother. The people are warm, the city is generous, et cetera—all that. Yet when I tell her that life seems softer in Cancún, she quickly responds with "Definitely!" When I ask if her family will be going back, she answers even more rapidly.

"Never!" she shouts, startling me with the force of her reply. "I still go up to visit my grandma, but Juárez is so violent. I saw a car get jacked right in front of me at a red light!"

THE INDIOS LOOK a little tired after the break. Road trips are grueling, as I've learned. Especially with a cross-country flight like the one the team took only yesterday. The humidity isn't making anything easier. The biggest factor has to be their play in the first half. It seems to have depleted them. They've given Atlante their best shot, and it didn't produce a goal. It's going to be hard to play with that same intensity, yet now is when they really need it. They cannot afford even a tie. Because they must play for the win, Gabino relaxes the defense a bit, telling his players to make more runs on net. It's a risky tactical decision. With the midfield and the forwards pushing ahead, the Indios are vulnerable to a quick counterattack, which is what Atlante pulls off perfectly. Ten minutes into the second half, the home team scores a goal: 1–0.

This is not good. Not at all. The Indios need to score two goals now. They have not scored two goals in a single game all season. Gabino has no choice but to double down, to push even harder. He pulls off Edwin, replacing the veteran with younger and fresher legs. Two more players are soon swapped out as well, to energize the attack. That's all the substitutions we're allowed. I find myself feeling nervous, my leg fidgeting like Gil Cantú's before the Monarcas home game. *If you're not nervous, then you don't care, brother.* I wasn't invested in the team when I moved to Juárez. I am now. I don't want the Indios to lose. I want Edwin's hard work to be rewarded. I know a loss will pain Marco tremendously. He needs a goal, from somebody. *We* need a goal. Check that: We need two goals. The team that scores next, though, is Atlante. Again. And again off the counterattack. Two-nothing. Juárez is done.

I can see the Indios deflate. The players still on the field—Marco, everyone—they just dissolve. It's over. They have been kicked into a pit of fiery skulls. Score three goals in the fifteen remaining minutes? Not even in a fever dream. The moment everyone in Juárez has been dreading—and everyone else in Mexico knew would come—has indeed arrived. Very late in the game, with any chance of a comeback already shot, our goalie Christian stops a breakaway the only way he can: by taking out the opposing player, a move that earns him a red-card expulsion. The Indios have no substitutions left. Someone on the field will have to step into the net. Maleno Frías gets the call. He's handed a pair of big white gloves and a fluorescent orange jersey that indicates he's the goaltender from here on in. His first job is to stop a penalty kick. Impossible. Embarrassing, really. His flailing stab at the ball—he comes nowhere close—is a fittingly ridiculous end. Three-nothing, then the final whistle. The Indios will drop to the minors next season.

On leaving: The players shine with sweat as they slump off the field. Marco strips off his Indios jersey as if he's disgusted to have it covering his chest. Just before he ducks into the locker room tunnel, he throws his uniform into the stands, wanting nothing to do with it. The sweaty shirt is caught by a man named Christian Sanchez. He's an architect. Seven years ago, after finishing up his studies in Mexico City, he moved to Juárez cold, not knowing anyone but confident the border's booming population would give him plenty of work. He found clients almost from the day he arrived. He landed so many commissions he was able to start on a personal project, a home of his own.

He gave his house a clean, modern look. Silvery steel railings and trim, walls painted rich cream or a deep, contrasting plum. He wanted the details of the house to signal quality. The garage door is like no other: two steel slabs that appear to be acid-washed. The front door is huge, maybe twice the size of a normal door. While the first floor of the house appears fortified, which is a traditional Mexican look, the second story is unusually public. Glass walls illuminate an upstairs living room. From the master bedroom, a wide porch overlooks the street. Even before construction started, the architect knew it would be the most striking house on his block. It was to be his calling card, the example to show prospective clients. But by the time the builders wiped a final polishing cloth across the granite kitchen countertops, the murder rate in Juárez had exploded. Who needs an architect with bodies stacking up in the street? Why pay for picture windows when they expose you to stray bullets? Families abandoned thousands of the finest homes in the city, flooding the market—if it could be said there was even a market anymore. Sanchez started planning his escape. He put his dream house up for sale, having never moved into it. He prayed someone would buy it.

Marco, after meeting Dany in the gym, began looking for a place where the two of them could live together. He drove all over Juárez, checking out everything available. When he saw Christian Sanchez's showpiece, he fell in love for the second time in a month. The list price: $180,000, less than it cost to build, but probably still too high, now that all property in Juárez is considered distressed property. Marco offered $140,000 in cash, the bulk of his savings account. The architect accepted the offer immediately, gratefully. Marco probably could have bought the house for a lot less, but he wanted it badly. It was perfect. He thinks it still is perfect, as does Dany. "I love my house," she's told me. With everyone else running away from the city, Marco sank into Juárez all he had in the world. At the closing, as he turned over his pesos and signed the deed and other paperwork, he saw himself as Juarense for the long term. At that closing, Christian Sanchez shook Marco's hand. And then he moved to Cancún to start over. He moved that very same day.

GABINO IS THE first Indio I find. The stadium has emptied—it was never that full to begin with—and the youth teams of both Atlante and Los Indios are on the field for their meaningless exhibition. I spot the head coach in a box seat, along with the Indios' goalkeeper coach and the team doctor. Gabino shakes my hand politely when I step into the box, but it's obvious he's in a bad mood, and not merely the kind of upset anyone might feel after a loss. He's angrier than that, very mad. He had prepared the team to play their best, he thought, had all his ducks lined up in a just-right row. Yet his forwards failed him, as usual. It's as if a few key players didn't care that the loss permanently kills the Primera dream and that everyone, including Gabino, is now stained with red stripes of stink. The goalkeeper coach signals to Gabino that it's time to go, that the team bus is about to leave. Gabino signals back that he's going to stay. The team can leave without him.

I slink out of the box as quietly as I can, heading to the parking lot to see if I can catch Marco. We're in different hotels, and I'm staying in Cancún yet one more extra day—why not, right?—so this might be my only chance to talk to him. I pass Domino's pizza vendors liquidating their inventories with slashed prices—a whole pie for about a dollar. Beer ladies who'd expected more fans at the game roll coolers full of unopened Corona bottles through the loose gravel

that rings the stadium. I watch a young female television reporter
navigate the gravel in five-inch stilettos. Her skirt is the shortest I
have ever seen in the wild, so mini I really, truly, and honestly cannot help but notice that her panties match her tight black tank top.
When she finally makes her wobbly way over to the dressing rooms,
Atlante players crowd around her, eager to be interviewed.

There's significantly less buzz outside the Indios' locker room.
I'm the only Juárez guy here, and only two Cancún reporters collect
the obligatory "We feel bad" quotes from the losers. "We knew we
were going down," Marco tells me. "We just hoped it would be longer before it was official." Marco and I both notice Alain N'Kong—
the top forward on my list of suspected quitters—signing autographs
and talking to friends he made when he played down here. He's upbeat, telling jokes, smiling and laughing. It makes me mad, his indifference. I want to pull an Oskar and crack one of those Corona
bottles over his skull. "Alain's living in the past," Marco practically
spits, angry too. He climbs on the bus, and a few minutes later Kong
joins him. They pull away from the stadium without their coach.
Atlante fans jeer as the bus slips through a guard gate. It rolls onto
the street, not to come back this way for a long time, if ever again.

"They lost the game, they lost the city, they lost the people,"
states the Indios' Ramón Morales in an especially melodramatic
press release that lands in my cell-phone in-box. I trade in the green
bib I needed to wear to sit in the press section, receiving my passport
in return. It's almost eleven P.M. I'm too worked up to go back to my
hotel, and I don't want to go to a spring-break nightclub. I walk Cancún in search of food, hopefully someplace far away from American
college students. I cruise up and down side streets until I come
across Rolandi's Restaurant Bar & Pizzeria. It might be a tourist
joint—the sign is in English—but when I step inside, everyone is
speaking Spanish and the pizzas smell so good and the crowd looks
local and I ask for a table. I'm seated near a man and woman enjoying
a date. Two women share a table across the room, under a TV showing a boxing match in Monterrey. Near me, a woman absently taps
the back of her toddler, his head resting on her shoulder. A family out
at almost midnight! I love it. "You're alone?" my waiter asks, concerned. Yeah, but I'm happy to be here. The ceviche is pushed, but I
want comfort food tonight. Those Domino's vendors at the stadium
got into my head. I order a pizza margherita topped with shrimp and

onion. The waiter brings me a Negra Modelo and pours it into a tall glass. I take a long first sip and lean back in my chair.

I don't know how to feel about the Indios. Obviously they were going down. Tonight is not a big surprise or anything. "Nobody thought we'd even reach the Primera," Marco told me once, same as that young woman I spoke to at halftime. It's been nice, for a while, to be in the fold, to be a city all of Mexico has to acknowledge is indeed in Mexico. However fleeting the coverage on ESPN Deportes, Juárez was still on ESPN Deportes. The Indios games against Santos and Toluca and Club América were broadcast across North America, sometimes even down to Colombia and Argentina. The city's name appeared in the league standings every week, if always at the very bottom. After tonight, order is simply being restored. Juárez will once again disappear.

It was clear they were going to be relegated. Of course. Not only did they need to beat Querétaro, and then Atlante tonight; they had to win five more games after that. This team that can't score needed to win seven games in a row. That was not going to happen. But we liked to think it could have. That the team would rebound just like Juárez can still rebound from this violence and become "like Las Vegas but Mexican, so better," a city where dentists are not shot at and where ambitious architects can build a practice. The end of any dream hurts. It forces us to take a cold look at where we stand. If we're being honest with ourselves, we know Juárez won't get better, not any time soon. We know it's probably going to get a lot worse, actually. Calderón's social programs will fix nothing. Some of the maquiladoras will pack up and move to China. Some of the bus drivers that serve the remaining maquiladoras will be murdered. In the morning, the Indios will return to a hemorrhaging city.

I think of a line by the author Charles Bowden, an American who's covered Juárez for nearly two decades. Before I moved down, I read his border big three: *Juárez: Laboratory of Our Future, Murder City*, and *Down by the River*. And then I put the books aside. I don't want to re-plow land he's already harvested, which is something many journalists who visit Juárez end up doing. I've even tried to dodge him physically, though, perhaps inevitably, I did run into him one Saturday afternoon at the El Paso Museum of Art. While I've kept my distance, lines he's written flash in my brain all the time. "The governments of Mexico and the United States are not waging a war *on* drugs, they're waging a war *for* drugs." Forty years in, illegal drugs in the United States are cheaper, more available, and of better quality. Proceeds from the sale of these drugs—perhaps fifty billion dollars a year—prop up the Mexican economy. NAFTA, Bowden argues convincingly, has been a social disaster, a prime reason why so many Mexicans are compelled to illegally cross into the States. (And, by the way, border fences aren't going to stop a desperate man or woman from crossing. Fences clearly aren't in any way stopping the flow of drugs). My favorite of his many sharp insights: People in Juárez are murdered twice. First they are killed. Then their reputation is assassinated. There are exceptions for victims like Pedro Picasso or those massacred students, but for the most part, if you're gunned down, it's assumed you did something to bring on the bullet. Why else would you be killed?

I recommend Bowden's books. Yet as I sit in the pizza parlor, I find myself dwelling on a line of his I've always disagreed with. "In Juárez you cannot sustain hope," he wrote in *Laboratory of Our Future*. No hope? Hope is all that Juarenses have. They overflow with hope. Hope is the ultimate coping mechanism. It is hope that drew so many to the border in the first place, eager to cross to the United States or, barring that, to land a factory job after the earthquake took everything or the drought evaporated their crops or NAFTA destroyed the only way to make money their family had ever known. The hope that maybe the maquiladora will work out, that the impossibly low wages—just do the math—will magically provide for the family they must leave every day. The hope that, after making the sensible and pragmatic decision to slip into the drug trade, they will be the one exception, the only man—or woman—to make it out alive: rich, honorable, loved, old. It won't happen. None of it will happen. But they can hope. There is nothing else. It is hope that repels the odor, that toxic stench as the shit they are drowning in bubbles ever higher.

Now *I'm* getting angry, like Gabino after the game. Bowden may be right after all. It's disappointing, the loss. It's truly too bad the Indios are going down. The team's failure feels like an argument against hope itself.

CHAPTER 16

The Dead Women

I ARRIVE BACK IN JUÁREZ IN A GOOD mood somehow. I can't be that upset about the Indios; I knew they were going to lose, same as everybody else. I've enjoyed one last day at the beach. And now I get to again see my supercool new dog, who was being watched by a friend. I get to sleep in my own bed, too. "It's funny how you miss this place when you've been gone," the bass player of an El Paso rock band said one night when I was clubbing with Paco Ibarra; the band had just returned from a California swing. The sentiment's the same on the Juárez side. Even after five days in Cancún, I'm jazzed to be back on my home turf, in such high spirits that I walk with my luggage from the Free Bridge all the way back to my apartment, maybe two miles. A choking dust floats in the air. I pass abandoned buildings and junker cars and I walk on roads bruised with potholes. None of this bothers me. When I step into my neighborhood, I hear little kids playing in their front yards. They look like animals caged behind iron bars, yes, but they are still little kids, and they are still playing. Buds green on trees lining my street. There's my apartment up ahead, and I melt a little when I see it. Home remains sweet, even in Juárez. It's funny how much I missed this place.

"Hey man, did you see that guy that got killed?" a neighbor asks me. "They killed him right over there, right at the dip in the road. I guess he was slowing his car because of the dip and they shot him. They shot up his car with a thousand bullets. It was in the news. It was right over there. He was the son of a woman who owns one of the houses over there. She was all crying. The police weren't even around."

My neighbor is excited to be breaking the news to me. He ducks inside his apartment to fetch a copy of *PM* published the day after the shooting. He saved the paper because our building appears in it, like we're famous. Yep, there's my usual parking space. That is indeed my apartment right there in the photograph. The man was executed maybe a hundred yards from my front door. "Liquefied by bullets" is how the newspaper put it. And if my neighbor hadn't told me about the shooting and saved the paper, I wouldn't have known a thing. All the evidence has been swept up, like it never happened.

THE VERY FIRST time Marco and I went to lunch, he gave me a somewhat surreal driving tour of the city. There's the new consulate flying the American flag. There's the mall, and there's the bowling alley, the only place we feel safe going out at night. Here's where I was carjacked. Oh, and you've heard about the dead women, right? That cotton field over there is where a bunch of them were found.

I'd heard about the dead women. Until it evolved into the killing capital of the world, Juárez was best known for one thing: the murder of women. The basic storyline has been disseminated in newspapers, via television and radio reports, even in the arts. There's Oskar's favorite book, *2666*. ("It concerns what may be the most horrifying real-life mass-murder spree of all time: as many as 400 women killed in the vicinity of Juárez, Mexico," wrote Stephen King in a review published in *Entertainment Weekly*.) There have been separate movies starring Jennifer Lopez, Jimmy Smits, and Minnie Driver. TruTV.com posted "Ciudad Juárez: The Serial Killer's Playground." *Ms.* magazine published "The Maquiladora Murders," linking the dead women of Juárez to free trade policies. Tori Amos wrote a song. Jane Fonda and Sally Field marched over from El Paso to read *The Vagina Monologues*. Juárez: It's where women are murdered just because they're women, and where authorities care so little about women they refuse to resolve the crimes.

I still see the religious iconography around town. Painted pink crosses, a little faded by now, cling to telephone poles along Avenida Colegio Militar, in view of the border and Texas beyond. A large wooden cross framed in pink and studded with the kind of spikes that crucified Jesus Christ guards the Santa Fe Bridge, the last thing a tourist sees before walking back to El Paso. With tourists no longer visiting, the spikes have been repurposed as hooks for plastic trash bags and as shelving for newspapers sold to Mexicans lined up to escape. Deeper inland, a pink cross welded from metal rebar protects the justice center. And there are still eight small pink wooden crosses huddled in that cotton field Marco pointed out to me, the site where the decaying bodies of eight young women were found.

Femicide, as the mysterious killings have come to be called, first received attention in Juárez close to twenty years ago. That attention has not abated, at least internationally, even as the city has undergone its dramatic upswing in overall violence. In the past few months, I've seen femicide stories in the *Christian Science Monitor*, in the *Los Angeles Times*, and on several news broadcasts. The dead women were a plot point on the television show *NCIS*. Drexel University in Philadelphia, in conjunction with Amnesty International, sponsored an "ArtMarch" to call attention to those being murdered in Juárez "simply because they're women." On International Women's Day (March 8), a group called Sydney Action for Juárez gathered in the center of their Australian city wearing pink-and-black clothes and carrying pink crosses.

"Most of the Juárez femicides have been young maquiladora workers," the group's coordinator told the *Sydney Morning Herald*. "The women seem to be targeted just because they are women."

Most significantly, just before I moved down, the Inter-American Court of Human Rights ruled that a pattern of gender-based violence in Juárez had been well established by the time the women's bodies were discovered in the cotton field, in 2001. The Mexican government was ordered, among other things, to continue investigating the cotton-field murders and to give $800,000 in compensation to the victims' families and their lawyers.

"This ruling is a landmark," Amnesty International's Mexico researcher, Rupert Knox, told me via e-mail. "It confirms that femicide has occurred and that the State's failure to prevent and punish the crimes is a violation of the State's responsibilities. This is important."

When Knox sent me that e-mail he was an ocean away, in London, where he lives and works. The court that ruled that a femicide has occurred in Juárez adjourned in Costa Rica, several countries south of Mexico. In my time on the border, I've noticed that when the topic of femicide comes up, the words locals use to describe the dead women often differ dramatically from those disseminated by Amnesty International over in Europe or by the court down in Central America. When I'm in Juárez I hear words like "myth." And "black legend." And "a great lie." When I showed a young Juarense a photograph I'd taken of a pink cross, she scrunched her face into a frown.

"Ugh," she said. "That's super cliché."

"FEMICIDE IS LIKE a religion," Molly Molloy told me the first time I met her. "I used to be a true believer. Then when I started looking at the real numbers, I changed my opinion. Now I'm a heretic. Now I'm like someone who has escaped from a cult and feels compelled to attack the cult."

Although she's not even five feet tall, Molloy has become one of the most visible people studying La Frontera. A librarian at New Mexico State University, in Las Cruces, she's spent almost two decades collecting and disseminating information about the border. She reads every newspaper published in Juárez, every morning, in an attempt to track every death in the city. Three, five, nine times a day, she updates her Frontera listserv with stories of fresh kills and with articles about Juárez published in the *Washington Post*, the *London Guardian*, and anywhere she finds them. When I went to visit her at the NMSU library, I found an *Onion* headline taped to her office door: KITTEN THINKS OF NOTHING BUT MURDER ALL DAY.

The Frontera listserv has given Molloy a platform she has not hesitated to use. In frequent e-mails, she slaps down any reporter who dares romanticize the border, perhaps by lamenting the sharp drop-off in business at the Kentucky Club. "I have a hard time balancing more than 28,000 dead in Mexico and nearly 6,500 dead in Juárez with the hard times of a few bars," she wrote after the airing of an NPR story.

Her biggest criticisms, the ones she marshals the most energy to launch, come when any journalist, academic, or filmmaker dares focus solely on Juárez's dead women. Her 2,600-word essay "A Perspective on the Murders of Human Beings (Women, Men & Children of Both Genders) in Ciudad Juárez" arrived in electronic mailboxes packed with stats and supporting a main point Molloy is increasingly comfortable espousing: What is happening in Juárez is much more than a femicide. It's a human-rights disaster.

"Those in the press and academia who have written extensively about the murders of women, those who coined the term 'femicide' to define the killing of women as a product of their gender, seldom acknowledge the actual numbers of victims of violence in Juárez and the fact that the killings of women are a small percentage of the total," she wrote. "And that this gender ratio in murder statistics is not uncommon, not in Mexico, not elsewhere."

In 2001, the year the eight bodies were found in the Juárez cotton field, 12 percent of all murder victims in Juárez were women. That's not a high percentage for any city in North America, and 2001 wasn't an anomaly. The rates have held steady since 1993. Since 2008, when the overall murder rate in Juárez accelerated, the percentage of women murdered has fallen below 7 percent. By comparison, close to a *quarter* of all murder victims in the United States are women.

Some of Molloy's other findings:

> It is not true that hundreds of the murders of women that occurred in Juárez between 1993 and 2007 are unsolved. The majority of the cases have been shown—by Mexican officials as well as by independent researchers—to be domestic violence cases: The killers are known, and they were known to the victims.
> Across Mexico, the number of women killed per capita between 1995 and 2005 has been highest in cities in the center of the country, not in Juárez or anywhere else along the border.

And then there's impunity. It's a core contention among femicide proponents that *machismo* has kept Mexican authorities from prosecuting crimes against women. The Inter-American Court for Human Rights specifically ruled that "gender bias" undermined the government's investigation of the cotton-field murders. Molloy counters, with sources, that 99 percent of *all* reported crimes in Mexico go unpunished, male victim or female victim. And only one in one hundred crimes are reported in the first place.

"I don't want to be misunderstood," Molloy later insisted to me via e-mail. "There's nothing wrong with people mobilizing, organizing and challenging the government in Juárez and Chihuahua to solve these murders. There's nothing wrong with these women [from the cotton field] getting a judgment against the State for not solving these cases. These cases deserve attention. The wrong thing is not what the Mexican activists have done. It's what the idiotic American and international activist and feminist theorizers and these Hollywood people have done in turning it into this mysterious untrue thing, this myth."

THE MYSTERY, EVERYONE agrees, began back in 1993. Amado Carrillo Fuentes took control of the Juárez Cartel. The murder rate in the city subsequently took off. The number of men killed doubled from the year before, from fifty to one hundred. The number of women murdered shot up from six deaths in 1992 to twenty-three, almost a quadrupling. A retired accountant named Esther Chávez Cano focused on the spike in female murders in a column she'd launched at *El Diario*.

Chávez became an exceptional advocate. She was never afraid to call up a journalist or a politician or anyone else she felt could prod the government into action. She criticized officials up to the state governor for, at least initially, blaming the victims for staying out late at night or for dressing provocatively. When her activism prompted reforms, Chávez insisted that the reforms never went far enough. Not one more murdered woman was her goal—*Ni una más*, to this day the rallying cry of the femicide movement. Chávez went on to found Casa Amiga, the border's first rape crisis shelter. She won the Mexican government's National Human Rights Award, specifically for her work on behalf of "the murdered women of Ciudad Juárez." She died of cancer on Christmas Day 2009.

"She literally changed the world for women in Juárez, bringing the struggle of the raped, the disappeared, the discarded women and girls to global attention," wrote *Vagina Monologues* author Eve Ensler, who performed her play in Ciudad Juárez in 2004, along with the actresses Sally Field, Jane Fonda, and Christine Lahti.

Hollywood actresses marching across the Santa Fe Bridge marked the high point of the femicide movement in Juárez itself, says Kathleen Staudt, a UTEP anthropologist. After that, at least locally, energy began to drop off. I stopped by Staudt's office one morning during a break between classes. An insect frozen in amber held down papers on her desk. A poster from Amnesty International hung on a wall behind her chair. The poster featured a green road sign embossed with the words WELCOME TO CIUDAD JUÁREZ. The overall population of the city was listed on the road sign, as well as the total number of men who live in the city. There was no corresponding number for women, only an arrow pointing to a graveyard.

"Away from the border, some would surely wonder how many border women were still alive," Staudt told me with a chuckle. "I don't know if they did that for fundraising purposes or what."

In her 2008 book *Activism on the Border*, Staudt credited Chávez with introducing femicide to a wider audience. Juárez proved conveniently malleable, a blank slate upon which anyone or any group could sell whatever agenda they pleased. With none of the crimes ever prosecuted, any theory behind the murders remained, technically, viable.

There are a lot of theories. Alicia Gaspar de Alba, the author of the dead-women-of-Juárez murder mystery *Desert Blood* and a professor of Chicana and Chicano studies at UCLA, connected the killings to the North American Free Trade Act. In addition to criticizing NAFTA in her novel—the plot revolves around a lesbian who adopts a child carried by a maquiladora worker—Gaspar de Alba also organized a conference at UCLA called "The Maquiladora Murders, or Who Is Killing the Women of Juárez?" More than a thousand people at the conference pondered the "disposability" of women on the border, in factories and in life generally. Amnesty International lobbied to sell pink scarves at the conference, Gaspar de Alba told me. "I think they were looking at femicide as a fundraising opportunity." The dead women as a global economic metaphor has been a powerful symbol, Staudt concluded in her book, but only after noting that just a small fraction of the women killed in Juárez had ever actually worked in a maquiladora.

If free trade isn't killing women, how about a snuff-film/pornography ring based in El Paso and run by Border Patrol agents? (That's a key plot point in Gaspar de Alba's novel.) Or how about serial killers? Prominent El Paso journalist Diana Washington Valdez claims that "two or more" of these serial killers currently haunt

Juárez. "Most of the victims, practically all of them, are young women, teenagers often," Washington Valdez told Al Jazeera in 2009. Yet when Staudt actually examined the murders, she found much diversity. There were young victims and old victims, poor and not so poor, their killers known more often than they were unknown. Rather than victims of snuff filmmakers or serial killers, the list of the dead features "the sort of routine sexualized torture associated with female homicide found in many cities and countries."

So why the emphasis on the fantastic? "People read mysteries like there is no tomorrow," Gaspar de Alba told me when I reached her by phone in Los Angeles. "It's one of the biggest-selling genres." Bolaño's *2666* features an American journalist trying to solve the murders of the dead women in "Santa Theresa," an obvious stand-in for Ciudad Juárez. "No one pays attention to these killings," the journalist says, "but the secret of the world is hidden in them." Argentinean filmmaker Lourdes Portillo starts her documentary *Señorita Extraviada* by stating that she has come to Juárez "to track down ghosts and listen to the mysteries that surround them." In *Bordertown*, a film released straight to DVD in 2008, Jennifer Lopez plays a crusading American journalist sent to Juárez to single-handedly solve the killings. (It was the bus driver!)

"A story can haunt you forever, whereas statistics fade," Gaspar de Alba elaborated. "'Facts' are not always 'truth' but rather pieces of well-crafted information that somebody wants you to know. If you base your opinion on so-called statistics and facts, before you know it you're spouting inanities like that Molly Molloy, and femicide becomes a fable instead of an ongoing slaughter of young, brown fertile women's bodies on the El Paso/Juárez border."

PEDRO ALBUQUERQUE IS a well-traveled anthropologist currently posted in the south of France. For five years, starting in 2002, he lived in Laredo, Texas, working at a branch of Texas A&M. The border intrigued him. He wondered why crime rates are so much lower on the American side of the Rio Grande than on the Mexican side, despite similar cultures and socioeconomic backgrounds. His research revealed that high levels of violence in Mexican border towns "originate from deficient law enforcement and legal systems, and from chaotic urbanization and high population densities." That

is, he found that a corrupt justice system and suddenly overpopu-
lated cites—the mix in Juárez, for sure—*cause* the violence.

Next he turned his attention to femicide. While noting that the
murders of women, especially in Ciudad Juárez, have received a
remarkable amount of attention, the vast amount of literature on
the phenomenon originated mostly from "radical scholars, interest
groups, international and nongovernmental organizations and political activists, usually with little regard to the evaluation of the
available data." Specifically, he cited "preconceived notions and ad
hoc statements not supported by empirical investigation."

So he and a colleague looked at the data. Because erratic numbers
are often the biggest problem in cross-border research, Albuquerque
avoided newspaper reports and even police statistics. Instead, he and
his colleague turned to the morgue.

"Coroner data is very reliable," he told me via e-mail from Mar-
seilles. "Because coroners do not have any incentive to hide the
work they do, and are relatively insulated from the criminal estab-
lishment."

Poring over the morgue's records, Albuquerque found that cities
with higher populations had higher male homicide rates. And cities along the border had male homicide rates that were higher still.
The female homicide rates in every city—including Juárez—rose
and fell with the male homicide rate. Women are being killed in
Juárez because men are also being killed in Juárez.

"Femicide rates in Juárez are high and worrisome," Albuquerque
told me. "However, general homicide rates in Juárez are even more
astounding than femicide rates, and the femicide rates are not especially high when compared with other Mexican cities, if studied
across many years. Perhaps even more important, the femicide
phenomenon is clearly much more significant in many American
large cities [and] particularly extreme in American inner city
neighborhoods."

Drexel University's ArtMarch was held in conjunction with Ni
Una Mas, a proudly activist exposition intended "to stop the Femicide." The goal, said the curators, was "to raise awareness about gender violence and, in particular, crimes against women in the Mexican
border town of Juárez." Yoko Ono contributed art. Amnesty International attached its name. Drexel's athletic director published an op-
ed in the *Philadelphia Inquirer* in which he escalated the terminology

in Juárez from *femicide* to *genocide*. By definition, he argued that someone or a group of people are trying to kill every single female in Juárez.

Before the exposition opened, its curators e-mailed Molly Molloy in Las Cruces, hoping she'd help them build a body of information. Their first question had to do with the total number of women killed in Juárez since 1993. Was it seven hundred, as they had read? Molloy responded that seven hundred sounded about right. (Her total at the time was 677.) "BUT," she added, "I have a problem with the whole definition of femicide, that is that all of these women were killed for sexual motives or BECAUSE they were women." She pointed out, as she does to anyone who mentions femicide, that ten times as many men have been murdered in Juárez over the same period.

A back-and-forth ensued. One Drexel curator replied that, from what he had read, "There remains a great deal of evidence that the majority number [of women] have been snatched off the streets and then raped and murdered. This makes the context of their deaths different from the many men who have died as a result of the drug trade."

Molloy countered that the phrase "snatched off the streets" is a myth—a myth that particularly grates on her. "It has been documented that the majority of the killings of women were always found to be domestic violence related," she wrote. The curator proceeded to question Molloy's statistics, doubting any figures coming out of Mexico. Molloy wrote back in great length and detail, arguing that there *are* facts everyone should be able to agree on, that facts matter, and that the folklore surrounding the femicide story in Juárez can be harmful.

She wasn't persuasive. As part of the exposition, the university produced this television commercial, which aired on the Telemundo network:

"Over 700 girls and young women have been murdered in Ciudad Juárez, México since 1993," says a female narrator. "Some as young as twelve years old. These killings are still unsolved. And they continue to this day. Because there is no penalty." On-screen, a woman in a pink shirt places her hand on the shoulder of a girl, the girl kneeling with her hands clasped in prayer. The girl also wears a pink shirt. "Our lives are being taken just because we are women." The commercial ends with information on the then-upcoming Art-

March, aimed at ending "this femicide in México and violence against women everywhere. Help save the girls."

The commercial did not say that girls are a very small minority of those killed in Juárez. It did not say that exponentially more men and boys are killed in Juárez every year, and that those male murders remain unsolved, too, and continue to this day. Most relevantly, Drexel did not say that, prior to the recent explosion of cartel violence, Philadelphia has historically been more lethal for women than Juárez, despite being about the same size.

In 2006 in Juárez, 253 people were murdered. Twenty of those killed were women, or 7.9 percent of the total. In Philadelphia that year, according to a database compiled by the *Inquirer*, 406 people were murdered; forty-seven of those were women, or 11.5 percent of the total. Furthermore, most of the women killed in Philadelphia were of childbearing age, a descriptor frequently used for the dead women of Juárez. The first woman murdered in Philadelphia that year was a twenty-one-year-old bludgeoned to death by a young man she'd broken up with over the holidays. That man also stabbed the victim, murdered her grandmother, and burned down their house in an attempt to cover up his crime.

DIANA WASHINGTON VALDEZ was the keynote speaker at the Drexel exposition. She's a reporter at the *El Paso Times* and the author of *The Killing Fields: Harvest of Women*, first released in 2006. In publicity materials for her book, Washington Valdez is described as "*the* expert on the ghastly border crimes." Drexel posted on its Web site a video of Washington Valdez's 2009 interview with Al Jazeera. The news network flew her to London, sat her in a studio, and described her on the air as "the woman who knows more about this story than anyone else."

On her own Web site, Washington Valdez documented her trip to England by posing in front of the Tower Bridge. She's spoken about the dead women of Juárez in not only Philadelphia and London but also Barcelona, Madrid, Rome, Cartagena, Mexico City, Los Angeles, Phoenix, Dallas, Nashville, New York, Washington, D.C., Portland, Seattle, Boston, and more than a dozen other cities. When I met her for lunch, she told me she'd just accepted an invitation to speak at the University of Colorado in Boulder. Expenses paid, as always.

"I check my calendar, and if I have room on my schedule and I think I can do some good, I'll go," she said. "Someone like me and others like me out there, we're going to continue to keep very focused on what's going on with the women, simply because we've made it our business to do so."

Washington Valdez got into the femicide business relatively late. Esther Chávez started tracking the murders of women in 1993, yet it wasn't until 2002 that Washington Valdez published "Death Stalks the Border," a series in her newspaper. That series led to her book, in which she claims to have solved the femicide crimes. I've read the book. Apparently, the killings of women were part of a circuit of orgies by prominent Juárez families. I say "apparently" because she does not name any of these families, nor any of her sources, nor any women specifically killed at an orgy. The book concludes in a Mexico City coffee shop. Washington Valdez meets with an unnamed source, a man talking in a shadowy way about a party he attended with unnamed powerful people. At the party, says the unnamed source, he learned that the state of Chihuahua had been sold to "bloodthirsty" Colombian narcos, some of whom "were known to practice human-sacrifice" rituals.

Washington Valdez's theories about the dead women of Juárez have evolved over the years. "The best information we have is that these men are committing crimes simply for the sport of it," she told NPR in 2003, in a story that was strongly criticized by reporters based in Juárez. In a British documentary from 2005, she nailed down the killers with great specificity, though she did not name names, nor did she name her sources. "Mexican federal authorities have conducted important investigations of their own already that reveal who the killers are," she says in the documentary. She pauses. She cocks her head slightly, her interviewer waiting quietly. Finally Washington Valdez delivers the goods: "Five men from Juárez and one from Tijuana get together and kill women in what can only be described as blood sport."

She adds: "I've discovered that these people that were revealed by these investigations were very important people. And some of the other people involved and named allegedly as killers are prominent men with important political connections that are considered untouchables."

She does not name any of these prominent men. In an article she wrote for Channel 4 news in London, she said that a "confidential source" had indicated that a number of women in Juárez were being murdered so their organs could be harvested and sold to Americans. She did not name anyone supposedly trafficking kidneys and hearts, nor did she name any gringo buyers. In her report, the "confidential source" said that murder for organ harvesting "had to be one of the main ways in which [women in Juárez] vanish."

I met Washington Valdez at a Mexican restaurant in El Paso, near her newsroom. I ordered beef tacos, and she sipped a bowl of tortilla soup flavored with avocado. When she spoke to Al Jazeera in London, Washington Valdez gave a list of "five lines of investigation" into the Juárez femicides "that even the FBI agrees with." I asked her, just so I could fact-check, who at the FBI had endorsed her list.

"I don't know that they're still there now," she answered, "but they can speak about it."

I again asked for their names and for some way I could contact them. I repeated that it was simply fact-checking, that I needed to make sure they actually existed. "There are a couple people you can ask, but they're not there anymore. And I'd have to contact them, okay?" she replied. Washington Valdez promised to contact them and get back to me. She has yet to do so.

That list she read in London also traveled with her to Philadelphia for her speech at Drexel. She reads from it on camera in a video posted on YouTube. Printed on the list are the five likely reasons women have been murdered in Juárez:

Drug dealers killed women with impunity, including to even celebrate successful crossings of drugs across the border.

Violent gangs that have killed women to initiate new members.

Two or more serial killers who are still loose, never been arrested.

A group of powerful men who killed women at different times for different reasons.

And then you have your copycats who have taken advantage of this situation to hide their own murders.

Powerful men killing women at different times for different reasons? That sure is broad. Serial killers? An FBI investigation in 1999 concluded that the sex crimes were probably committed by many different men who did not know each other. "It would be irresponsible to state that a serial killer is loose in Juárez," the agency reported. Reading her book and her articles on femicide and watching all her videos on YouTube, I started to wonder if maybe Washington Valdez is being pranked. That perhaps one of her unnamed sources told her that a serial killer from Tijuana was murdering women for blood sport just to see if she'd run with it. Orgies involving *los juniors*, the offspring of the wealthy elite? Harvesting of organs? Her published theories lack any possible path to reinvestigation. They can't be checked out in any way.

"It's not my job to solve the crimes," she told me at lunch. "It's the investigators'. They know who did it."

Three times in our interview, she said she couldn't answer a specific question because it would put her in too much danger. She told me she can't go into Juárez anymore for her own safety, that she's grown too high-profile. Spookiness, I suspect, is central to her appeal. She's invited to travel the world on the femicide speaking circuit because she hypes the mystery. Since none of the murders have been prosecuted, none of her theories can be proven wrong. And her theories are much more exciting than what has been documented to be behind the majority of the murders, at least before 2007: domestic violence. Given what Washington Valdez includes in her list, it's worth noting what she leaves out. She never mentions the word "boyfriend." Or the word "husband."

"There are reporters in Juárez who actually think it's a myth," Washington Valdez told me at lunch. She was referring to the whole femicide phenomenon. From the expression on her face, I gathered that I was supposed to find this unbelievable. This reporter—who has blamed the dead women of Juárez on villains ranging from orgy throwers to "blood sport" psychopaths to organ harvesters to two or more currently active serial killers—looked at me as if the idea that there never has been a femicide in Juárez was the craziest thing she'd ever heard.

"People are interested in the dead women of Juárez because it's a way not to look at Juárez," Charles Bowden said in an interview broadcast on NPR. "If you say it's young girls, sixteen to eighteen, being killed by a serial killer or rich guys for fun or whatever, then you have a finite problem and you don't have to look at the city. And you can ignore the fact that while one to three hundred women have vanished, depending on who's counting, 2,800 *people* have died. You can ignore the fact that seven hundred men have disappeared in the same period. You can just pretend that really the only problem in Juárez is this bizarre slaughter of young girls, and then you're safe."

Bowden was one of the first journalists to bring wide attention to the dead women of Juárez. In *Murder City* he eulogized Esther Chávez as a champion for justice. Yet he regards his initial writings on femicide with some regret.

"I created a Frankenstein's monster without even knowing it!" he told me. "Suddenly there developed this cottage industry."

The longer I've lived in Juárez, the more I feel the city's problems have little to do with gender. Girls are not being snatched off the street by serial killers or kidnapped and killed by U.S. Border Patrol officers making snuff films or whatever it was Gaspar de Alba conjured up for her mystery novel. The problem is that life itself in Juárez, across the board, has been devalued. Murder is effectively legal. You can kill almost anyone you want just about anytime you want. To separate the killings of women from this larger truth is to misdiagnose what is really wrong.

"Mexicans who have tried to solve cases of murdered women have actually taken real risks," Molloy tells me. "They've organized and criticized the government. And they have suffered retributions of one kind or another. They've been harassed. That doesn't mean the focus on this should be based on something false. The truth is bad enough. It's just more mundane."

I believe her. I believe that what happened to the dead women of Juárez is bad. It is horrible! But it isn't all that mysterious. What happened to them—what is still happening to women in Juárez—is what would be happening to a percentage of women in any city in the world where the government has given up on law and order. It's remarkable, actually, considering the mayhem in this town, that more women aren't among the dead.

THE COTTON FIELD isn't far from my apartment. At midday, the field broils in the sun. A woman walks past me, shaded under a pink umbrella. She swings a bottle of Coca-Cola in her free hand. A friend walking with her flips through *PM*, the daily documentation of fresh kills. They pass old cement blocks piled into mounds. I spy a box of aluminum foil with some foil still on the roll. An old cup of *Danonino* drinkable yogurt molds on the ground next to a flattened plastic Sprite bottle. And the fender from a truck, one work glove, a crushed Marlboro box, and countless squares of Styrofoam. This remains a place where things are dumped.

Every documentary about the dead women of Juárez includes a scene filmed out here. Diana Washington Valdez, in both the author photo on her book and the profile photo on her Facebook page, is standing in the cotton field, in front of eight wooden crosses painted pink. The crosses have changed over the years. In some photos I've seen, the crosses are tall and feature the names of each woman found here painted in cursive letters. The crosses in the field this afternoon are shorter, have the words NI UNA MÁS stenciled on them in black paint, and feature a stenciled fist inside the symbol of Venus. Three of the crosses stand in the dirt, their stability bolstered by small piles of rocks. The five other crosses have toppled and lie in a pile.

"Even if they were not statistically significant (ever) they are certainly significant in human rights terms," Molloy once told me in an e-mail. She was referring to the women found in the cotton field and also to the court case their families fought. "The fact that the families were ignored and spurned and even ridiculed by the government officials is really important. Esther's work in calling upon the government to do something was so very important. She called the government on their impunity. And that was a good, important and risky thing for her to do.

"I'm not against anyone," Molloy added. "I don't want to seem flippant. I respect what people think, I really do. If it was my daughter murdered, I'd be crusading the rest of my life."

I understand that. I understand why these mothers of the murdered women keep fighting, why all the activists aligned with the mothers fight, too. In a city where nobody gets justice, they have collectively convinced an international court to pay attention to their cases, and convinced that court to demand that the governments of Mexico, Chihuahua, and Ciudad Juárez pay attention to the cases, too. It's token. Nobody, especially not the families, expects the government to ever solve these crimes. But attention means something. Women from Philadelphia to Sydney are marching in the streets. Cash reparations have been ordered. If it takes a murder mystery to keep the attention flowing, then, well, fine.

Driving back from the cotton field, I stop at my apartment to feed my dog and pick up a pile of laundry. It's a short drive on to the Rio Grande Mall. There's a *lavandería* there, and I need to wash my dirty clothes for the week. I turn north up Montes de Oca, crossing a handful of east-west streets. At *Avenida Vicente Gurrero*, at a red light, I notice two fliers pasted to a yellow utility poll. Such fliers are common in this city, yet they are something I usually, almost deliberately, try not to notice. The fliers are for a missing girl. They are taped to a utility pole the way someone in another city would advertise a lost pet. She happens to be young and female, this missing person. I know she does not represent all the dead. I know there are many other people besides girls who go missing in Juárez. But still.

The light changes to green. I don't want to move, but there are cars behind me. I touch the gas and roll through the intersection. Extortion, murder, fliers for missing girls—it's all in our faces every day. At the *lavandería*, I throw my clothes inside a couple machines, separating the colors from the whites, adding soap and dropping tokens to start the wash. I watch suds bubble up. I think about the girl's parents doing everything they can to get their daughter back. Everything—anything—though we all know there's little chance she's still alive. I imagine them taping up the fliers, hoping for some response, and . . . the sadness is more than unspeakable. I feel so sad, thinking about it. It is so utterly sad.

CHAPTER 17

Good Sports

Semana Santa. Holy Week on La Frontera. Gyms and restaurants close up early or shut down altogether. Teenagers lug wooden crosses around Juárez, reenacting the passion of Jesucristo. A massive sandstorm settles over the valley, ramping up the biblical feel. I can no longer see Franklin Mountain from the rattling windows of my apartment. Sand scratches my sheets, my tile floors, and the old couch in the living room. An almond grit coats my kitchen counters, even gets inside my refrigerator somehow. The murder rate drops dramatically. On Holy Thursday, only two people are killed, both of them before sundown. This leaves the vampires on Channel 44 scrambling for something to cover. They need blood to survive.

"*Juárez está tranquilo*," reports Gaby, their main newswoman out in the field. The anchor—that Crypt Keeper guy—cuts over to another reporter driving around streets empty of all traffic. This second guy has nothing to relay, either, though he tap-dances impressively for close to four minutes. Eventually they cut back to Gaby, who has found an awning that has blown down in the strong wind.

On Easter, the Son of God rises from the dead. The Indios remain in their grave. They lose at home to Pachuca, a championship team from a relatively small town—think of them as the Green Bay Packers of Mexican soccer. The final score is 2–1, a competitive enough game. The real battle is taking place off the field. A full-on mutiny brews. Players, with no more season to save and nothing else to lose, openly grumble about not, you know, being paid. The papers run with the complaints, building a case against Francisco Ibarra. He's a terrible businessman, apparently, a soccer screwup. Surely he'll be forced to sell the team. So loud is the grumbling that before the Pachuca game kicked off, Ibarra took to the field with a microphone. Don't listen to the stories, he implored the fans. I'm not going to sell the team. The Indios aren't going anywhere.

"I have such a headache, brother," Gil Cantú tells me when he shows up at the Yvasa complex for the next practice. "I only got four hours of sleep last night, and the whole time I was dreaming about the Indios." He says that Kappa, the uniform provider, hasn't sent the Indios a promised check. Even S-Mart is withholding funds; the supermarket chain wants to distance its brand from Gil's team of confirmed losers. At S-Marts throughout Juárez, everything Indios has been reduced to half price. Jerseys, hats, water bottles, and even, in the automotive aisle, Indios-logo air fresheners to hang from rearview mirrors.

"It's hard to pay the players if our sponsors don't pay us," Gil tells me before stepping onto the pitch to address the team, hoping to quell the mutiny. "But we need to pay them their money. How can we ask them to do all these things, to work so hard, if we don't?"

Marco stays relatively quiet. He doesn't want to publicly complain about Francisco or Gil or his missing pay because, while the team has been struggling, Marco's professional stock is on the rise. He starts every week, without question. His stress-free defensive play is in no way responsible for the Indios' descent. (That would be the lack of goals.) Even though he has no agent nor a grand plan beyond finishing out the season as best he can, he's hoping someone will notice him, and will rescue him from this mess.

"Have you seen how people are tearing their Indios stickers off their cars?" Marco asks me, stretching at midfield after Gil wraps up his briefing. I have noticed a few cars with soccer-ball-shaped patches of glue where logos used to be. I've also noticed that the groundskeepers at the Yvasa training complex have taken down the JUÁREZ: LAND OF CHAMPIONS banner. "Everything was great here," Marco says. "I was happy here. Then it went down."

Practice is extra crowded this morning. A crew from the Canadian

Broadcasting Corporation has descended for a story on the Indios' sad end. The Canadians arrived in two trucks, with two camera- men, a producer, an interpreter flown up from Mexico City, and a correspondent flown in all the way from England. The correspon- dent tells me she rode in a truck with *federales* last night, but they didn't come across a body, to her disappointment. I tell her she should have gone out with Channel 44. No better way to find a corpse, unless it's Holy Thursday.

With no dead bodies on their B-roll, the Canadians have brought to the practice some live ones: boys from Colonia Altavista, Maleno Frias's old hood. The cameramen film the boys talking to Maleno. Indios sign jerseys for the kids, and that's a wrap. The CBC packs everything up, I wish them well, and they drive off. Marco scur- ries to the locker room; he's got a pre-wedding obligation to attend with Dany. Head Coach Gabino steps into the interview room, it being his turn to take questions from the press. The local report- ers follow him inside, eager to ask about the financial crisis. I stay outside to bathe in a sun that's emerged for the first time in a week.

There's another visitor at practice today, one not brought by the CBC. She's a young girl missing a leg. She lost it when a Mexican soldier shipped to the border to make Juárez safer got drunk and crashed his truck into her family car. Her metal limb is painted pink. A white sock decorates its false foot, which tucks into a clunky black Mary Jane. The fake leg is a little too long for the girl's body; I guess she'll grow into it soon enough. It juts out to the side a few degrees when she hobbles after the soccer ball the team gave her. The ball has been autographed by all the players, but when the girl received it, she immediately bounced the ball on a concrete sidewalk; a toy is more fun to a seven-year-old than a col- lectible. The team gave her a jersey, too, also autographed, but she peeled it off as soon as the sun emerged. She's really cute, and of course more than a little heartbreaking.

Her presence isn't a media stunt. The CBC didn't even notice her. Someone in the front office—Wendy, I think—simply thought the girl would enjoy a morning with the team. It's cool how the Indios give attention to kids like her, victims of the violence and the military buildup. The girl hobbles around and shoots on Christian the goalie. He's on his knees, grunting with her every kick as if it takes great effort to stop the ball. When a shot rolls past him, he howls in disappointment, which makes the girl smile. She puts her all into each kick, planting her artificial limb so she can swing with her live leg. On her approach, she hops twice on her good leg, once on her limb, twice more on her good leg, and then she kicks.

Team captain Juan de la Barrera walks over and asks if he can join the game. *Claro que sí!* she shouts. Of course! She asks him to hold her hand so she can put more torque on her shot. Sometimes she kicks the ball with such force she topples over, even with Juan holding her. She always bounces right back up, always laughing. Neither Juan nor Christian has been paid in months. With practice over, their responsibilities to the team have been met. Yet they play with the girl for close to an hour. They're not doing it to burnish their images or the fading reputation of their team. If they even think of me as a reporter, they can't tell I'm watching. They just do things like this. Although they play for the worst team in the history of Mexican soccer, they know they can still make people happy. It's a role they're pleased to still play.

"IT WAS THE most awkward text I've ever gotten."

Arson Loskush is telling me about his brother's murder. We're at a Texas Roadhouse on the far west side of El Paso, just off the interstate and close to the yellow-and-red signs welcoming drivers to New Mexico, the Land of Enchantment. His brother, Charlie, had sent the text. What it said, the text of the text, wasn't so odd: "Call me back!" It's the timing that makes it hard for Arson to forget. The text hit his cell phone around midnight on an evening when everyone was celebrating a Mexico win in World Cup qualifying. About an hour later, Arson learned Charlie had been shot.

"I didn't find out through the police or anybody. I found out through this girl. She was in Juárez celebrating the win with everyone else. My mom had gone earlier that day to visit Charlie, and he told her he was going to watch the game at a bar with this guy he knows. When Charlie texted me, I tried to call him back, but I couldn't get through. At around one, that's when this girl rang my phone. She said there was a shooting at Bongos on Lincoln. The crime scene was a mess, she said. It was dirty with glass and bullets and lots of blood. She thought maybe Charlie's truck was involved—the truck was the same model and color as Charlie's. I asked her if there were a bunch of stickers on the back window. She looked and said, 'Yes.' I asked if one of the stickers said 'El Kartel.' When she said yes, that's when I knew for sure Charlie had been shot."

Arson's just finished up a shift at his father-in-law's warehouse, restoring big wooden spools built to hold copper wire. I happened to be on the El Paso side, so we've met up. We've been running into each other quite a bit lately, an indication Arson is hanging around El Kartel more often these days. His story of Charlie's murder lines up in fundamental ways with the version first relayed to me by Saul Luna. The main differences: Arson never brings up La Línea. Or drugs—trafficking, or their consumption. Also, Arson never mentions a fat man named J. L. Those details, in his memory, aren't relevant.

"My mom used to work at the Bowie Bakery, in El Paso's Segundo Barrio. She'd cross over from Juárez through this tunnel. Lots of people would do it, every day. She'd work a full shift, and then she'd walk back to the tunnel and return to Juárez. When I was three months old, we all crossed over and just stayed. We came over illegally. That's the attitude: Get here first, then figure it out. We got permanent residency cards the year I turned seventeen. Charlie would have been nineteen. Right after we all got residency, that's when Charlie got busted robbing a house. They deported him back to Juárez. He'd sneak back over to see us sometimes, but he got caught doing that, too. He was a screwup. He had bad luck his whole life. So he was over in Juárez for good. My mom, she would go visit him every three days. She'd bring him money and clothes and food.

"Being deported really does fuck with you. He'd embrace people, anyone, and that's how he got linked to bad shit. Like the night he got shot, he went to watch the Mexico game with this guy we'd never heard of. We don't know where they met. We know only that the guy had called him up and asked if he could catch a ride to the bar to watch the game. Everybody wanted to watch the game, right? Before they go over to the bar, Charlie swings by this mechanic he knows. The mechanic tries to warn him to be careful, that the dude he's with is dangerous. We later find out that the mechanic saw a gun.

"When that girl called me, I called my mom. I went home and woke her up. I said, 'Something's happened to Carlos; we're going to Juárez.'

"We went to the clinic where they told us they'd taken Charlie. In the waiting room there was a path of blood from where they were bringing in the bodies constantly. We can see blood dripping from one guy. We can hear him, too, still alive but choking on blood, gasping for air. The doctors told my mom there was nothing they could do for Charlie but wait for him to pass away. 'Wait?!' my mom yelled. 'What the fuck does that mean? You can do something!' They gave my mom the runaround. As she's arguing with the doctors, I'm listening to that one guy choke on his blood. I'm looking at him and suddenly I realize that it's Charlie, that he's the one choking on his own blood!

"We need somebody to transfer Charlie to a hospital as quickly as possible. We have to find an ambulance. But we can't find one willing to stop by the clinic. We eventually get an ambulance to show up, but when it gets there, the driver asks what had happened to my brother. When we said he'd been shot, the driver wouldn't transport him—he doesn't deal with victims of gun violence. We had to beg and then sign forms and also pay the driver in cash up front. It takes us two hours, but we finally get Charlie to the best hospital in Juárez, Hospital Angeles. When we get there, the doctors tell us the same thing: that they don't take shooting victims. My mom yells and argues and finally they say they'll take Charlie, but we have to pay five thousand dollars in cash right then and there, and then they're going to charge us a thousand dollars for every half hour after that. And Charlie ended up staying in the hospital for two weeks!

"Military and federal police guarded the intensive care unit. They set up two roadblocks. Two municipal police stood outside Charlie's room. One of the first things a soldier says to us was that from here on out we shouldn't speak to any of the municipal guys. 'Don't give them addresses. Don't share with them any personal information. These people are involved in all this,' the soldier said. 'We can't trust them. They already know what happened. They

know more than you do. So don't tell them anything.' The municipal officers who were guarding the door started asking me about
my brother. That made me suspicious. Why are they so interested
in finding out about him if they've just been assigned to guard the
room?

"We actually thought Charlie would make it at first. The doctors gave us hope. Even though he'd been shot in the head, his mind
seemed to still be working. He was reacting to sounds and voices.
But he got really sick that second week. He started getting blisters
in his mouth, infections in his mouth and down his throat. The
infections spread into his lungs and made them collapse. He passed
away on the sixteenth of September. It was ironic to me that he had
been celebrating Mexico's win.

"A lot of players sent condolences. Guys on the team called me
up to say they were sorry. I heard that Juanpi [Uruguayan midfielder Juan Pablo Rodríguez] was out driving to a restaurant with
his wife when a teammate called him and told him somebody from
El Kartel got killed. Juanpi just drove around. He didn't eat. Instead of
going to a restaurant, he ended up returning home. He called the El
Kartel office and left a message for me. He wanted me to know he was
sorry.

"I stopped going to games. I didn't want to see anybody in Juárez
anymore. I had a wristful of El Kartel bracelets that I had to cut off.
I couldn't take them, physically or mentally. The day after the funeral I cut them off and gave half of them to Charlie's girlfriend
and half to my mom. I was really angry at Juárez. I said, 'You know
what, I'm never going back.' There's nothing to go back to. The city
I love so much is the same city that took one of the people I love
most. So why go?

"It's the team that made me go back. Not the city but the team.
They're my therapy. They're what made me get better. I missed all
last season and missed the beginning of this season. It was really
hard. But when I went back it was comforting. The fact that the
players had called me. The fact that all my friends were at the
games, and they were all so happy to see me back. It helped me a
lot.

"It's causing a big conflict with my family. My mom doesn't
want me going to the games. She's been so happy every time the

Indios lose. She knew that every loss was one step closer to my never returning to Juárez. My mom and my stepfather, they don't understand that it's a big part of my life. I don't know what else I would be doing if I wasn't going to games. I don't know what I would be doing without it."

"I DIDN'T THINK it could happen!" Marco shouts, wrapping my hand in a watery grip. A white towel winds around his waist. All the Indios whoop and sing in the visitors' locker room at Estadio Cuauhtémoc. They have won again. They even scored two goals in a game for the first time this season, one goal more than the home team from Puebla. A cheer erupts as Edwin returns from the field, followed by Christian the goalie. Make that Christian the *winning* goalie. Maleno Frías looks blissful even as he ices a hamstring he pulled during the game. Banda rhythms oompah from a boom box. It's nice to win. A lot of fun, even if the elation is tinged with melancholy, a feeling, as Marco puts it, of "Ah man, we could have done this all season."

We traveled to Puebla on a budget. The skeleton crew in the locker room doesn't include even the goalkeeper coach, who had to watch the victory on television back in Juárez. Money is so tight in the organization that before I could tag along, I had to deposit into the team's checking account the full cost of my hotel room, airfare, and even the four meals I'll share with the players. I always pay my own way, but in the past I've settled up a day or two after we've returned home. After I made the deposit and returned to the Yvasa training complex with a receipt as instructed, the power to the Indios offices had been shut off.

Despite the money troubles looming over everything, this road trip has been almost pure fun. With the stress of possible relegation lifted, the trip has felt like those two days at the mountain resort: time with friends and a chance to play outside on a field of green grass. On our way down, Juan de la Barrera raided an Abercrombie & Fitch at the Mexico City airport, not yet too broke to keep current. Two fans asked forward Tomás Campos if they could take his picture. Marco and Edwin bought lottery tickets. "If I win, then the whole team gets paid!" Marco told me with a smile. We chartered a bus over to Puebla, watching most of *The Hangover* on the eighty-mile ride. At the hotel, we all watched Barcelona play El Clásico against Real Madrid.

El Kartel made the trip, too. This morning we woke up to discover a hardcore crew of Karteleros camped out in the hotel parking lot. When we sat down to breakfast in the hotel restaurant, they watched us through a window, looking hungrier than stray dogs. (They'd invested all their money in the bus, leaving nothing to cover even food.) I invited a couple of them in to eat whatever they wanted, my treat. Edwin, Marco, and other players came over to the table to kick in enough pesos to feed the rest. Juan de la Barrera added money plus a stack of tickets so everyone could watch the game for free.

The breezy feel of the trip carried over to Gabino's pregame strategy session. In a conference room at the hotel, minutes before we rode over to the stadium, the head coach did not play any maudlin movie clips, nor did he air video montages of the horrors unfolding back in Juárez. He cracked jokes, and laughed along at the jokes cracked by his players. Puebla features the league's leading scorer, Las Vegas native Herculez Gomez. Gabino told Marco and Juan de la Barrera to mark him closely. But to have fun, too. It's a nice day, everyone, a big stadium, a pretty city.

Herculez Gomez scored no goals. The Indios' game winner was a long, arcing shot from way outside the penalty box. The Indio who shot it, one of the Argentineans Gil Cantú had imported, surprised me with the blast; I didn't know he had it in him. When the ball rippled the net, the shooter ran toward the El Kartel section of the stadium. Red shirts rushed down to the fence to return the affection. One of the Juárez fans held up a banner that stated MY LIFE IS YOURS. The Indios and El Kartel, in love once again.

Showered and dressed, Marco walks to the bus, crossing himself when he passes the stadium chapel. Edwin steps into the chapel to say a few prayers, finding Kong already on his knees. Juan de la Barrera gives an interview to ESPN, then steps on the motor coach. El Kartel slaps the side of the bus when we slowly pull out of the lot. The players signal back with upturned thumbs. Lose 7–1 to Atlas and the bus ride is somber. Beat Puebla on the road and the ride is a party all the way back to the Mexico City airport, where we'll be spending the night in a sweet hotel. Banda on the stereo, the rest of

The Hangover playing on video screens. Marco sits beside two brown boxes, gifts from his grandparents, who'd driven from Mexico City to watch the game. They own a printing shop in the capital. In the boxes are the invitations to his wedding.

CHAPTER 18

Chivas

AFTER THE PUEBLA WIN, AS THE TEAM and I fly up to Juárez from the airport in Mexico City, Francisco Ibarra flies the other way, down to the capital. He's going to address the media, to tell them that relegation is a setback for his team, but it's not the end. In a rented conference room at a hotel near the airport, he will report that the Indios aren't going anywhere. Ciudad Juárez needs soccer. His club will forge through its economic struggles, and will solve its problems on the pitch, too. He will sit alone at a table draped in white cloth facing reporters from Fox Sports, ESPN Deportes, and all the newspapers that matter, none of which are the papers in Juárez. *Juárez doesn't exist.* Cameras will flash as Francisco reads a script he hopes will inspire a government or two—the state of Chihuahua? The Calderón administration?—to step in and back his "social program." What he will actually end up doing, from the moment he opens the floor for questions, is make the situation on the border look more hopeless than ever.

Yes, he will admit, he feels unsafe in Juárez. Police have stopped him—with guns drawn—at least six times. And, yes, a goalie quit the team after *ladrones* threatened to kill him, a story we all know in Juárez but which will be news to the national press. The violence is probably the main reason why the team dropped down, he'll speculate. When asked to elaborate on how the violence has affected the squad, Francisco will let slip that *extorsionistas* have demanded money from at least a dozen of his players. While he feels lucky that he personally has not yet been shaken down, he's afraid to even investigate the people threatening his strikers and midfielders and goalies.

"I'm not naming names; it is very delicate," he will say, hopelessly off-script. "I do not want to know where it comes from. If you live in Juárez, the last thing you want to know is who is behind the bullet."

The still-unpaid Indios players and I return to a city crowded with even more police. Calderón has dispatched another surge of *federales* to the border. More than fifty of the new officers have moved into my complex. I always thought my place looked like an army barracks. Now it definitely looks like military housing, a police academy. Officers sleep and watch TV on both sides of my unit. They're below me, too, and crowded into apartments in all five of the complex's buildings. Two officers—the poor bastards— have even been assigned to Alaska, my old digs. My new neighbors march around in blue uniforms and black boots and flak jackets, automatic rifles in their hands or slung around shoulders. Blue Dodge Ram police cruisers occupy every parking space in front of my building. Any thought that I might be safer with these cops around vanishes when six *federales* are murdered, ambushed while on patrol. The referees at the Associated Press recently declared that the Sinaloans have won the game, that El Chapo and his cartel now control the Juárez Plaza. J. L. and La Línea killed the *federales*—in a spectacularly cinematic way that reminds me of an Italian mafia hit—to refute the article. Their letter to the editor—a *narcomanta* painted on a wall near the ambush site—said, essentially, "We're still here." Game still on.

My apartment building is now a big fat target. Great. The violence in my neighborhood is already on the rise. Somebody dumps a dead body a couple streets up, the male corpse crammed into a pair of women's panties and a bra. Another man is decapitated and strapped to a fence next to my regular burrito place. (His head is found a block away.) A *federale* is murdered down my street. Also on my street: Gunmen break into one of the finer homes and kill the owner, his wife, and their eldest son. Oh, and still on my street, three more people are massacred outside a different apartment I came very close to renting. Walking Benito the morning after I got back from Puebla, the neighbor I've come to know best asks if I'd heard the bullets. Which ones? She'd been walking her dog in our little park when shots rang out. She ran over to the giant Zaragoza mansion and pounded on its security door until she was let in.

"It was funny," she says.

THE SKY IS just starting to lighten at seven in the morning, which is when Ramón Morales likes to meditate. The temperature will probably climb into the nineties today, but at dawn, in the desert, it's crisp enough for sweatshirts and sweatpants. We first walk a few languid laps around a dirt track hidden behind a Wal-Mart and close to the Rotary Bridge. Ramón, the head of the Indios' media department, used to start his day with thirty minutes of jogging. He's powered down his routine on doctor's orders, something about an old hip injury. As we walk, a sprinkler system turns the track's sandy infield into milk chocolate mud. Three ladies in wide-brimmed black hats—almost bonnets—power past us, one of the women wearing those sneakers with the curved soles that supposedly tone the legs. A man with the hood of his windbreaker pulled tight around his face really grounds out the kilometers, lapping us twice before Ramón points to a quiet spot near some bleachers and underneath the thin canopy of two shade trees.

Ramón's job with the Indios was his destiny, he tells me. He grew up in Juárez, leaving only because he wanted to get ahead professionally. Puebla first, where he helped out a minor league soccer team. Then on to Guadalajara, a city he loved so much he planned to stay there the rest of his life. An unplanned pregnancy brought him back to La Frontera. "I won't even say she was my girlfriend," he shares, "but I wanted to do the right thing by her so we got married." She was a Juárez native, too. Because she wanted to raise their child near her family, she and Ramón returned to the border. Yet the marriage dissolved almost immediately, and mutually: They both felt staying together would make their newborn daughter miserable. Ramón divorced, moved in with his parents, and delved deeper into meditation, a relaxation habit he'd discovered in Guadalajara. While meditating one morning, a vision of Indians popped into his head. Soon afterwards, Francisco Ibarra announced he was bringing soccer back to Juárez, and that the team would be

called the Indios. It struck Ramón as fate. He applied for the head
media job and got it.

I see Ramón almost every day, either at the Yvasa complex or up
in the press box at Olympic Stadium. He looks like a professional
when he's at work, like he's the right guy for his position. He wears
blazers and dress shirts, keeps his hair short and his brown beard
always trimmed tight. The lenses on his fashionable eyeglasses
darken when he steps into sunshine. This facade of proficiency
cracks a bit when he's writing up press releases. As he types, he
likes to blast his favorite Canadian classic-rock power trio, which
always makes me laugh. *Juárez loves Rush!* Ramón and I connected
pretty quickly, just as people. He was the first to call me El Gringo
Loco, a nickname that caught on way too quickly in the press box.

"Are we going to talk or are we going to get started?" Ramón
asks. Have I been posing too many questions? I stop my interroga-
tion and sit Indian style, as instructed. Ramón tells me to touch
my sacral chakra, three fingers below my belly button. Together we
pray for kindness, to let our anger go and to let love in. It's Reiki, a
specific style of meditation Ramón's been practicing for about two
years and which he's been delving into deeper and deeper as the
season has progressed. He flips through Reiki study books while in
the office. A red kabbalah string circles his right wrist. Recently,
after sending out the Indios press release of the day, Ramón has
started following up with a second e-mail full of quotes from Gandhi
and tips on how to release stress. This second communication goes to
every reporter on the Indios' mailing list, though Ramón makes sure
to send it from his personal address.

"Breathe in," he tells me. "Big breaths." On Ramón's lead, we claw
the energy from our right arms, using our left hands as the claws. We
switch arms and then we shake out both hands (claws?) to release the
bad energy. On the dirt track, a trio of older men start into their own
slow laps. One man sports a hat advertising Chivas, the Mexican su-
perteam and the Indios' opponent tomorrow, Wednesday, an unusually quick turnaround after the Puebla game, which was played only
two days ago.

"Embrace love," Ramón commands. "Let anger out . . . Breathe
deep . . . Just sit." Ramón hits a button on one of his cell phones,
which sounds a melodic gong. He stands up and circles a palm near
my forehead, gliding his hand close to my arms and down my back

as he follows an invisible aura. "Out with the bad energy," he says. "Think about love."

We end the session by chanting five-word phrases I know I won't remember later and am too much in the moment to write down now. I try to chant just loud enough to let Ramón know I'm participating, but not so loud as to be showy. I'm a humble meditator. Or I would be if I did this sort of thing regularly. I don't. A large part of me can't help but think that as relaxing as this is, it would be even more relaxing to have simply stayed in bed. I showed up today because I've been curious about Ramón's growing spirituality. And because Ramón has been signaling that he wants to talk about his frustration with the Indios. He has some bad energy he needs to let out.

"That press conference disappointed me so much," he says after a final chime sounds on his phone and after we salute the sun one last time. He's referring to Francisco Ibarra's disaster in Mexico City. "Talking about extortion was such the wrong thing to say." Everyone in Juárez gets extorted over the phone, he reminds me. As crazy as that sounds, it's true. A poster on the door to my gym warns of criminals working their way through the phone book, calling people at random as they phish for someone gullible enough to divulge personal information. It's not much different from the mass e-mails sent by supposedly wealthy Nigerian businessmen. The only people who end up actually extorted are the one in five thousand who engage with the callers. Francisco's highlighting of this crude con is only the latest in a long string of bad decisions, Ramón insists. The main reason the Indios are struggling financially is not because of the violence, as Francisco claimed in the press conference. It's because Francisco doesn't know what he's doing, and he won't listen to anyone else. Ramón tells me he might have to quit the team, just on principle.

"I'm kind of pissed off that we let this happen," he says, referring to Juárez's expulsion from the Primera. It was not even a year ago that the Indios needed a miracle to beat Cruz Azul and stay in the majors. "And yet we didn't learn from it. We were almost relegated back then, but we got this synergy going with the fans and the media and the internal work we did, work that [Francisco's] not doing now. We had to go to all these meetings in El Paso because he couldn't come here. When he was trapped over there, it was better in a way, because we had the power to make decisions."

Ramón and I walk over to the bleachers and sit down, normal style. I'm feeling exceptionally chill, relaxed. I've just let out a lot of animosity and let in love and clawed the anger out of the veins in both my arms. Ramón, in contrast, is unusually riled up. "Gabino and Gil, they know the right things to do," he continues. "But Francisco, he won't give up the power. He has to be in control. And he doesn't make the right decisions."

Ramón's not the first person in the front office to say this to me. The team's lawyer, Mario Boisselier, once told me that the Indios' big victory over Cruz Azul had disappointed him greatly. Not the victory, which thrilled him, but what happened immediately afterwards. The team had been struggling to make payroll even back then. The win earned Francisco enough bonus money to cover the gap between revenues and operating expenses. If only he hadn't handed it all over to the players in fat bonus checks. That generosity made Francisco popular with Marco and Jair and everyone else on the team, for a while. But it exacerbated the problems that are making the players so angry now: There's zero money left to pay them. The miracle win over Cruz Azul also presented the Indios with lucrative endorsement opportunities that Francisco never capitalized upon, the lawyer complained. Francisco Ibarra, basically, is getting all the blame.

"Where is he?" Ramón asks, referring to the team owner. "Have you seen him lately?" I haven't, actually. Not for a while. "I'm angry because we invest so much in the team. I don't mean money, but I've invested my time, my labor, my experience to make this team successful. I want to do my best for the Indios. We were on the same level as the greatest teams in Mexico, and yet our media office has only two people? That's crazy."

Ramón needs more than just a larger staff, he insists. There must be a travel budget, too; if he'd gone to Mexico City with Francisco, he could have prevented his boss's self-destruction. Other people close to the team have told me that Francisco "suffers from attention deficit disorder," that "he's difficult to work for," "he's anxious," "he's hyperactive," and "he likes things done his way and only his way." It's a rare instance when the scapegoat label hangs on the guy at the top.

"This team isn't just for him," Ramón concludes. "He says that it's not for him, that it's for Juárez. We all believe it. But then it doesn't seem like it's for the city when he makes decisions that benefit only him. He says it's for the city, but it's clearly not. This team doesn't belong to Francisco Ibarra or the Ibarra family. Not anymore. They started it up, but this is for the city."

THE MIGHTY GOATS of Chivas check into the Camino Real hotel across from Central Park and close to Las Misiones Mall. It's the same hotel Felipe Calderón prefers when he's in town, and security is as tough for the team as it is for the president. Several guards, all armed with assault rifles, grill me for three minutes before they let me in. *Let's see your passport. Now your Indios media credentials. What paper do you write for?* I don't write for any paper, which causes a problem. Luckily, a reporter for *El Mexicano* steps in to vouch for me, El Gringo Loco. Left out in the parking lot are a hundred Chivas fans. They sing team songs and wave team jerseys over their heads like red-striped Terrible Towels. Chivas is beloved. If they played baseball in the States, they'd be the Red Sox and the Yankees and the Cubs and the Cardinals combined. Maybe even the Dodgers, too. No team in Mexico is more popular. Number two, Club América, in Mexico City, is way back there. Chivas is so adored in large part because only Mexicans are allowed to wear the team's striped shirts. The club charter forbids imports from Argentina or Brazil or Gringolandia. Even though Marco Vidal's only passport was issued by the United States, his innate Mexicanness was certified when Chivas signed him back when he was twelve.

I enter a conference room crowded with reporters from around the country. The Chivas team videographer records a segment he'll post online. He's one of five people here from their press office alone, a glaring contrast to the two Indios—Ramón and Adir—who handle everything, and who can't afford to travel. Local *periodistas* grab free cans of Coke, the journalists already caffeinated just from sharing a room with Chivas's famous (in Mexico) president and with the team's even better-known (in Mexico) head coach. Before the press conference starts, they ask for autographs, a move strictly forbidden in the United States. (Try it and a team will ban you for life.) The Juárez reporters, excited as they are to have Chivas in their town, are also a little bummed that the team's emerging superstar, Javier Hernández, is not here with them.

"Chicharito will be missed," says Chivas's head coach when the press conference starts, referring to Hernández by his nickname, which means "little green pea." Only two days ago, Hernández signed with English power Manchester United. "But we are a team, not just one player." The second question isn't even a question but a thank-you to the celebrated squad for visiting Juárez, a city "with a bad reputation in the wider media, but it is a nice city."

"We're happy to be here," the team president says, voice recorders humming on a table in front of him. "Juárez is beautiful. It's the people who are ugly." The local reporters smile with pride; they know he means only the killers are ugly. "We're happy to be playing tomorrow. We will play our best, and we are confident we will win."

They most certainly will. While the Indios went winless in their first eight games this season, the stars from Guadalajara won *all* of their first eight. Outright wins, not even a tie, the best start in league history. The talent and glamour of mighty Chivas generates a sellout on Wednesday night. Olympic Stadium overflows way beyond the official seating capacity. There's no place for me to stand in the press box. I can't sit with Gil Cantú, either, as his usual seats are occupied by men I don't recognize. I end up in a walkway, crushed up against a cement wall whenever *Clamato y cerveza* vendors pass with their trays. I'm on my toes watching the action when I realize that one of the many people along the wall with me happens to be Gil. Not even the general manager gets a seat tonight.

It's an electric crowd. The roar is supersonic when Jair Garcia scores the game's only goal. The Indios beat Chivas. Chivas! Gil Cantú, El Kartel, the vendors of the beer that everybody threw in the air when Jair scored—the whole city is ecstatic. Or almost the whole city. I race down to the locker room, expecting a party like the one after the Puebla win. I find the players slumped over in front of their lockers. They pull off their shin guards quietly, showering and changing into their civilian clothes without talking. That same melancholy that tinged the Puebla celebration has blown pandemic. We've won two games in a row. We just beat fucking Chivas. Chivas! We can play at this level. We're good. It hurts to think about what might have been. What obviously could have been.

Jair, the hero, lies exhausted and dehydrated on the massage table, attended to by the team doctor. After dressing, Marco goes out to sign autographs, which he sees as his duty. Dozens of fans crowd around him. Karteleros reach out to touch Marco as if he were an apostle, one of the eleven holy champions of Ciudad Juárez. *Va-mos Indios! Va-mos Indios!* I step off to the side, where I bump into Dany.

"It's because the pressure is off!" she shouts above the cheers and the team songs. "They were trying too hard. They were playing tight all season. They were too nervous!" She's as frustrated as Marco. I feel her pain. I'm frustrated, too. They didn't have to go down. It didn't have to end this way. We look over at her husband, a legitimate star. Marco's Sharpie flies across jerseys, T-shirts, and souvenir photos. The backlog of fans spills off the sidewalk out into the parking lot. Dany allows herself a smile.

"I miss this, the way he signs autographs afterwards, everybody coming up to him," she says, sweeping her arm across the crowd. The fans are smiling, too, happy to simply stand next to a civic hero. "It's positive, you know?"

CHAPTER 19

Everything Must Go

BEFORE THE KICKOFF OF THE CHIVAS game, the entire Indios team marched onto the pitch holding a large and professionally printed banner. Marco anchored one corner. Equipment manager Whisky held down the other end. Everyone else lent a hand or two to hold up the middle.

THANK YOU FRANCISCO IBARRA FOR YOUR HELP! WE ARE WITH YOU AND WITH JUÁREZ!

The banner was signed by *"Los Jugadores."* The Players. When I saw them walking the banner to midfield, my jaw dropped. The players hadn't been paid in two months. At the last practice before the game, a walk-through at the stadium, they bitched to Gil Cantú so forcefully that Head Coach Gabino asked me to leave the team alone for a while. I knew they hadn't been paid since. So why were they thanking the team owner, and so publicly? When the players reached midfield, everyone in the stadium turned to Francisco to gauge his reaction. He stood up in his box seat and raised his right arm twice in a gesture of gratitude. The very next day, he cut the players a check. It covered only about a fourth of what he owes them, but it was an appreciated start. *Los jugadores* know how to negotiate.

I've started seeing a new and creative Indios bumper sticker. Instead of the traditional soccer ball with a red sash around it, the new sticker features the red sash circling a brown paper bag, as if the ball is ashamed to show its face. That I've seen this new sticker in the parking lot of the Grupo Yvasa training complex is an indication of how low club morale has dropped. Even Francisco Ibarra's longtime personal secretary has been laid off. She'd served as the office manager, too. It's shocking how few people are left to run a team that, for at least a couple more weeks, remains in the Mexican major league. After one practice, when I visited the media office to check my e-mail, the receptionist was the only other person in the building. The Wi-Fi still worked, so I stuck around for an hour, maybe two. And nobody showed up the whole time. Francisco Ibarra's office sat silent, as always. The sales department sat silent, too, along with the business office. I may have actually been in charge.

Gil is the most burdened by the low morale. He tells me it's starting to affect his health. With Francisco nowhere to be found, Gil's the one dealing directly with the players. They're still angry. It's leaked out that Francisco just booked three weeks in South Africa to watch the World Cup. He's bringing five members of his family along, Paco included. Hotel, food, a safari or two, and tickets to all the Mexico games. He's charging everything to the Indios, the team that can't pay its players. Gil tries to temper this news by announcing that Francisco will cut a second set of payroll checks this week. That'll leave the players only a month behind, which Gil insists to me is no big deal, something common at all levels of Mexican soccer. ("It's not *that* common," Puebla star Herculez Gomez tells me when I ask him for some context. "My heart goes out to those guys on the Indios. I know this is their livelihood.") Even if late paychecks *are* standard operating procedure in Mexico, the players' grumbling is understandable. Like, why stay with a team this inept in a city this violent?

"If you want to leave, let me know and we'll make an arrangement and you can go," Gil tells the players after practice as they sit at midfield. "If you're going to stay, focus and play like men, like professionals."

Marco isn't one of the malcontents giving Gil problems. He continues to keep his head down, his mind on little more than his upcoming wedding. After practice, he hands Gil an invitation. The cover is a white jigsaw puzzle with four pieces dislodged and glued to the surface. One piece is "D" for Daniela and another is "M" for Marco Antonio, the name his family calls him. On the other two pieces are printed the wedding date. The space where the pieces fit is a vibrant green upon which are handwritten the words *"Nos*

Casamos!!!" We're getting married! On my invite, I'm addressed as "Sr.," for *Señor.*

"I thought about putting 'Mr.,'" Marco tells me when he hands me my envelope. "But you've been here long enough."

The Indios lose their last away game, down in Chiapas, near Guatemala. So much for the winning streak. The final score is 1–0. The start of the game was delayed by a massive hailstorm, a deluge that gave way, almost instantly, to punishing tropical sun. Jair Garcia earned a red card on the sloppy field, meaning his Indios career is over: League rules require anyone with a red card to sit out the next game, which for the Indios will be the last game of the season, at home against a team called Pumas. I'd made plans to watch the Chiapas match with Francisco Ibarra, on television at his house in El Paso. He canceled on me right before kickoff, after I'd already crossed the river. He had his brother call me to say a *quinceañera*—a niece's fifteenth birthday—had come up at the last minute.

"I knew it," Ramón Morales cackled when I told him I'd been stood up. "I knew he was going to do that to you!"

IN THE RUN-UP to the last game, El Kartel rents out a nightclub and hires three live bands to play what might as well be the EK prom. I get a lot of mileage from the lines I learned in Cancún—that sophomore year sucked, but junior year has been awesome, and next year we're going to rule the school! The rented club is in the Pronaf District, on the third floor of the same building as Vampires Karaoke. The decorating committee goes all out, inflating balloons and draping the ceiling, the stage, and even the windows in red and white satin. *Maybe El Kartel really is an arts-and-crafts club.* One band goes garage to cover the Doors and the Rolling Stones. They're followed onstage by a sixteen-piece orchestra slinging salsa, which draws Saul Luna onto the dance floor. That's followed by banda, of course, the tuba-centric music of the North. One of the Kartel girlfriends collects ten dollars from everybody at the door. Her lockbox overflows with cash; the whole *barra brava* shows up. The kids who pound bass drums at the stadium on game days, the 915s in El Paso and the young guys in Los Fabulosos Muertos, all the subgroups, a ton of people. Saul Luna buys me an icy bucket packed with bottles of *cerveza* Sol. I buy Saul a bucket of *cerveza* Indio.

Oskar buys me a shot and I buy a shot for Oskar, and then I buy a shot for Ken-tokey, too.

"Hey man, I've got Marco Vidal on my instant messenger and he doesn't even know me," Ken-tokey says, laughing and showing me his phone. "I'm sending him messages about the Pumas game. And he keeps responding with 'Who is this? How did you get this number?'"

Everyone's upbeat, enjoying the social event of the season. Big Weecho is here. Arson, too. Don Roberto, Chuy, Sugar, Angel, Sofia and her sister. (Kinkin and his girlfriend have moved to Cancún.) One guy limps by, one of his legs noticeably shorter than the other. He fell off a fence at an Indios game, and it was a miracle that he lived, Saul Luna tells me. He also killed his son in an accident. I'd heard he was a drug dealer, I tell Saul. "Not anymore," Saul responds. "He got his act together."

Chicharrón (her permanent name since her arrest in Monterrey) smokes a cigarette and sips from a can of her beloved Coors Light. She tells me her visa to enter the United States expires in three months. Fortunately, she adds, her daughter, born in El Paso, will turn twenty-one over the summer. "So she'll be able to pull us all over." Over to Texas, and permanent residency.

"I see these people in El Paso on the ramps to the highway, and they have these signs saying 'anything will help' and such," Chicharrón tells me. "Doesn't the government take care of them? They are lucky to live in a country with social security." I find it cute, her misconceptions. She's not the only one here who believes the United States mothers its citizens for life. Medicare, enough welfare to live on. I want to tell her about the big check I cut every month for health insurance and how my insurance is functionally useless; a simple broken arm would wipe me out. Social Security does nothing for me now and will probably implode before I turn sixty-five. (If I even get there.) But then she brings up the Statue of Liberty and how badly she wants to see it. I let my grievances slide. I should probably step back and appreciate how attractive my country is, misconceptions or not.

We all get really drunk. So drunk that Oskar talks freely about his side job. He's disgusted at the young generation of *sicarios* coming up, unskilled boys who kill for as little as fifty dollars and who spray cars with gunfire rather than leave a tight circle of bullet holes, like a real professional. Oskar sports a German army jacket over a hoodie, the jacket olive green with a patch on the shoulder of yellow, red, and black stripes. He injured two knuckles last night in a fight, he tells me. The other guy bumped into him. Oskar told the guy, "Hey man, I don't want to fight." The other guy goaded him, so they fought.

"*Boom*, one punch, the guy goes down!" Oskar recounts. He followed up the punch with a flurry of boot kicks—he's been studying kickboxing. There was another fight a week before that, with one of his cousins and some Mexican soldiers. I kind of lose the thread of who was fighting whom in this earlier skirmish. Whatever happened, Oskar's cousin ended up in Juárez's city jail. It took seventeen hundred dollars to spring him. Oskar said if his cousin had been sent on to federal prison, Oskar would have killed the soldiers who'd started the fight. When he kills, he tells me, it's for real money, for ten or twenty thousand dollars. Not like these kids today. They give it away. They have no pride in their craft.

I leave the party around four in the morning. It's very windy out, and very cold. I walk down López Mateos, cutting into my neighborhood of Colonia Nogales a little early because the side streets leave me less exposed. I laugh out loud as I close in on my apartment. Oskar, man. It's not funny at all, what he said, but I can't stop laughing. I laugh and laugh. That twenty-thousand-dollar claim really cuts into his credibility. I could have the *mayor* killed for a fraction of that. Ha-ha. No way he's telling the truth, right? Obviously he doesn't really kill people for money, firing his bullets in tight clusters like a professional. I mean, no way. Right?

PUMAS REPRESENT UNAM, the Universidad Nacional Autónoma de México, a major university in Mexico City. They're school ambassadors exactly the same way the Wolverines football team represents the University of Michigan. Except Pumas players are paid above the table, and none of them go to class. The team Estudiantes, in Guadalajara, is sponsored by a university, too. Ohio State, Auburn, and USC should take note. UNAM graduates root for Pumas on game days, just as if the players were so-called amateurs. And no one has to pretend the team and the players—and the school—are engaged in anything other than a business.

The last full practice before the Indios' last Primera game is bittersweet. It's a light workout, as usual two days before kickoff. Maleno Frías sits on some aluminum bleachers, a bag of ice wrapped around his still-torn hamstring. I'm on the bleachers, too, along with Edwin's two young daughters, who are holding teddy bears. While the rest of the team plays soccer volleyball, old man Coco Giménez confronts the reporter from *El Diario*. The newspaper, in an article about the future of the club, printed that Coco is unlikely to be re-signed, as he is at least six years older than his stated age of thirty-four. That's a fair claim, even conservative; my eyeball carbon dating continues to reckon Coco is no younger than forty-two. Coco jokes around with the reporter, but he also crowds the reporter's space, leaning in close. He pokes the reporter in the chest to make a point. It's all light and friendly, but there is an undercurrent of *Hey, amigo, this is my livelihood here.* I recall a series of photos of Lyndon Johnson convincing a Senate colleague to bend to his agenda.

When practice ends, Edwin's girls run out to greet him on the field, holding hands as they leap off the last bleacher step. Edwin hugs them both, but his mind is elsewhere. He stares at the construction pit, then up at a clear sky. He turns to inspect the stone walls that fortify the complex and then he looks down at the grass. Edwin was a charter Indio. He scored the first goal in team history. He's probably going to be released from his contract, same as Coco. I know he wants to stay in the Primera if he can. A boy, the son of another player, approaches Edwin for an autograph, which Edwin gladly signs. Coach Gabino snaps a photo with the reporter from *El Diario*, who remains the best journalist here no matter what Coco thinks. Marco splashes his face with water to rinse off the sunblock, then poses with the reporter, too. Jair Garcia lingers on the grass longer than anyone. He asks the team masseur to help him stretch out his back. He spreads his legs and alternates deep bends toward one knee and then the other, limbering up even though he can't play against Pumas. His career in the Primera is over. He's not a young guy, and he scored only twice all season. It's unlikely a Primera team will pick up his contract. So this is his last practice in the major league, ever. He stays on the grass for a very long time, loitering, really. I notice him take an especially deep breath at one point, as if he's committing to memory the acidic tang from the gravel pit. As if he'll miss even that.

LITTLE YELLOW LEAVES color the trees that ring Benito Juárez Olympic Stadium. Twenty-four hours before the final kickoff, workers blow desert sand off the stadium's bucket seats. A woman steps into the empty press box to mop grit off the concrete floor. The refrigerator in the owner's box is restocked with bottles of Coca-Cola and Tecate. Advertisements for the Home Depot and Gatorade are reattached to the billboards ringing the field; most of the ads blew down in a sandstorm earlier in the week. The grounds crew lines the pitch, using buckets of white paint and the same common brushes you'd use to paint a windowsill. The field has already been cut in a crisscross of light green and dark green squares. "We've got a great field, I'm really proud of it." Gil tells me as he surveys the preparations. The cauldron sits unlit, waiting for an Olympiad. A few students from the university sprint laps around the track. In the parking lot, vendors of T-shirts and tacos set up their booths.

Marco checks into the Hotel Maria Bonita, in Juárez, as required the night before a home game. He and Maleno Frías watch soccer on television in the room they share. El Kartel's arts-and-crafts brigade stays up all night sewing banners and cutting cardboard into huge red squares to be flashed during the game. Someone in the *barra brava* secures the use of a *rutera*, and it is on this school bus that El Kartel arrives at the stadium in the morning. They ride inside the bus. They also ride on top of the bus like the Indios did back on that night when the team rose to the Primera. Karteleros who can't fit in or on the bus march alongside it, pounding bass drums and spitting into dented brass trumpets. Everyone wears jerseys. They've all got their flags and big cardboard squares. Sofia and a dozen other Kartel girlfriends wear jester's hats and red-and-white pantaloons sewn from the same satin used to decorate the nightclub for the EK prom. Sofia has painted a huge red star on her face, centered on her right eye. VOLVEREMOS, state at least a dozen banners. *We will return.* One hand-painted banner I see: I AM JUÁREZ, I AM INDIOS. The banners float into a parking lot already full with cars and pickup trucks. Above the stadium, a giant white flag—a *megabandera* to rival the Mexican tricolor—announces that it's game day on La Frontera.

Los jugadores warm up under a sun that's on the cusp of intense. Marco and his teammates wear all-white uniforms to reflect the rays better than the navy-blue tops worn by Pumas. Juan de la Barrera and Marco and everybody else zig and zag around flat orange cones. Christian deflects soft shots lobbed by the goalkeeper coach. Referees check the nets to ensure there are no holes. Pretty girls advertising a cell-phone company walk a lap around the track, wearing blue spandex outfits. They are followed by the Home Depot dance team, in orange spandex, and then the Tecate beer girls in tight red. Groundskeepers straighten vinyl banners for Sony and Office Depot positioned just off the field, near the goals, where they will be seen by television viewers across the continent. Municipal police in riot gear set up a line in front of El Kartel, just in case. Someone lobs onto the track a roll of toilet paper. A Border Patrol helicopter buzzes the river.

It's a sellout crowd, of course. Nobody's going to miss this one. The north bleachers fill with fans of Pumas, a popular team. The tunnels to the dressing rooms inflate maybe fifteen minutes before kickoff. The Indios jog through their tunnel, back to their cramped lockers. Liniment stings the air. Candles burn under the Virgen de Guadalupe. Everyone changes into their game shirts and Gabino calls the team into a huddle, showing more passion than I've ever seen him display. This is it. We can do it. A prayer is offered to the Virgin. The team name is shouted in unison. Marco, just before running out to the field, shakes the hand of the team priest who works the locker room every home game.

Up in the press box, Ramón and Adir assist the national correspondents covering the Indios' descent. I turn toward the owner's box. Francisco Ibarra is not in it. He has not shown up for the final game. *What is up with this guy?* As mystified as I am by his absence, I'm more surprised by who sits in Francisco's regular seat: Paco. The son who said Juárez could drown in its own shit for all he cares. He motions for me to join him, so I do. I watch the game in the owner's box, sitting between Paco and Lorenzo Garcia. Girlfriend Karina Garcia rounds out our row of extra-wide padded seats. Paco orders me a beer before I even ask for one, asserting himself as the host.

"I'm thinking of maybe moving to Mexico City," he tells me. "I've got a lot of new projects. As for the Indios, my dad's ideas are probably too big for people from Juárez. He presents ideas to the mayor, to the governor, and they don't dare to dream big. In Mexico City, they're more receptive."

On the field, Coco Giménez gets the start, sort of an honorarium for all his years (and years) of service. I watch him stand still, conserving his energy as the ball caroms around the field. But when the ball randomly lands on his boots, he does get off a nice shot on goal, which the Pumas keeper barely deflects out of bounds. An Indios corner kick follows, and Coco heads it in. Coco has scored. Take *that*, *El Diario*! We're winning 1–0, and then 2–0 when Coco—old man Coco!—scores again, one of the best goals I have ever seen. First, he knocks down a long pass with his chest, and then he spins 180 degrees to face the Pumas goal. Although he's well outside the penalty box, he doesn't wait for the ball to hit the ground before kicking a long shot that arcs over the goalie's outstretched hands and into the far top corner of the net. It's world-class, the goal of the year in the entire league. And with the goal, his second of the game and his second all season, Coco ties Jair for the dubious title of team scoring champion.

The Indios hold on for their third win in their last four games. They've knocked off another top team, shut them out, even. El Kartel spills onto the field, mostly in gratitude. I see Weecho. I see Saul Luna. Arson Loskush's gray tank top reveals a colony of tattoos: DIRTY SOUTH scripted on his left shoulder, a thick EK gunsight logo on the biceps. Red stars shine on his chest, and the name of his son is inked on his neck. The police want to beat El Kartel back into the bleachers, but Gil Cantú calls them off. The fans can stay on the field. Gil runs into the locker room to ask the players to head back out to sign autographs.

Marco is one of the first to emerge. I follow him through the tunnel. He's showered already and dressed in a red Indios polo shirt and an Ed Hardy baseball hat, worn backwards. El Kartel collapses onto him, asking him to sign everything in sight: a T-shirt on which are printed the words EL KARTEL: OUR BLOOD IS FOR YOU, a photo for a teenage girl, another T-shirt. A Kartelero asks Marco if he can hook him up with some merchandise, and Marco takes the polo shirt off his back, signs it, and hands it over. This only excites

El Kartel further. They push on Marco so aggressively I start to worry for his safety. Can someone be crushed to death standing up?

"Robert, hold this for me, will you?" he cries out, handing me his messenger bag. It's the last I see of him for three minutes. Everyone wants a piece of Marco, perhaps a piece of his flesh. It's as if El Kartel had been zombified in the hot sun and now they must feed on an Indios midfielder to survive. Marco's buried in there so deeply that Adir from the press office calls in the police to pull him out and back to the locker room, to safety.

"That shit was crazy," Marco says when I hand him back his bag.

The zombies march out to the parking lot, where Gil is liquidating the Indios' inventory. He's set up a red tent in which everything Indios is available at bargain-basement prices. Everything. All the surplus uniforms, shorts, socks, the remaining cold-weather parkas, duffel bags, red polo shirts exactly like the one Marco just gave away, and more. It's official stuff, the real deal. A Primera game jersey that might cost seventy-five dollars online, you can have it for twenty. What color do you want? White? Black? Red? Long-sleeved or short? *Grande o pequeño?* The other T-shirt vendors working the stadium pack up shop, unable to compete. Gil is sorry to cut into their sales, he tells me, but he's gotta do whatever he can to make payroll. The few remaining front-office staff rifle through boxes to fill the orders, which fly in fast. Just about everyone in El Kartel stands in line, pesos in hand.

"They're actually pretty cheap," Gil tells me, trying to convince me to buy some stuff, too. "I bought a whole set of uniforms for this youth team I have in El Paso."

I see Big Weecho in the tent, searching in vain for any jerseys sized extra, extra large. What's next on the El Kartel itinerary? "Drink, man!" he tells me. He points to a live band setting up in a corner of the parking lot, near the *poliforo*, an arena where Weecho has wrestled in the past. A vendor serves *hamburguesas* to a growing crowd of Karteleros. I walk over and fall into conversation with two Kartel girlfriends.

"Life is better when something is on the line," one of them says. "The league is better when a team has to descend. It's just too bad that team is Los Indios."

"It's emotional," her friend adds. She's wearing a brand-new

Indios jersey, white. "You cannot cry, because the experience was positive. But you want to cry."

"Tienes que soportarlo," concludes the first girl. You have to bear it. I stay with the girls and the rest of El Kartel through two sets of salsa standards and two orders of hamburgers with onions and jalapeño peppers. We all stay even after the band stops playing and packs up their trumpets and amplifiers. The setting sun stretches shadows across a mostly empty lot. My cell phone rings.

"You're still at the stadium, dude?" Marco asks. He left four hours ago. Yeah man, I'm here with El Kartel. We're doing what Jair Garcia and Edwin did at the last practice. We're loitering. We're remembering. We're reluctant to leave.

CHAPTER 20

Wedding

SOFIA AND KEN-TOKEY APPEAR ON the front page of all the newspapers: she in her jester's hat and face paint, the two of them holding up an I ♥ INDIOS banner. They are the faces that best represent the sadness, resolve, and *amor* of *la gente*. The morning after the game, on the way to the Grupo Yvasa complex for a last team meeting, I buy every paper with their picture: *El Diario, El Mexicano, Norte,* and *PM*, which despite its name usually hits the streets before noon. Photos from the Pumas victory make *El Diario*'s society page. Also in the society page: coverage of the *quinceañera* of fifteen-year-old Frida Lara. Her coming-out party is described as "an unforgettable experience." Her dress is white and puffy. A tiara sparkles in her black hair as she leans against a couch. For a theme song, the paper reports, she chose the pop anthem "Bittersweet Symphony" by the Verve.

"Cause it's a bittersweet symphony, this life. Trying to make ends meet, you're a slave to the money then you die."

The players have been called to the complex largely to clean out their lockers. When I get there, I find Marco wearing his Ed Hardy baseball hat, gray capris of unknown label, white canvas Izod tennis shoes, and a gray Aéropostale T-shirt. A red Ferrari backpack hangs from his shoulder. He offers me a raspberry-flavored breath mint as he thanks Adir from the media office for printing up directions to the wedding, this Saturday. From his locker, Marco pulls a tube of hair gel and presents it to the goalkeeper coach, a joke because the coach is bald. The coach laughs and asks Marco to sign a jersey for him.

The clubhouse is located in the same building as the front office and the media-relations department. It's understood to be for players and coaches only. In addition to the lockers and showers, there's a big lounge with a computer for checking e-mail and also a microwave, a refrigerator, a coffeemaker, and a large table where the players like to play cards. Official team photos line the walls, along with jerseys signed by every player that particular season. Dozens of framed copies of *Vamos Indios!* magazine show captain Juan de la Barrera touring a maquiladora while wearing plastic safety glasses or Edwin Santibáñez screaming down the pitch with his long hair flying behind him. A leather sectional couch faces a TV that's usually showing live soccer. (There's always a match somewhere.) Occasionally a couple guys fire up the Xbox to play FIFA as themselves, against themselves. Edwin strolls into the clubhouse wearing a tight green Ed Hardy T-shirt. King Kong follows him inside, pulling off mirrored sunglasses. Kong is greeted warmly; all is forgiven. It feels like the last day of school, like exams are over and time off awaits. The meeting, called by Gil Cantú, is quick.

"We just talked about the money and our vacation time," Marco tells me when we stop afterwards at a roadside stand for gorditas and orange soda served in bottles embossed with pictures of luchador *Rey Mysterio.* Two more players join us at the stand, a quorum that decides to upgrade to Los Bichis for a full lunch. Marco gets on his phone to invite more players. By the time we get to the Sinaloan seafood restaurant, nine Indios are already there, with more on the way. Waiters pull tables together and rope off a section of the dining room. Christian the goalie asks for a spicy shrimp cocktail. I order the fish tacos on Edwin's recommendation. Marco calls for the first of what will be many, many rounds of Tecate Light.

"We're just chilling," Marco says. "It's the first time we've ever done this in a restaurant where people can see us. Normally we try not to drink in public. But now, you know, why the fuck not?"

Highlights from the Pumas victory flash on a television, and Edwin winces when he's shown absorbing a hard foul. I notice the wrinkles around his eyes, evidence less of his age (he's thirty) than of a life spent working outdoors. Defenseman Tomás Campos orders enough oysters for everyone to share. Marco selects a smaller serving of marlin tostadas and shares them anyway. Christian calls for another round of Tecate Light. The goalie tells me he's outta

here. He only came to the border to jump-start his career. He'd
been languishing on the bench of the Monterrey Rayados when Gil
Cantú offered him a short-term contract and a chance to start.
Christian had just married. He didn't want to leave his new wife,
and she most definitely wouldn't join him in Juárez. But they
prayed—he's as religious as his name—and God told them Christian
should go to Juárez anyway. He played so well that several Primera
teams want him for next season. It was a good decision to come here,
he acknowledges. The city gave him an opportunity. But he is so
very gone. He orders yet another round of Tecate Light.

"No más Tecate Light," says the waiter. We've drunk them dry.
I think of a T-shirt that Pittsburgh Steelers quarterback Ben Roeth-
lisberger was photographed wearing at a party: DRINK LIKE A CHAM-
PION TODAY. The Indios may be minor league losers in soccer, but
nobody comes close when it comes to Tecate Light consumption.
Christian switches the order to *cerveza* Modelo and the liquid
lunch continues. A liquid dinner follows. The players stay into the
night, allowed to continue drinking whatever liquor remains even
after the restaurant's normal ten P.M. closing. It's a serious binge,
but it's only one night. *Why the fuck not?* The rest of the week,
Marco's sobered by all the wedding prep he's juggling. Where will
his parents sleep? What time does he need to be at the church? How
will his sisters get to the church? He calls me one afternoon in a
panic. Do I know any place where he can buy live butterflies to be
released after the ceremony? Dany still wants those live butterflies.

WEDDING SEASON IN Ciudad Juárez. On the morning Marco and
Dany are to marry, the papers chronicle a wedding from the previous evening. Just five minutes after the bride and groom had vowed
to stay together until death, gunmen stormed into the Lord of
Mercy Catholic Church, ordering everyone to the floor. The groom,
his brother, and his uncle were whisked away. A man outside the
church was shot. The groom and the two others turned up dead
in the bed of a stolen pickup truck. Their bodies showed signs of
torture.

"I'm confused, frustrated and in despair," the father of the groom
told the *El Paso Times*. "My wife, she is devastated."

Marco and Dany also marry in a Catholic church, Our Lady of Peace, located behind the torta restaurant I visited my first week in Juárez, the one where a man was shot more than a hundred times. The church is blond bricks stacked in a style that, in 1974, looked contemporary, perhaps ultramodern. It has a relatively low roof and walls that were never designed to meet at right angles. Although we're deep in the city—I can hear car horns in a Wal-Mart parking lot—Marco rides up to the church on a white horse speckled with gray spots. The horse's saddle is brown leather atop a colorfully striped wool blanket. Marco wears all black—his suit, his shirt, and his shiny black tie. "Rock & Republic," he tells me with a big smile, "narrow cut." He knows I was curious about the designer label. Sharp sunlight glints off the diamonds in both of his ears. His uncle pins a red rose to Marco's lapel, right above his heart.

Dany says her strapless white wedding dress was the first one she tried on. Upon further questioning, she admits it was really the first one she tried on at that particular store; she'd previously rejected six other dresses at two other shops. Her black hair sweeps off her face, held back at her ears, which are pierced with pearls. Her narrow white veil is visible only from behind as she walks down the aisle. The youngest of her nephews fidget in wood pews to her left, Marco's family from Dallas and Mexico City sit on the right. Several Indios hang in the back. Gabino in a suit. Edwin in a suit and his daughters in dresses. Juan the captain wears blue jeans and a T-shirt from Abercrombie & Fitch. Francisco Ibarra doesn't show up, but his bodyguard does. The main image on the altar is Jesucristo levitating outside the tomb where he'd been buried three days earlier.

The priest tells Marco and Dany to love everybody with Jesus Christ in their hearts. Dany is specifically instructed, in a lecture that lasts almost fifteen minutes, to obey and cherish her husband. Marco's uncle—chosen because his marriage is the example Marco and Dany want to emulate—lassos a jeweled silver necklace around their necks, symbolically uniting them. Marco and Dany recite their vows into a microphone so everyone can hear. Toward the end of the ceremony, the necklace is removed and the newlyweds carry a rose over to the church's glassed-in shrine to the Virgin of Guadalupe. They kneel and say a private prayer. When they return to the altar, Marco kisses his bride. Outside, in bright sun, family and *futbolistas* shake Marco's hand and tell Dany how beautiful she looks. Live butterflies, I'm sorry to report, are not released.

"I'm happy for you!" cheers Wendy, from the Indios' sales office.

"I'm happy, too!" Marco replies.

No blue jeans allowed at the reception, though winter coats will be tolerated. A cold front has swooped in so suddenly that it snows in Chihuahua city. The outdoor wedding reception is going to be chilly, a holiday on ice. I'm hoping to tough it out in only my best suit, which I'm wearing on Marco's strict orders. The directions Adir provided lead me to the house where Dany grew up and her parents still live. I enter through what is technically the garage, though you wouldn't know it. Gauzy white drapes hide the automatic door so well I feel like I'm in the Delano hotel on Miami Beach. True to Dany's vision, the garage and the backyard it opens onto have been transformed into a nightclub. White leather couches and ottomans cluster around illuminated white cubes. Palm trees bathe in pink light. Ice sculptures try to melt into a swimming pool that has been turned into a fountain, streams of water arcing into the air and somehow landing back in the pool without making a splash. Daisies swirl in the hot tub. Laser lights fire onto the side of the house next door, forming patterns that swirl and change colors, like at a disco.

Waiters aggressively push drinks—"What do you want? Beer? Bourbon? Really good red wine? We've got everything!"—while shuttling guests to their proper places. Marco's parents and sisters control a round table covered in champagne-colored fabric, just like Dany wanted. Teenagers recline on a cluster of couches near the garage. Even the youngest kids, ages six and seven, have their own lounge. I'm steered to what I choose to believe is the VIP section, where the famous soccer players of Ciudad Juárez sit on one set of couches while their wives talk to each other on white couches of their own.

I take note of who shows up and who doesn't. Juan the captain attended the wedding, but he's skipping the reception. Adir from the press office is here. Ramón Morales is not. Whisky the equipment manager has made it. Team owner Francisco Ibarra has not, which I know hurts Marco's feelings. Even Gil Cantú fails to attend—*Drive in Juárez at night? Are you crazy?!*—but at least Gabino the coach is here in his stead. Paco Ibarra has known Dany longer than even

Marco has, yet Paco has skipped out as well, same as his father. "I don't like weddings," he will tell me afterwards. Some of Dany's cousins, as threatened, stay in El Paso.

Huge mistake. When the band takes the stage promising to keep the party going till six in the morning, they mean it. I salsa with Wendy as best I can. Gabino two-steps the achy breaky *corazón* with his tall wife. A full dinner is served, and the drinks keep on coming; there's a dedicated bartender just for shots. As the night unfolds, I discern a circus theme. Mimes show up at one point, slinking around the lounges as silently as the human statues Dany ordered up for the yard. The dance floor is crowded, but I have no problem spotting two guys dressed as jesters and walking on stilts. When the band takes a break, out come a trio juggling fiery batons, kids hired right off the street, where they spit fire in exchange for pesos from passing cars. Marco grabs one of their batons and spins it overhead. The guy's a natural. No one is burnt to a crisp. No leather couches are incinerated. Marco's Rock & Republic narrow-cut suit is not even singed.

"Have you seen the monster you created?" Indio Jair Garcia shouts at Maleno Frías.

"I didn't do anything," Maleno shouts back. "He was this way when I found him!"

Dany's sister dips a strawberry into a chocolate fountain while mariachis serenade a pack of her nieces. Marco shuttles from couch to couch, posing for pictures. By two o'clock in the morning women are wearing their husbands' suit jackets for warmth and some of the youngest kids nap on the couches. Just when I'm thinking the party might be winding down, the band takes the stage for another set and the kitchen produces a full second feeding. Menudo, a hearty soup, bubbles in steaming cauldrons. I accept a bowl and then a second, dunking chunks of warm bread into the thick broth. Edwin invites me into the house for shots of Don Julio 1942 tequila. "There is none better," he assures me. Dany slips past us, wearing a puffy ski jacket over her wedding dress but also wearing flip-flops with her name inked on one foot and Marco's on the other. She steps onto the dance floor so we can tape pesos and dollars to her veil. Her girlfriends all dance with her while wearing blinking red plastic devil's horns, which apparently is a Mexican tradition.

"They've done this at every wedding I've ever went to," one of her friends tells me.

Edwin hands me an apron, telling me to tie it around my waist like the other men are doing. Okay. Before the garter is thrown, the single men are ordered to run figure-eights around the dance floor. I'm dizzy by the time I spin back to one of the leather couches. Dany's mother encourages me to enjoy another shot. Adir slaps me on the shoulder.

"You see what I was telling you, Robert? It's not all violence here."

Of all the weddings I've been to, this is the best by far. As a night out, it beats even *lucha libre* with Fussion and the gang from El Kartel. This is family. It's life. *Mexicans are a happy people.* There is a terrific energy here. I feel substantially more alive just by witnessing it all, by sharing this night with Marco and Dany and their families and my friends. The Indios players take over the dance floor, pulling Marco into the center of their pack.

Right now, in this city, a bride mourns the murder of the man she was married to for only five minutes. That happened here. In Juárez. Same Catholic religion. Same holy sacrament Dany and Marco shared with us this afternoon. Is it luck no bullets have found us? Providence? Earlier tonight, after Edwin poured me a shot of that superfine tequila, one of Dany's uncles pulled me aside in the house. He told me I'm crazy to be living in Juárez. He has no choice anymore, he said—he *cautioned*. His family is here. His work is here. But since *I* don't have to be here, it'd be insane for me to stay.

"In Juárez you can be a good person and the violence comes to you," he warned.

The Indios players hoist Marco into the air. I'm told this is another of the traditions. He falls back into their arms and they toss him again, up into the cold night. His legs go akimbo. Even above the cheers of his teammates and his family I can hear him laugh. He's not coming back, I think to myself, and what I mean is to the United States. His house is here. Now his family is here, too, and so is his work; he's still under contract with the Indios, and the last anyone heard from Francisco Ibarra, the team isn't going anywhere. Marco made all these choices with his eyes open, and on a night like this I can understand why. He's staying in Mexico. He's staying in Juárez.

MAYBE IT *IS* providence.

Marco and Dany honeymoon in Europe. Five cities in fifteen days, a whirlwind so exhausting they fall asleep in public at one point, on the steps outside a church, their heads resting on each other's shoulders. Marco had proposed a gambling junket to Las Vegas, but Dany put her foot down. This, she said, is the time in life to think big. So it's Spain first, just so Marco can tour Santiago Bernabéu, the home stadium of Real Madrid. From there a boat to Athens for one day and one night. Then to Rome, to toss one coin each in the Trevi Fountain, and up to Venice for not much longer than a gondola ride. In Paris, Marco insists they case the entire Louvre in an afternoon, warning Dany to keep up because he has the money and the passports and she doesn't have a phone. Paris, they discover, is expensive. Four beers cost sixty euros the one night they visit a disco, when they climb onto platforms and gyrate as crazy as they want because they know no one there will ever see them again.

And when they return to Juárez, Marco finds out he's been traded to Pachuca. Down near Mexico City. One of the best teams in the Primera.

CHAPTER 21

Politics (or, About Those Money-Laundering Allegations)

CROSSING INTO EL PASO IN MY CAR is an ordeal. It almost always takes a long time. With the summer here, and if I make the mistake of trying to cross at midday, the blacktop bakes so hot my power steering can fail. The worst part of crossing is the way drivers cut me off, constantly. If I leave the slightest space between the car or truck in front of me, someone will dart into it. Maybe they'll throw only a front bumper in there, but that'll be enough to force me to let them in. It's wickedly antisocial. Like, dude, you see me, I see you, we're in this together, and you're still cutting me off? Everyone I've met in Juárez has been so generous and friendly. And every Juarense I encounter in line to El Paso is ruthless. Male or female, young driver or old. Even if the bridge is so backed up it takes hours to inch toward customs, I can't relax for a second. I can't glance at the headlines in *El Diario* or *PM* I won't even change the radio station. I have to be on my guard the entire time.

"*No tranza, no avanza,*" Paco Ibarra tells me when I moan about the phenomenon. "It's a saying in Mexico that my dad likes. It's one of his favorite phrases. *No tranza, no avanza.* If you don't cheat, you don't get ahead."

TOLUCA WINS THE title. As I predicted. Santos comes in second. Mexico does not win the World Cup, though you wouldn't know it from the passion around here for the national team. An opening-round defeat of France inspired hundreds of Juarenses to run laps around the *megabandera* in 113-degree heat. I can't imagine what they'd do if Mexico ever won a game that actually mattered. (Facing Argentina in the first knockout round, Mexico lost 3–1.) Soccer steps off the field. The political season steps forward. An election approaches fast, on July fourth. I watch countless ads about the importance of voting, of the integrity of the process and why everybody should participate. One commercial features an upper-class family finishing up a meal in a restaurant while concluding that every vote makes a difference. In another ad, a family more middle-class decides that voting is good citizenship. Two poor laborers till a field, debating whether their votes matter before agreeing that they do. All these ads really try to sell it, the idea that the public is empowered.

"That's all just so people vote and think they're living in a democracy," Paco insists. He's been joining his father at private meetings with the candidates for mayor and governor and other offices. "But it's all just a front. It's about giving jobs to functionaries, doling them out like a short-order cook."

There's no question who will be elected Juárez's next mayor. Teto Murguía already served as mayor, three years ago, for the one term allowed in Mexico. After sitting out the term of current mayor Reyes Ferriz, who himself is now required to leave office, Teto's come back for a second stint in power. His victory is so assured, it didn't look like he was going to bother campaigning. But then one day in May, boom, the city woke up covered in his posters and billboards. Teto's smiling face adorns seemingly every single telephone pole along La Frontera. His banners drape from every bridge. It turns out he owns the strip mall where I lift weights a few nights a week, and that's where he's set up his campaign headquarters. The entire mall has been shrink-wrapped with that same smiling face.

All projections have Teto returning to office in a landslide. "The guy running against him, he's a lightweight," Mayor Reyes Ferriz tells me. Teto could probably defeat a heavyweight, too. He's a skilled populist. At his rallies in the poorer barrios, Teto hands out free bags of cement, for home repair. In one of the posters his campaign has glued all over the city, Teto squeezes the shoulders of two gray-haired grandmothers, both of whom hold their thumbs high. He's a shoo-in. One pollster has spotted him a twenty-six-point lead.

Yet there's this:

"It's going to be a disaster for the city if Teto is elected," Reyes Ferriz tells me. When I remind the mayor that he and Teto share a political party, Reyes Ferriz says it doesn't matter. Teto back in office would "send exactly the wrong message."

The Mexico City newspaper *Excelsior*, citing a U.S. Drug Enforcement Administration document, has alleged that Teto's successful first campaign for mayor was funded by La Línea. During his original term, seven companies that formed only days before Teto took office ended up winning a full third of the city's business, according to an article published in *El Diario*. A man named Saulo Reyes Gamboa was a partner in three of those instant—and instantly successful—companies. Reyes Gamboa was already the owner of a chain of hamburger restaurants, a chain of Japanese restaurants, and a chain of Subway sandwich shops. Teto was so close to Reyes Gamboa he named him his chief of police. Three months after Teto's term expired, DEA agents caught Reyes Gamboa trying to transport more than a ton of marijuana into Texas. Teto expressed complete surprise that this man he had trusted and had worked with so closely turned out to be a major drug trafficker. He insists that this in no way means he, Teto, is connected to the drug trade.

There's no doubt Teto has made out quite well for himself, especially for a civil servant. They say in Mexico that a politician who is poor is a poor politician. Teto is such a good politician he owns homes in (at least) Juárez, El Paso, Mexico City, and the vacation town of Ruidoso. He claims that his wealth comes not from politics but largely from side businesses, like a family paint company. His brother heads Juárez's chamber of commerce, and his cousin owns Barrigas, a restaurant chain. When I pulled public records in Texas, I learned Teto holds an ownership stake in a pharmacy concern of some kind. He's obviously well-off. I learned just how well-off he is on that road trip with Francisco Ibarra.

At first it was only supposed to have been a day trip, to the apple town of Cuauhtémoc and right back. But Francisco is known for impulsive decisions, and we ended up staying the night in Chihuahua city, Francisco covering my hotel room and paying for my food, too. The next morning, instead of returning to Juárez as planned, he wanted to fly down to Guadalajara. His family owns several homes on the Pacific coast. Francisco suggested a trip of five days to a week—we'll bring Paco, we'll hit the beach and live large. That is an outing I would take anytime, except when I'm in the real world. I had obligations back in Juárez I absolutely could not break or reschedule. And besides, I couldn't afford to fly to Guadalajara anyway.

"Don't worry about it," Francisco said, campaigning for the trip. "We'll take Teto's jet."

I didn't go to Guadalajara. I returned to Juárez instead, as I needed to do. Francisco stayed in Chihuahua for at least another day, and may have continued on to the beach after that. Two questions stuck in my brain on the long bummer of a ride back to the border:

(1) The mayor has a private jet?
(2) He lets Francisco just use it?

PACO IBARRA HAS told me his family was not rich back when he was a kid. They weren't poor, but they hovered no higher than the Mexican middle class. But by his teens, his family grew so wealthy, so suddenly, that a high school friend was taken aback the first time he visited the family's private, ten-mansion compound. Sculptures pranced on the lawns, as they still do. A bridge arched over the pool in the backyard of the house where Paco lived with his parents. Indoors, a waterfall gently cascaded from the second-floor bedrooms down to a grand foyer tiled in marble.

"C'mon, Paco," the classmate said, "you have to admit you guys are loaded." And Paco did. He admitted it. It was true.

The great expansion of the Ibarra family fortune coincided with the first Teto Murguía administration. Grupo Yvasa, a company that had started out with a lone taco stand, won a contract to build an entire highway. Yvasa also won contracts to fabricate hundreds of houses on land provided by the city. Some sixty public works projects doled out by Teto were divided between only four companies, Yvasa among the lucky few. The Ibarras remain grateful, and close. How close? Teto sat next to Francisco at the Chivas game. Mario Boisselier, the Indios' attorney, is Teto's campaign manager.

Not six months before I moved to Juárez, the U.S. Drug Enforcement Administration released the results of a wide-ranging investigation into Mexican drug cartels. Project Reckoning, they called it. Among many other findings, the DEA indicated that soccer teams in Mexico's second and third divisions may be laundering cartel drug profits. Several teams were identified by name. The agency also fingered one team in the Primera: Los Indios de Ciudad Juárez. Francisco Ibarra's social project was tied to agents of La Línea, the Juárez Cartel.

"They mention that the Indios were victims of 'agents' that are linked to the cartel," Francisco responded. "I don't know if there are agents that are linked, but we are not dealing with agents. We deal with the players directly."

I wasn't aware of the DEA report when I moved to Mexico, just like I wasn't aware of the murder of Pedro Picasso. I had no idea, basically, what I was getting myself into. Ibarra, when he responded to the allegations, added that an examination of possible wrong-doing in Mexican soccer is a good thing, and will leave the game in a healthier state. To my face he said pretty much the same thing, about a year after the initial report, when I finally got up to speed. He doesn't know what the DEA is talking about. Which makes him pretty much the only one who doesn't.

"You have to remember that Chihuahua is a narco state," Channel 44 news director Edgar Roman told me one evening when I went body hunting with one of his station's cameramen. "The government and the cartels are one in this city. Picture a triangle. The drug dealers give the money to the government, and the government gives the money back to the people."

I *have* noticed how the government subsidizes much of Juárez's aboveboard business life. I admire and generally trust *El Diario*, yet how independent can the newspaper ultimately be when it floats on page after page of ads from the federal government and the state government and the city government, every day, just like every other paper in town? All those government-sponsored "Please Vote" commercials that have annoyed me since February have certainly padded the bottom line at Channel 44. I shared a beer at a party one night with a guy who told me he was an actor. The next day, at halftime of a Primera match I was watching on TV, the guy showed up in a commercial for the Todos Somos Juárez social program, his acting underwritten by Felipe Calderón.

None of that qualifies as money laundering in the traditional sense. It's more common, I've since learned, for money to be laundered through chain restaurants, or, even better, through pharmacies, fronts that can cloak the purchase of processing chemicals. I've read in a dozen places by now that drug money, if it's not the backbone of the Mexican economy, is at least one of three legs— along with oil and tourism—that keep the country upright. The profits from drug sales touch everything in Juárez, and everyone. (And of course everything and everyone in El Paso, too. As Tony Payan, a professor at both UTEP and UACJ told me, those Juárez drugs don't end up in Chicago without crossing through El Paso first.) Even someone as naive as me can figure that out. A person who wants to survive in this city—and, God forbid, if they want to actually thrive—will mingle with the drug underworld somehow, in some way, wittingly or unwittingly. If the news director at Channel 44 knows Chihuahua is a narco state, then the lucky con- tractors paid millions of dollars by the state know full well where their money is coming from. They'd have to be totally stupid *not* to know.

And that, incredibly, turns out to be Francisco Ibarra's best de- fense. I don't like even calling it a defense, because that implies that Francisco is up to something nefarious, which not even the DEA has substantiated with hard data. Francisco doesn't run the Grupo Yvasa construction business. He has brothers who run it, with their powerful father supervising everything. Francisco is the son in the family who likes soccer, likes it so much he worked with the team called Cobras instead of concentrating on construction, as his fa- ther wanted. Francisco likes radio, too, enough to build a popular AM station. Radio, really, is his career these days. The Indios are his toy. He bought the minor league team that became the Indios because the millions of dollars he needed to buy them had come his way, somehow.

"Francisco Ibarra is a good man," says the doctor who prescribed me Xanax. "*Muy sincero.* Decent."

Francisco sure isn't stupid. I've used that word as a crude short- hand. *Ignorant* is a better adjective. *Willfully ignorant.* Kind of *ex- actly* the same way Marco Vidal remains stubbornly clueless about the violence surrounding him in Juárez. The violence that killed one of his club's coaches. That inspired his wife and her family to flee the country for a while. He doesn't think terribly hard about why his dream house came on the market at such an affordable price. He stays in his soccer bubble. Ask Marco about drug running or money laundering or cartel hierarchies and you might think he's an airhead, or a child. *What? Huh?* The less he knows the better. Marco's smart enough—and he's very smart, super sharp—to be as dumb as possible.

Just like Francisco. Agents of La Línea? I don't know anything about La Línea. Or about cartels. Agents? Like sports agents?

"My dad is the most honest person I've ever met," Paco told me when I asked him about the laundering allegations. "I'd bet my life on it. If it ever turned out he wasn't honest, my world would be turned upside down."

One can't expect an objective take from Paco, of course. Is Paco aware that the house where he lives with his family, the brand-new house in El Paso's upscale West Side, belongs to the owner of Peter Piper Pizza restaurants linked in a chain throughout Juárez? And that the owner lets the Ibarras stay in the house rent free? *Who has a brand-new spare house to lend out?* Why would Paco look into something like that? What's in it for him? And yet, even if a blood relative can't certify a man's character, I think Paco's telling the truth about his father. I think Francisco may very well be the most honest man he knows. Ramón Morales, who grumbles about Francisco's business acumen, still describes him as sincere. Indios lawyer Mario Boisselier, when I last visited him at Teto's campaign headquarters, told me Francisco is "incompetent, lazy, and distracted, but he's not a bad guy."

One reporter who covers the Indios informed me that when Ibarra stepped forward with his plans to build that superstadium for his still-minor-league team—four hundred luxury skyboxes!—a red flag unfurled as tall and wide as the *megabandera* that flies over the valley. Some newspapers outside of Juárez ran with the story, asking the itchy questions. And then the project died. It was the falling economy and the rising violence that killed the stadium, Francisco told me, not the persistent questions about money laundering. I believe he's probably right.

"If we were laundering money, the Indios would be the best team in Mexico," Paco argued with me, somewhat playfully, with a smile on his face. "We'd have the best players in the league, my father would have his new stadium, and every one of my film projects would be totally funded!"

That, really, is credible. If the Indios were fundamentally corrupted, they wouldn't be this bad. They wouldn't have been kicked out of the Primera, they wouldn't have laid off almost the entire staff, and they wouldn't have launched their last doomed campaign with a motley crew of old men and castaways, otherwise unwanted players bonded by such a desperation to play soccer—to work—that they were willing to do it in the deadliest city on the planet. Marco doesn't have to worry if he's being paid by drug profits because, well, he hasn't been paid in more than a month. If the Indios were a money-laundering front—and we're talking specifically about the Indios here, only the soccer side of Grupo Yvasa—they'd be a much better team.

THE FOURTH OF July. Capitalize that "F." It's also a Saturday, the day I try to run long. Instead of jogging up and down the river like I usually do, I cross into El Paso, it being an American holiday and me being an American and all. I get in eight miles at Ascarate Park, in the Central Valley. Even though I started out early to beat the heat, families already crowd the barbecue pits and picnic pavilions. A poodle chained to a tree snarls at me whenever I complete a lap of the park's modest lake. A young girl snaps gunpowder pop-'ems on the sidewalk. Two workers on a golf cart carry the equipment for making snow cones over to a refreshment stand. Standard American stuff even if the park sits right smack on the border fence. The whole time I'm running, I can see directly into Juárez, a city celebrating, or perhaps enduring, a holiday of its own: Election Day, the return of Teto.

He wins easily. His opponent claimed at every opportunity that Teto was the candidate of La Línea, but that argument, on the cartel's home turf, swung few votes. Mario Boisselier tells me the victory party will start around six thirty P.M. When I arrive at campaign headquarters at almost seven, not much is going on, at least not yet. Only a few people stand around, none of them looking primed to party. I opt to stroll Juárez for a while. Almost everything is closed. Election Day is a federal holiday in Mexico. No lights flicker inside the Pronaf District clubs; all the bars shut down for the night, by law. At OXXO and Bip Bip convenience stores, black trash bags drape over locked beer coolers, alcohol sales having been prohibited since yesterday so the electorate could vote in

sober confidence. I walk up to Chamizal Park, where Mexican families unfurl blankets to watch the fireworks, same as their American
cousins unfolding lawn chairs in *their* Chamizal Park, right across
the river. I head back into the city, past a polling place where I can see
workers cleaning up. A huge sign over the door to the gymnasium
where the voting took place announces that the gym was built, four
years ago, by the administration of Teto Murguía, deft gamesman-
ship a politician in Chicago might admire.

It's dark by the time I make it back to campaign headquarters.
The party has started. There is a band. There are some more people,
and a few reporters on scene to cover the news. The first fireworks in
El Paso launch into the sky. From the parking lot I can see the flares
of red and blue and, at one point, red, white, and green, the colors of
Mexico. Gunpowder smoke wafts over from Texas. Teto's party is not
nearly the wingding I'd expected. The band sounds as if it's going
through the motions. The crowd is relatively modest, and its mood
approaches sedate. *Muy tranquilo.* But everyone knows their role,
why they are here. Gaby, the main reporter from Channel 44, sets up
a feed. When she goes live, a couple dozen boosters shout Teto's name
and wave Teto cardboard cutouts, along with flags colored green and
red. It makes for a nice visual. On TV it probably looks as though a
lot of people are happy that Teto won, that it's a good thing.

CHAPTER 22

The Last Straw

A *FEDERALE* IS MURDERED AND DISMEMBERED, his body parts scattered—a leg here, an arm there—along my regular jogging route near the river. The officer's head lands close to the stadium, right where I'd finished up a run that same afternoon. While watching the news that night, I calculate I must have missed the body-part dump by no more than five minutes. The next day, I return to run the same route.

Marco and Dany registered at Liverpool, Mexico's Macy's. *Ladrones* invade the Liverpool at Las Misiones, the same outpost where I'd bought the newlyweds a set of towels and a wastebasket. "This was supposed to be a safe space," a store clerk tells *El Diario*. Kids in day care at the mall's Total Fitness gym, where Marco and Dany first met, hide in the women's bathroom until police give the all-clear.

Two more men are shot dead on my street. Again outside my apartment. I don't witness their murders. I somehow don't even hear the bullets, although I'm home at the time. I look up and blue federal police trucks clog the street. I step out to watch the technicians contaminate the crime scene. It struck me, the first time I saw those two dead bodies at the convenience store, how casual everyone had acted. Now, I'm mostly annoyed. I need to drive to the Laundromat to wash my clothes for the week, and my car is boxed in by all the trucks. I'm going to have to wait until the whole scene is cleaned up.

My running partner Manuel, the Baptist pastor, talks about getting out. Is there a right time to leave? How much closer does the violence have to get? We jog our usual loop from his townhouse to the U.S. Consulate and back. We run slowly, sweating only because in the summer it's hot even before dawn. He thinks it'll take twenty years to get the violence under control. He'll be in his seventies by then. Can he make it that long? What might finally prompt him to move? A kidnapping attempt? His wife being shot? Manuel worries that his church will drown if he leaves. He feels obligated to stay, as long as he possibly can. He reminds me I have other options.

"What will it take?" he asks. "What will be the last straw?"

"I'm pumped," Marco tells me. He's excited to have signed on with Pachuca. Marco's new team recently dethroned Atlante as CONCACAF club champions, which means Marco will be flying to Dubai for the FIFA Club World Cup, possibly to face Italian stars Inter Milan. He's going to have to fight for playing time in Pachuca, he acknowledges. But he's optimistic.

"They wouldn't have bought my contract if they didn't think they have a use for me," he says. Marco's back in Juárez for one last week, training with his old team to shake off the rust from his honeymoon. He hasn't exercised for a month, not once. That's actually a good thing, a chance for his body to recover. He still feels guilty for letting himself go. The summer sun roasts at 107 degrees already, an hour before noon. Marco jogs a warm-up lap alongside faces that are mostly unfamiliar. Jair is missing. So are Edwin, Kong, Coco, and a starting lineup of other mainstays. I'm selfishly pleased to see captain Juan de la Barrera is still here, still an Indio. Maleno Frías remains, too.

"At first I wanted to leave, but they wouldn't let me," Maleno tells me after practice. "So maybe it's for the best. I love Juárez. I'm going to defend my jersey with all my heart."

My follow-up question is a disaster. I ask Maleno if any progress has been made in the investigation of his brother's murder. The question, as soon as it comes out of my mouth, sounds flip, like I might be making a joke at his expense. Of course no one has investigated the murder. I'm horrified at my gaffe, but Maleno cuts me some slack.

"I just leave it to the law," he tells me. "I put it behind me and I've moved on."

The Indios sell off their youth team. Ramón Morales quits, as expected, telling me he'll be devoting his full attention to his Reiki practice. Federal agents arrest Jesús Armando Acosta Guerrero, alias "El 35," identified as the operational leader of La Línea. A report on his arrest indicates that J. L. remains La Línea's top man. I hear a radio story about Juárez focused only on "the young women targeted for sadistic killings." Other news, other once-big events, fade from our consciousness. We moved on from the consulate murders long ago. We've forgotten about the boy shot by the Border Patrol. Our attention is currently trained on a dead woman, actually, a pretty sixteen-year-old girl who fits the classic profile. She wasn't snatched off the street, though. She was murdered by her boyfriend. He led investigators to her dismembered body and he admitted his crime in open court. It was a very rare case of a killing making it as far as the courtroom. Yet right after he told the judge he was sorry, the judge—a woman, if it matters—dropped all charges, citing "a lack of evidence." She released the murderer, free to go. The victim's mother fell to the floor in tears.

We are so moved by her pain, we give her a name: "Rubi's Mother." We follow her crusade. She marches all the way to Chihuahua city to meet the governor. He grants her an audience, but nothing else is done. She continues marching. In Chihuahua city. In Mexico City, too. I've driven slowly past her as she marches across Ciudad Juárez. A sandwich board around her neck demands punishment for her daughter's killer. We admire her courage. And we will not be surprised, a few months later, when she's shot dead, assassinated on a busy street, back in Chihuahua, right outside the governor's office. *She'd stepped off the line.* No one will be charged with her murder, even though we all know exactly who is behind the bullet. Her tragic story will disappear, almost instantly. Her daughter's murder, the also-tragic story Rubi's Mother agitated to keep in the news, will fade away, too. That's why they kill.

I PARTY WITH Paco at his family's mansion in Juárez. He crosses the river to host a relaxed little welcome-home-from-the-World-Cup get-together. A dining room table displays the booty: game tickets, signed jerseys, wood carvings, plastic vuvuzelas. The party moves outdoors to the poolside cabana. Cooks from Tacos El Campeón unpack warm tortillas and stir a tray of spiced ground beef. I'm happy to see Paco's girlfriend, Karina, is here, along with her brother, Lorenzo; the three of us went out for my birthday, in June, when Paco was in Africa. Lorenzo tells me that I'm Juarense, that I qualify by now. Everybody in Juárez is from somewhere else, he says, and I've put in more than enough time. This makes me feel surprisingly happy. It took me more than ten years to define myself as a Miamian. Here in Juárez, I'm already in. And not just nominally in, but *in*, really in. I do feel like I belong here. That I am not only in Juárez but *of* it. I love this city, totally.

"But if you stay here longer," Lorenzo cautions, "you're going to start to know the people who are killed. You'll know them personally." Another guy at the party tells me that when you grow numb, when the murders stop affecting you, that's when you know you have a problem.

I read this story on CNN.com:

"The bodies of two men—both decapitated and showing signs of torture—were found early Sunday in Ciudad Juárez, Mexico, the state attorney general's office said.

"The victims were found in the Colony of Los Nogales neighborhood in Ciudad Juárez, Chihuahua. Their hands and feet had been bound with duct tape."

In El Paso one afternoon, I strike up a conversation with a soldier stationed at Fort Bliss. He's just back from Iraq. He can't believe I'm living in a city as dangerous as Juárez. Actually, he says, Juárez is just like Iraq. Same houses. The people look the same and they act the same, too. Only difference is, in Iraq you have to watch for bombs.

THE FIRST BOMB explodes just after halftime. It explodes while I'm sitting in a sports bar on Avenida 16 de Septiembre, just east of El Centro. It explodes while I'm watching Marco's new team, Pachuca, open a preseason tournament in Houston, against the Dynamo of Major League Soccer.

The game airs only on cable, which I don't have at my apartment. Not even the satellite dish at Applebee's pulls in the channel, so that's how I ended up trying this place for the first time. I've driven by here many times on my way to Olympic Stadium, but I've never been able to tell if it's open for business or not. When I pulled up tonight, the lot sat empty, as usual. When I jiggled the bar's front doors, they were locked. But then a waiter emerged to unlock the door, let me in, and then quickly lock the door behind me. I half expected to find cobwebs and dust, but a full staff stood ready to serve me: waitresses and waiters, a kitchen crew and a bartender governing a big central island of beer mugs and liquor bottles. As I look around now, two men sit at a table, talking. They may be customers. Or maybe that's just the bar manager and his friend? I can't tell. It's not even seven P.M., so it's early for a night out. Are the front doors locked because of security? That would make some sense. Locked doors make it harder for *ladrones* to storm the place. Is business down, in general, because of the violence? Or do the owners not really care if any customers visit? Is generating a profit the main objective of this place? The game flickers on all of the bar's many TVs, just for me. I'm sitting by the windows, as I usually do to keep an eye on my car. A waitress brings me a fresh bottle of Tecate Light.

Marco's not on the field, which isn't a surprise. He needs to learn a brand-new system, directed by different coaches. It usually takes him a while to work his way into any lineup. I study the faces and numbers of his new teammates. I want to learn their names, because with the Indios out, Pachuca is my new favorite team in the Primera. At halftime I order a plate of chicken wings. About ten minutes into the second half, Houston scores off a corner kick. Maybe two minutes after that comes the first concussive shock. Silverware clangs on the tables. A mug falls off the bar. The windows overlooking the parking lot vibrate almost out of their frames; they don't shatter, though in the first microsecond it seems as if they might. Through the glass I watch the bar's *parquero* dash over to the street. An ambulance and a police truck race past. More police trucks follow, one after the other after the other, shooting west, even though the avenue is normally a one-way running east.

The second explosion is minor, a concussive aftershock. Now every police car in the city zooms past our door. Some of the kitchen staff rush outside to see what's happened. There goes Channel 44, confirmation that we've got a dead body, which I'd already deduced. A second surge of federal police trucks. Then another ambulance. Then a convoy of green army trucks. Then finally the *transitos*, city traffic cops, blocking off the street in every direction.

I watch the rest of the game. It's amazing how unfazed I am by the explosions. I see cops running around, but there's Herculez Gomez on the TV, about to sub into the game. The American was traded to Pachuca, too, and is Marco's new roommate on the road. I watch last season's Primera scoring champ dart around the field, and I'm disappointed when he fails to put the ball in the net. The game ends 2–1, the Pachuca loss not really a bummer—it's preseason. I leave enough pesos on the table to cover my bill, then step outside. I walk toward my car, planning only to drive back home. But it's a nice evening, and still light out. All those cops have clustered only a few blocks away. I decide to walk down and check it out. What the heck.

The closed road has a block-party feel. Kids swoop past me on bicycles, laughing at their freedom. I stroll to the ornate, block-long mansion of the singer Juan Gabriel, the most famous Juarense until Maleno Frías came along. The rock star reporters at Channel 44 set up a feed outside the mansion, attracting a crowd; everybody's excited their neighborhood will be on TV. A black husk of what once was a federal police truck smolders in the middle of the road, just beyond the mansion. The burning shell of another vehicle, an old car, also litters the avenue. I see a couple bodies, charred and bloody. Was there an accident? Why are so many police around: a hundred or more total officers—city, state, and federal—along with army soldiers in green uniforms? I see a photographer I know and ask him what happened. Bomb, he confirms. Two *federales* killed, retaliation for yesterday's ambush of two city police officers. *Federale*: Sinaloa. City police: La Línea. The bomb is a new twist, but it's an old and well-established battle.

I'm intrigued by the word "bomb," but not enough to stick around. You've seen one dead body, you've seen 'em all. As I walk back to my car, the street remains abuzz, perhaps even happy. I almost feel like I should be licking an ice cream cone. Men ask me what I know and share with me what they've heard. I don't watch the news when I get home. I wind down the night thinking mostly about the Pachuca game; I bet Marco sees some playing time in the next match. The bombing doesn't strike me as a particularly big deal.

IT DOES HIT me, though. Real emotion. Devastation and shock. For maybe half a day. When I open the paper in the morning, I learn that the bomb was a much bigger deal than I'd realized. Much, much bigger. By the time I make it over to El Paso to meet Paco for lunch, my American cell phone is blowing up like it has several times this year. Family, friends, distant friends, colleagues who'd warned me that moving to Juárez was my stupidest idea yet. I meet Paco at the Subway by UTEP, near his house. He arrived first, and when I walk in, we give each other a hug. Because we need to, because it feels heavy, what we we're carrying. I hand him a copy of *El Diario*, with the screaming (and justified) headline *"Narcoterror!"* The main photo shows blasted body parts and the once-blue police truck that's exploding in bright orange flames. A *federale* runs away from the fireball to save his life. "World-class" are the words that pop into my head when I look at the photo. This is world-class terror. This is as bad as it gets anywhere. They're going to reprint this picture in Tokyo and Berlin and Cape Town, and they should. This is a major event, a big deal.

Paco shows me a video on his iPhone. One of the TV stations got there before even the first blast. A camera broadcast back to the station what appeared to be a routine crime scene, nothing special, not even a dead body. Just a police officer shot and lying in the street. A paramedic attended to the wounded officer. Technicians unrolled yellow caution tape. And then the first blast—the first one to rock the sports bar—blows everything orange, including the camera, which stops transmitting. The jolt is severe, even on a four-inch screen. We can feel it. We both jump a little even the third time Paco replays it.

We catch up on the details. It was the first cartel car bomb in Mexican history. Twenty-two pounds of C-4, all packed into that old car I saw, the bomb activated via cell phone by someone who must have been in the line of sight. La Línea orchestrated everything, perhaps J. L. personally, in retaliation for the earlier arrest of cartel leader El 35. (The initial report from my photographer friend was a bit off.) First they kidnapped a man and dressed him in a police officer's uniform, wounded him, and dumped him in the street, knowing an officer down would draw attention. An ambulance arrived first. A doctor who'd happened to be only a block away rushed over to help. The first explosion killed the decoy, the paramedic, the volunteer doctor, and a *federale*. That initial and lethal blast attracted every remaining officer in the city, the parade of trucks zooming past as I continued to watch the game. *As I continued to watch the game!* The second explosion, it is presumed, was an igniting gas tank.

It sinks in, the horror of it. The doctor, the paramedic, the original victim they'd dumped in the street. I was really close, too. Not so close that I could have been killed. But it went down just a couple blocks away, on the same main street. World-class terror, and I was right there. And I didn't even realize it, really. I brushed it off like it was an everyday happening, routine anarchy. In my car, as I cross back into Mexico after lunch, I ponder how detached I've become. When I get home, I feed Benito and change into nylon running shorts. I pull on my racing flats and head up to the San Lorenzo Cathedral. By the time I get there, to the starting line of a 10K road race, I've moved on. The two-phased narcoterrorist car bomb is pretty much out of my system.

SAN LORENZO IS the Indios' church, the cathedral where fans lit candles for the team before the big game against León, and where the Indios threw the victory party after the win. Exactly 104 runners join me in a small plaza outside the church. It's the entirety of Juárez's running scene, most everyone familiar to everyone else. They try to hold twelve races in Juárez a year, including a marathon in November. I hand over my entrance fee of twenty pesos, which is less than two dollars. My name is recorded in pencil in a small notebook and I'm handed back a cheap digital wristwatch so I can track my time. An air horn sounds and we start running.

We move in a pack for safety, navigating major roads still live with traffic. A motorcycle cop usually—though not always—stops cars on cross-streets. We run right up to the border, turning at the university, where a family has hung a banner seeking information about their missing daughter, who must have been a student. Volunteers hand out baggies of drinking water at Olympic Stadium, where that *federale*'s severed head was found the other day. We run right past City Hall and the still-dented light post where the two Americans from the consulate crashed their car and then were murdered. From there we duck under the Santa Fe Bridge, proceeding to the Puente Negro, the railroad bridge where the U.S. Border Patrol shot that kid dead. Finally we turn into a residential neighborhood and the race's last leg. For a short while we run on Avenida

16 de Septiembre. The same street from last night, the same avenue as the bombing. A woman with a garden hose sprays water to cool us off, and we climb a hill and in a hundred more yards we cross the finish line. I give my name to the race director, who records it in his notebook. He hands me a T-shirt printed with a silhouette of two runners in stride and, below them, an image of the Virgin Mary holding the baby Jesus.

We've ended up at another church, joining a festival in full swing. Vendors sell corn slathered in mayonnaise and chili pepper, that no-thank-you snack I first saw for sale down in San Luis Potosí. Shaved ice makes a cooler alternative, and I'm tempted. Church workers serve up burritos, frittatas, and taco platters. Rickety amusement rides clatter and clank in a parking lot. It's a good crowd, a lot of people out and about. A man weaving thread into bracelets crafts me one in red, with the white letters CD. JUÁREZ. I decline to buy one of his other options: green and red thread embroidered with the word SINALOA and an image of two pistols. I bump into the head groundskeeper from Olympic Stadium, and we're both a little discombobulated; we've never seen each other away from the field. He gives me a hug even though I'm all sweaty. This is his neighborhood, he says. He goes to this church.

I haven't been up here before, at this church or on this hill. Below us unfolds the whole valley, both sides. I take in Franklin Mountain and the Wells Fargos and Chase banks of El Paso. There's the river and, closer, in Mexico, El Centro. I can see the Rio Grande Mall, where my *parquero* friend Mario is still watching cars at this hour. Two blocks south of the mall, green banners continue to cloak Teto Murguía's campaign headquarters. I can make out the pastel paint of my apartment complex, which sits an unfortunate ten kilometers due east. (That's the rub when a road race heads in only one direction.) The light of the setting sun gives everything a warm tint. All of it looks pretty, even Juárez. A band plays on a stage set up in front of a pink cross and a banner with the single word PAZ, or *peace*. All in all, not a bad afternoon. I got in a workout, earned a cool T-shirt, bumped into a friend, bought a new bracelet, and toured a neighborhood I'd never visited before. So I can't say the race itself was the last straw.

*   *   *

THE LAST STRAW drops a few days later, and the race is part of it. The car bombs exploded on a Thursday. The race and the church festival took place on Friday. The following Tuesday evening, I'm in my apartment doing nothing much, just watching a telenovela, when my Mexican cell phone rings. It's Manuel, the pastor. He's very emotional, almost crying. He's just driven up to the bomb site. He had to do it, he tells me. He had to go there. He needed to see the black scars in the asphalt and the jagged glass of storefront windows shattered in the double blasts.

"Everybody's acting like nothing happened!" he shouts. It's five full days after the bombing, an eternity. I ate at McDonald's only one day after the consulate murders. I went running along the river just one day after they dumped *federale* body parts up and down my normal route. When they finally cleaned up the two dead bodies off my street last week and I could drive in my car again, I raced to the Laundromat worried only that I had but a half hour before closing time to wash all my clothes. Five days is five lifetimes in this city, yet Manuel is dismayed to see everything already back to normal. They've cleaned up the bomb site. Traffic flows again. Manuel had to wait for breaks between cars before he could dart into the road in search of fragments of glass or charcoal scorch marks from the blast or red streaks of blood from the murdered first responders or something. "Something!" he tells me, still shouting.

I'm not sure why Manuel gets through to me. Why I don't just tell him to get over it and move on like the rest of us. So much of what I've seen has dribbled off my psyche. I'm Teflon by now. I'm tough. Manuel's a grown man, a native who'd left for a while but returned, Chihuahuaense. He's the father of two adult children, a pastor with a church he's trying his best to keep alive. A man who once told me it was a dream that brought him back to Juárez, a dream of doing good, of bringing God to the city. He may have broken through because a man of his age and stature, at least around here, isn't supposed to be affected, to show weakness or fear. He tells me it's not even that the car bombs went off, as unspeakably horrible as they were. It's that we *are not speaking about them!* We're acting as if it was no big deal. As if *nothing happened!*

"I started to doubt it myself!" Manuel cries. "I look on the TV and there's no stories about it. I look in the papers and they're writing about something else already. That's why I went up there. I had to see the scene. Did it really happen? And it did, Robert. It really happened!"

He gets through to me. His words—his plea for me to wake up, for all of us to wake up—pierce my calcified skull. Everything hits me. Months and months. They murdered Pedro Picasso. They dropped two bodies in the drive-through lane of a convenience store and the store stayed open for business. They murdered that crusading mother, and while we admire her, we remember above all to *stay on the line*. They murdered Maleno's brother only a few months ago, and he acts as if it happened twenty years in the past— like, whatever, gotta keep moving forward. They shot up a house full of high school students. They kidnapped, tortured, and murdered a groom on his wedding day. I was this fucking close to a car bombing, right down the same fucking street where I was drinking a beer and watching soccer and finishing off a plate of chicken wings. Chicken wings! And I ran a road race on the same street not twenty-four hours later, after they murdered four people! That's what I ignored during my nice afternoon outside, my solid workout. They murdered a doctor who'd rushed to the scene because he felt he could do some good. They killed him. They fucking killed him. J. L. killed the goddamn doctor and the ambulance driver and whoever it was La Línea dressed in a policeman's uniform in the first place when they set the whole murderous mousetrap. And I ran a 10K on that same street the very next day. A 10K! A road race! How ridiculous is that?! It all hits me, and it hurts me, and I'm feeling pain, and the pain is telling me that I'm not yet dead. That somewhere inside me I'm conscious and human and still sane. And by the time Manuel and I end our conversation, I'm feeling my own tears. And when I click off the phone they just come, the tears. I start to cry. I open up and I cry and I cry and I cry. And my face is so twisted and ugly even my dog is wondering what's wrong with me, what the fuck is going on, and Benito licks the tears that fall onto my arms, and I know I've got to get out. I can't stay here. I've got to go.

CHAPTER 23

Exodus: Part 2

KEN-TOKEY THROWS ME A FIST BUMP. "Hey man, good to see you again." I spy Sofia and Juvie from Las Cruces, along with Chuy and Sugar and the grandmother forever to be known as Chicharrón. Big Weecho's in San Diego attending a Tool concert, but Sugar's sister, the nurse who doesn't drink or take drugs, is here, and she kisses me on the cheek. Tonight's tailgate feels like a class reunion, or perhaps more like the first day back at school after a long summer break. I buy the El Kartel shirt-of-the-week. The *barra brava's* arts-and-crafts subcommittee hands out long, thin red balloons for everyone to carry inside. The white flag flying over Olympic Stadium signals that once again it's game day—actually game night—on La Frontera.

Federales patrol the parking lot, which is a new development. They search every truck and car, hunting for bombs. (Though I don't know what they'd do if they found one, other than die on the spot.) They pat us down as we file into a stadium that's not even half as full as the last game I saw here, the Primera swan song against Pumas. The federal police don't make us safer. Just the opposite, actually. *Federales* are bomb magnets. They're the ones La Línea wants to blow up. But even though we've been taught there are no neutral zones in Juárez, no safe spaces removed from the war, we're not worried as we watch the now-minor-league players take the field against some team I've never heard of. There's very little chance La Línea will try something at an Indios game. We know J. L. is a fan.

Maleno starts at striker, his hamstring injury healed. Gabino, still the head coach, wears his same black suit from Marco's wedding. On the chest of the Indios' jerseys, the S-Mart logo has been replaced by the logo of the team's new sponsor: Peter Piper Pizza. Free advertising—a straight trade, I'm told, for Francisco's free house in El Paso. Beer flies through the air when Juárez scores the first goal. El Kartel cries *"Puto!"*—Asshole!—whenever the visiting goalie punts the ball into play. A Border Patrol helicopter buzzes the stadium, and shadows stretch across the grass until the sun— the desert sun, the summer sun—finally falls behind the Juárez Mountains. When the referee blows his whistle to signal halftime, the temperature remains 103 degrees Fahrenheit.

Stadium floodlights flicker on. I check in with Adir in the press box. He's in charge of media relations now, a staff of one, handling everything. He offers me a potato chip drizzled in Valentina hot sauce. I inquire about his wife, pregnant with what will be their first child, a girl. *You have to believe in the future to have a baby, right?* When the Mexican national team plays the United States, Adir promises me, his daughter will root for the men in green. But she'll be born in El Paso, a U.S. citizen at birth, just in case. The game restarts and the Indios score again, taking a 2–0 lead.

"This is the best Indios team we've ever assembled," declares Gil Cantú, shaking my hand when I find him in his usual seat. He tells me he was up late last night talking to a prospect in Spain, a midfielder unaware of how violent Juárez has grown, of the club's money troubles or of the press conference where Francisco Ibarra said extortionists are terrorizing his players. Although Gil wishes he still had Marco to anchor the midfield, he's proud his reclamation project has moved up to such a good club. I tell Gil it's a little sad to see the Indios down in the minors. He nods his head in agreement.

"But what a beautiful run, brother. What a beautiful run."

I don't see Francisco in his regular seat. He's here, I've been told, but it takes me a while to finally spot him up in the stadium's one luxury box, walled behind glass and all alone. He waves for me to come up and join him. As soon as I step inside the box, a cool blast of air-conditioning washes over my skin, making me understand why Francisco has sequestered himself. At the same moment, just as I step into the box, the Indios score again, taking an incredible 3–0 lead.

"*Gracias a Dios!*" Francisco cheers, pointing his fingers at the heavens. "*Gracias a Dios!*" he slaps his palms against the glass. He spins in a circle and then points his hands toward the sky one more time. "Please excuse my passion," he asks me before returning his attention to the good news unfolding on the field. His team is rewarding his faith. He can see how it's all going to play out. The Indios will return to the Primera, and quickly, within the year. The team's redemptive journey, from disgrace back to glory, will inspire his hometown. The violence will fade away. He'll be able to sleep in his mansion on this side of the river. Juárez will thrive once again, evolving into a new Monterrey or Guadalajara or Las Vegas only Mexican, so better. God wants his Indios to win, Francisco believes, mistakenly.

The team will play solid ball in the first of the two annual seasons. Good enough soccer to reach the playoffs but not quite good enough to win a title. In the second short season, they'll fall back big-time. They won't make the playoffs. They'll look like candidates to drop down yet another rung, to division three. The air will deflate from Francisco's big dream as if it were a soccer ball ruptured by a bullet. He'll sell the club, something he has been saying he'd never do. His health is suffering, he'll announce at a press conference hosted at an Applebee's restaurant. And he's tired of the constant criticism. He'll move more and more of his life over to El Paso. At the World Cup, his second son, Paco's younger brother, rooted for the United States.

The Indios' new owners will appear to be the state of Chihuahua, though that's not entirely clear. "It's an absolute mystery," the reporter from *El Diario* will write. The team's new executive committee—Gil Cantú and Gabino will lose their jobs in the transition—will say only that, in addition to receiving substantial state funding, the team is owned by "entrepreneurs," none of whom they care to identify. One of the first things this new and mysterious ownership group will do is entice the league's most talented striker, the scoring champ from the previous season, to transfer to the border.

If we were laundering money, we'd have the best players in the league.

You have to remember that Chihuahua is a narco state. The government and the cartels are one in this city. The drug dealers give

the money to the government, and the government gives the money
back to the people.

If the secretive new Indios owners return to the Primera, they
will join the top league's newest team, the Xolos of Tijuana. That
club's owner, a gambling magnate named Jorge Hank Rhon, served
as Tijuana's mayor at the same time Teto first ruled Juárez; they
share a political party. In 1995, Hank was arrested at the airport in
Mexico City and charged with smuggling. In 1988, two of his bodyguards were convicted of murdering a newspaper columnist who
had criticized Hank in print. According to the Associated Press, a
"1999 report by the U.S. National Drug Intelligence Center singled
Hank Rhon out as an associate of drug smugglers." It was Hank's
father, also a prominent public official, who first said the famous
line "A politician who is poor is a poor politician." One month after the Xolos joined the Primera, Hank was arrested in a predawn
raid of his Tijuana mansion. Army soldiers found a large cache of
illegal weapons, including forty rifles, forty-eight handguns, 9,298
bullet cartridges, seventy ammunition clips, and a gas grenade. Two
of the guns were linked to earlier murders. Hank spent ten days in
jail before all charges were dropped, for lack of evidence.

Before the car bombing, Marco and Dany rented out their Juárez
dream house. After the bombing, they sold all the furniture inside
it. They're not coming back. A *rutera* driver working for Dany's
family will be murdered. "He was a very good man. A very extraor-
dinary worker for us," Dany's mother will tell me. "And he was
innocent. I don't know why they killed him."

It won't take long for Marco to crack Pachuca's starting lineup. In
a profile posted on an American soccer site, Herculez Gomez will
rave that Marco "brings a calmness to the game." But then Pachuca
will switch head coaches and Marco, as always, will land back on
the bench. Although he will fly to Dubai for the Club World Cup, he
will not play in any games. He'll ultimately end up in León, of all
cities, of all teams, starting every game for the Esmeraldas and trying to play his way back into the big time.

Mayor Teto will return the bullfights to La Frontera. He will also
change the official name of his town to Heroic Ciudad Juárez. I will
be told J. L. is dead. Definitely dead. Gunned down in Chihuahua
city. Those who tell me this will admit that no super-fucking-fat
dead body has yet turned up. Other people will tell me J. L. is still

alive. Most people will tell me he's dead. I'll decide he's dead. Once a week, as if visiting the Stations of the Cross, Arson's mother will continue walking to the police station in Juárez to ask if they've made any progress in their investigation of Charlie's murder.

And I will leave. Before my original visit to the border, the plan had been—hopefully, if it could be done—to make Juárez my permanent home. Juárez is energizing. To live in a city where you can be killed at any moment, as Ramón Morales first put it, is to answer, every day, a fundamental question: How badly do you want to remain alive? Just answering that question, just saying that you want to live—very much so, please—is a kind of gift. It's natural to take life for granted sometimes. It's impossible to do it in Juárez. When I'm on La Frontera, I'm conscious that I'm alive, and that I want to stay that way.

The city's inspiring, too. At least the people are. The ultimate purpose of government, I've been taught, is to protect us from ourselves. In a state of nature, man is inherently wicked, all selfish id, out to kill and fuck and terrorize. Juárez challenges this lesson. The city is a failed state, obviously. The most wicked of all crimes, murder, is legal. *Go ahead! Have at it!* Yet almost nobody in this town is a murderer. So many people—almost everybody here— pursue remarkably normal lives. They go to work. They marry, they raise their kids, they follow soccer teams. It's not lightly that I drop the name Anne Frank, but when I think about this city, she keeps popping into my mind. Juárez has made me believe that, deep down, people are fundamentally good. Juárez is where my neighbor tells me her mission in life is to help others and to love.

And the food here is the best. I wanted to stay. But Manuel made it obvious the endgame could not be avoided. Over the phone, he shook my shoulders and slapped my face and pinched my skin to prove I'd gone numb. And when you go numb in Juárez, that's when you have a problem.

It won't seem wise to start over somewhere else in Mexico, much as I've grown to love this country. Eight are killed at a bar in Cancún. Ships from Princess Cruises stop docking in Puerto Vallarta. My initially rosy take on Monterrey is proving way wrong, very naive. "Monterrey is becoming the new Ciudad Juárez," reports the Associated Press. Extortions are up, as are carjackings.

Fifty-two people are killed in a casino firebombing. Cartel assassi-
nations fuel a murder rate that, while not yet on par with Juárez, is
climbing rocket-ship fast. President Calderón sends in the *federales*, and we know how effective that'll be.

"The day-to-day reality is a violence that is out of control," the AP
concludes. Drug killings scar Guadalajara as well. Even in Pachuca,
Marco and Dany's home for a season, someone tosses seven dead
bodies down a well.

*Juárez is the start of what will end up being a second Mexican
revolution.*

I'll again pack up my car with everything I own, adding a small
Mexican dog to the pile. My landlady will say she's coming over to
retrieve my keys, but then she'll call to report there's been a shooting on her street and she can't leave her house for a while.

"I think it's getting worse," she will tell me.

I'll drive across the river, back into my country, heading ultimately back to Miami. An hour after I cross, maybe two hours this
time, *poof:* Juárez will vanish, as if the city never existed. Except I
can't forget Ken-tokey, who's unable to cross the border like I can. I
can't forget Lorenzo and Karina and their father who still drives
every morning to the machine shop where he was kidnapped. I
can't forget Ramón and Adir and and my landlady and the Karteleros and my dog-walking neighbor and everyone else living life as
best they can. The city really happened. Juárez does exist.

"We are going back to the Primera!" Francisco shouts. He's again
pounding the window of his luxury box with both palms, making
me recall the way the windows at the sports bar vibrated from the
car bombs. Juárez has scored a fourth goal, the game a blowout.
One of the Indios left from last season fired a low shot that slipped
under the visiting goalkeeper's arms. "This is good! This is good!
We're going right back up to the Primera, I assure you!"

He turns to make sure I'm listening.

"We're going to stay as long as God permits," he adds. "We will
continue here as long as God gives us the strength!"

A professional soccer team runs around one of the best-maintained
fields in Mexico. I can hear the drums of El Kartel thumping even
up in the luxury box. A hoppy tang hangs in the air from so many
beers tossed aloft in this runaway win. As long as people continue

to believe in the team, Francisco tells me, then the Indios are doing their job, which is to help people. The man who brought the Primera back to the border for a few beautiful years looks down upon his creation as if what he's seeing—as if a soccer ball finding the back of the net—were the sweetest thing happening in his city.

Acknowledgments

My thanks to just about everyone on La Frontera. That includes anyone associated with UTEP, with the El Paso Public Library, with the Juárez Maquiladora Association, and with a hundred other border outfits including, while I'm at it, the many Whataburger restaurants I patronized on the El Paso side. Beyond the people already mentioned in the text, I want to recognize the contributions of Ben Adams, Kesse Buchanan, Ilean Di Raz, Steve Dudley, Pat and Carolina Flood, Victor Foia, Kyle Haas, Chris Higashi, Nate Knaebel, Tristram Korten, Chris Lopez, Janet Lopez, Kirk Nielsen, Will Palmer, Chris Parris-Lamb, Randall Patterson, Johnathan Rendon, Aurora Rivera, Linda Robertson, Aaron and Sarit Schneider, Kirk Semple, Jessica Sick, Janine Sieja, Jabari Smith, Tom Trahan, Alberto J. Treviño and Steven Yore.

The *New York Times* commissioned my reporting on the dead women; a longer and unedited draft of the femicide chapter originally appeared as a Kindle Single. This book first took shape in the Scandiuzzi Writers' Room at Seattle's Central Library. Profound thanks as always to my family, especially this time to Nathan and Shea Bastian for their help in Dallas, and to Corin Jorns in Seattle for inviting me to his fourth birthday party, and for taking Benito on a good, long walk.

A Note on the Author

Robert Andrew Powell is the author of *We Own This Game*, a story of race, politics, and youth football. His journalism has appeared in the *New York Times*, the *New York Times Magazine*, *Sports Illustrated*, *Slate*, *Mother Jones*, *Inc.*, *5280*, *Runner's World*, and the *Kansas City Star*; on public radio's *This American Life* and in *The Best American Sports Writing* anthology. He lives in Miami.